Social and Literary Satire in the Comedies of Tirso de Molina

Ottawa Hispanic Studies

General Editors: José Ruano and Nigel Dennis

Published Titles:

Forthcoming:

P. R. K. Halkhoree

Social and Literary
Satire in the Comedies
of Tirso de Molina

Edited by

José M. Ruano de la Haza

and

Henry W. Sullivan

Ottawa Hispanic Studies 5

Dovehouse Editions Canada
1989

Canadian Cataloguing in Publication Data

Halkhoree, P. R. K. (Premraj R. K.)
  Social and literary satire in the comedies of Tirso de Molina

(Ottawa Hispanic Studies ; no. 5)
Includes bibliographical references.

ISBN 0–919473–60–1

  1. Molina, Tirso de, 1571?–1648—Criticism and interpretation.
2. Spanish drama (Comedy)—History and criticism. 3. Spanish
drama—Classical period, 1500–1700—History and criticism. I. Ruano,
de la Haza, José M. II. Sullivan, Henry W., 1942–   .
III. Title. IV. Series.

PQ6436.H34 1989   862'.3   C89–090206–2

Copyright © 1989, Dovehouse Editions Inc.

For orders write to:

Dovehouse Editions Inc.
32 Glen Ave.
Ottawa, Canada
K1S 2Z7

For information on the series write to:

General Editors, Ottawa Hispanic Studies
Dept. of Modern Languages and Literatures
University of Ottawa
Ottawa, Canada, K1N 6N5

Typeset by HUMANITIES PUBLISHING SERVICES, University of Toronto

Manufactured in Canada.   Printed by Imprimerie Gagné Ltée.

Acknowledgments

The Editors gratefully acknowledge the financial help provided by the Faculty of Arts of the University of Ottawa and by the family of the late Premraj R. K. Halkhoree, without which the publication of this book would not have been possible. The Editors also wish to thank Dr. Marcel Hamelin, Dean of the Faculty of Arts of the University of Ottawa, and Professor Nigel Dennis. Their faith in and support for this project have been unflagging since its initiation some six years ago.

Contents

Abbreviations

B.A.E.: Biblioteca de Autores Españoles.
BBMP: Boletín de la Biblioteca Menéndez Pelayo.
BC: Bulletin of the Comediantes.
BSS: Bulletin of Spanish Studies.
BH: Bulletin Hispanique.
BHS: Bulletin of Hispanic Studies.
BRAE: Boletín de la Real Academia Española.
CHA: Cuadernos Hispano-Americanos.
Est: Estudios.
Fi: Filología (Buenos Aires).
FMLS: Forum for Modern Language Studies.
HBalt: Hispania (Baltimore).
Hispl: Hispania (Indiana).
HR: Hispanic Review.
LR: Les Lettres Romanes.
MLF: Modern Language Forum.
MLN: Modern Language Notes.
MLQ: Modern Language Quarterly.
MLR: Modern Language Review.
N.B.A.E.: Nueva Biblioteca de Autores Españoles.
NRFH: Nueva Revista de Filología Hispánica.
PMLA: Publications of the Modern Language Association.
PQ: Philological Quarterly.
RABM: Revista de Archivos, Bibliotecas y Museos.
REH: Revista de Estudios Hispánicos.
RF: Romanische Forschungen.
RFE: Revista de Filología Española.
RFH: Revista de Filología Hispánica.
RoN: Romance Notes.
RPh: Romance Philology.
RR: Romanic Review.
S: Symposium.
Segis: Segismundo.

Editors' Foreword

This book is a slightly abridged and revised version of the doctoral dissertation "Social and Literary Satire in the Comedies of Tirso de Molina" which the late Professor Premraj Radhe Krishna Halkhoree (1941–1978) deposited with Edinburgh University in partial fulfillment of the requirements for the Ph.D. (1969). The editors have been prompted to publish Halkhoree's work posthumously for two reasons: firstly, as a memorial to a much mourned colleague whose brilliant career was ended in its prime by leukemia; and secondly, because today, after two decades, it is still unsurpassed in detail and scope as the most painstaking analysis to which Tirso's dramatic craftsmanship has ever been submitted. In this, it stands clearly under the influence of the dissertation's director, Professor Alexander A. Parker, and may be placed in a well-attested tradition of British "thematico-structural analysis" (Pring-Mill) or post-war "British New Criticism" (Cohen). But Halkhoree's work on Tirso brings this tradition to its apogee and, inasmuch as he tackled the neglected Mercedarian with a virtual *tabula rasa* of critical literature to guide him in the mid-1960s, the achievements of this book are uniquely his. To put the work in perspective, a brief editorial word on Halkhoree's career, on the nature of the excised passages and chapters, as well as on the work's overall significance, would not be out of place.

Premraj Halkhoree was born on April 21, 1941 in Trinidad, West Indies, amid affluent circumstances. His family was of Hindu extraction and his sensitivity to diversity of cultural traditions drove him early to study other languages and literatures, notably those of the principal Caribbean ex-colonisers: Spanish, French and English. He attended Queen's Royal College, Trinidad, from 1953 to 1959, where he distinguished himself in the three subjects mentioned, and won the School's Stollmeyer bronze medal (1959). From 1962 to 1967 he attended the University of Edinburgh, where he was a Stevenson Exchange Scholar (Salamanca University, Spain), as well as a Richard Brown Scholar. He gained the M.A. degree in 1965 and the Ph.D. in 1969. From 1967 to 1975, he was a much valued colleague as Lecturer in Spanish at Westfield College, University of London, where he gained the friendship and esteem of Professor John E. Varey and the other academic members of the department of Spanish. In 1975, after an initial year as Visiting Professor at the University of Ottawa, Halkhoree accepted an Associate Professorship there and taught at Ottawa until his death. Halkhoree's fundamental reorganisation—with Professor Nigel Dennis—of Ottawa's Spanish curriculum, and initiation of an M.A. degree in Spanish, marked the turning-point in the transformation of the Section from a popular, service-oriented sideline into one of Canada's most serious centres of Hispanic research. He is survived by his widow, whose gracious permission to publish her husband's doctoral study is gratefully acknowledged at this point.

In its uncut form, Halkhoree's dissertation covers 606 double-spaced A4 folios. This was felt by the editors to be of unpractical length for commercial publication, and perhaps not even desirable on *a priori* grounds. Dissertations fall mainly into two categories: those that document the process of research, and those that document only the results. Halkhoree's work falls clearly in the former category. Fourteen plays of Tirso are analysed, often in minute detail, and some measure of repetition can doubtless be avoided by cutting. The omitted chapters on *Por el sótano y el torno* and *Ventura te dé Dios, hijo* may be read, virtually *verbatim*, as "Satire and Symbolism in the Structure of Tirso de Molina's *Por el sótano y el torno*" in *FMLS*, 4 (1968), 374–86 and as "The Foundations of Nobility: An Interpretation of Tirso be Molina's *Ventura te dé Dios, hijo*," in *FMLS*, 9 (1973), 379–402. The chapter on *El vergonzoso en palacio* is brief and, in Halkhoree's self-deprecating words, has "little to add" to existing criticism on the play. This has been cut, along with the discussion of *La elección por la virtud*, since most of the latter's points about social conflict are as well, or better, exemplified by Halkhoree's analysis of *Amar por arte mayor*. To these excisions should be added those quotations in Spanish from Tirso's texts which serve only to vindicate or illustrate the claims made in Halkhoree's English commentary. The very long and detailed Endnotes of the original have also been reduced to the bare minimum. An appendix on *La mujer por fuerza* is omitted (though not on the grounds of its disputed authorship—the editors agree with the author about its Tirsian paternity); and we have also ignored a bound-in reprint of the *FMLS* article on *Por el sótano*.

To compensate for the loss of these folios, we offer here a summary of the essence of the four omitted chapters. They all, in varying degree, illustrate the main thesis of Halkhoree's investigation: that Tirso applied satirical nuclei for construction of some of his best comedies. Halkhoree wished, firstly, to refute the traditional view that Tirso's comedies are immoral or carelessly constructed and, secondly, modify that traditional view by regarding the comedies as satirically conceived. There is a close marriage here, then, of form and content, which may surprise some readers. A second consequence of the dissertation's methodological approach is the major polemical burden which the terms "satire" and "wit" are obliged to bear. Halkhoree intends them "in their widest sense."

By "satire," for example, Halkhoree does not mean the formal literary genre *per se* (as, for instance, the satires of Juvenal or Dryden), but rather the ridicule of a social or literary convention. Or again, to quote him: "In so far as Tirso's ridicule of conventions is intended to convince his audience of the validity of his point of view, he is a satirist." Halkhoree also uses the term "wit" in a thesis-bearing sense akin to the seventeenth-century Spanish *ingenio* (conceptual astuteness) or the eighth meaning offered by the *OED*: " . . . apt association of thought and expression, calculated to surprise and delight by its unexpectedness." For Halkhoree, wit, like satire, has a structural implication and is used by him as a novel argument in defense of Tirso's orderliness in dramatic construction. He characteristically champions *El amor médico*, for example, with the words: "The use of *wit* to link scene to scene and to provide the conceptual opposition in the play with an ultimate synthesis does not, however, mean that the principle of causality is ignored."

The first two omitted chapters of Halkhoree's thesis may be summarised very briefly, since they are both fully available in print. The chapter on *Por el sótano y el torno* falls under the general heading of "The Abuse of Religion: Good and Bad Ends" in the dissertation, and Halkhoree believes that its action may have been inspired by a real-life incident. Bernarda is responsible for the virtual enclaustration in a convent of her sister Jusepa, whom she has "sold" in a marriage contract of which Bernarda is the principal beneficiary. The aim of the play, then, is "to satirise and partially frustrate cupidity." The symbolic *torno* of the title is the revolving dumbwaiter which permits goods to be delivered into the convent, but provides no exit for its inmates; the *sótano* is the "earthy," underground passage that admits Jusepa's true lover. Halkhoree concedes that the *sótano* is a *deus ex machina* in the plot: "This, however, is a fault in the action, not in the theme, and an analysis of the symbolism employed in the play will establish that the comedy has a sound structural unity. Character and parallelism have produced the plot-structure of the play; the symbols provide the logic which establishes the unity of that structure." Halkhoree concludes his essay by saying: "Love and marriage, for Tirso, must be frankly based on the physical. Celibacy is an ideal only for real nuns, leading a real spiritual life; it should have no place in the love of man for woman, and sexual frustration, outside real convents, should not be falsely endowed with spiritual value and dignified by the language of religion." *Ventura te dé Dios, hijo* was placed by Halkhoree in its own section entitled "Social Aspirations and their Effect on Personal and Class Relationships." According to him, the play shows, in the first place, that learning is inadequate to cope with actual situations in real life. Césaro's education has produced in him a mechanistic mentality, which renders him incapable of coping with the unpredictable in life. This is partly due to the fact that his knowledge is superficial book-learning, absorbed by the intellect, but without any beneficial influence on his soul. Césaro, for all his learning, lacks nobility of soul. If anything, his learning is what exaggerates and brings out his moral flaws. And it is precisely in these flaws in his character rather than in any incidents of the play that Halkhoree sees the explanation for his failure.

Otón, on the other hand, has neither wealth nor learning as positive advantages, and loses the advantage of birth because of pride. The one thing he does possess, however, is *ventura*. But he possesses this *ventura*, which Césaro lacks, because he has earned it. And this, in Halkhoree's opinion, is the real point of the play. Otón is fortunate not because he is ignorant or poor, but because he is good. Virtue is the basis of all true nobility. Now, Halkhoree contends, the structure of the play becomes easier to understand. The absence of direct causal links in the plot-structure seems to be deliberate: it is an implicit humourous comment on the dramatic principle of causality with its underlying philosophical assumptions.

Halkhoree's discussion of *El vergonzoso en palacio*, originally under the heading of "Love and Class Barriers: Shame and Absurdity" stresses a) the social thesis of the elevation of the shepherd, and b) the figure of the timid lover. As the author points out, the links between the obtrusive disguise motif in the play and the identity theme illustrates that clothes, or noble disguise, here actually reveal the true character of Mireno. This thesis tests the entrenched *status quo*: "Whereas the point the play makes is that the name should befit the person, for the Duke, the person should befit the name. Status is all." As to Mireno's timidity, the Petrarchan-cum-courtly love conventions supposed that a lady simultaneously encouraged and discouraged the suitor, in order to egg him on. But Mireno takes Magdalena's discouragement too seriously, and the exasperated heroine assumes a far more aggressive role than normally expected from the Petrarchan woman.

Rejecting Hartzenbusch's charge that the first fourteen scenes in Act I of *El vergonzoso* are not obviously connected to the main action, Halkhoree now reaffirms his thesis: "As I have been trying to argue, it is an essential feature of Tirso's dramatic technique to use an asyndetic plot-structure in order to concentrate on the thematic motifs of the play." In his pro-Tirso argument based on asyndeton, Halkhoree intends this key term not in its grammatical sense of absence of connection or coherence of parts, but in the expanded rhetorical sense of "a figure securing energy by omitting connectives" (Funk and Wagnall).

La elección por la virtud, originally discussed under the rubric "Authority and the Individual: The Abuse of Power," interested Halkhoree because of a) its typically episodic structure in the main plot, and b) its constantly recurring Tirsian theme that the individual's position in society is to be determined by his intrinsic worth. The main plot dramatises the rapid and miraculous rise of Fray Félix, the future Pope Sixtus V, to the rank of Cardinal (his papal career was to have been dealt with in a non-extant *segunda parte*). The three acts chronologically highlight distinct periods of this career: a continuous rise in Act I; fall and rise in Acts II and III. The fall in Félix's fortunes is always caused by intrigues and obstacles maliciously placed in his way by high-born, ecclesiastical enemies; the rise is caused by the spiritual intervention of God through miracles. In the end, Félix's intellectual qualities and moral virtues (especially filial piety) are rewarded; hence the title.

But his character, his aggressive pride in his lowly shepherd origins, his ambition, belief in signs, and despairing passivity, all stand in curious contrast to his moral virtues. According to Halkhoree, the resolution of obstacles by divine intervention also robs the play of genuine conflict. The real weakness of the play, however, is the dramatist's failure to distinguish between genuine aspects of character-drawing and formal, structural devices such as the "cataphoric" (i.e., galvanising matter in the direction of flow) use of belief in omens and audience reminders that the papal tiara lies in the future. For Halkhoree, this confusion is compounded by Félix's speeches being the vehicle for both of these aspects. It would have been better to have other characters stress the inevitability of the progress of his career.

The sub-plot has a stronger storyline and deals with the secular, rather than ecclesiastical, aspects of social prejudice. Here, Sixto's sister Sabina and the truly noble Césaro wish to marry, but encounter rigid opposition from both Sabina's father, Pereto, and Prince Fabriano. When Césaro is imprisoned and the situation seems headed for tragedy, Sabina takes the matter into her own hands and succeeds in giving the rope to Césaro, who uses it to escape from his cell. The lovers are not passive characters, but tenacious of purpose in their resistance to irrational parental pressure. In both plots, therefore, the noble echelons (including influential clergy drawn from the nobility) are presented in a very bad light and, in general, bitterly condemned for their envy of rising talent and violent abuse of the lower orders. If, as Cotarelo asserts, *La elección por la virtud* was revived in early 1622 (shortly after the centenary of Sixtus's birth in December 1621), then it would be hard to avoid the conclusion that the play was put on by palace factions hostile to the Olivares regime (March 1621) who wished to condemn the nobility's abuse of their social power.

Whether the reader ultimately agrees or not with Halkhoree's thesis seems a minor issue besides his overall achievement. The writing has a sustained level of intellectual discipline and Spartan articulacy that is rare in Hispanic criticism. Halkhoree possessed one of the keenest analytical minds of his generation, but reined in any excess of judgement through modesty. His opinions are always worth having, therefore, and with even greater reason when he illuminates Tirsian comedies that even the majority of Golden-Age specialists have not read. The cultural upheavals of the 1960s arguably spurred a revival of interest in the topsy-turvy universe of Tirsian drama. Prior to that era, scarcely any book-length treatment on the Mercedarian playwright existed at all. If published back then, Halkhoree's work would surely have given more weight and points of reference to the "Tirso-boom" that never quite seemed to materialize in the 1970s. As it is, his work is available at the end of the 1980s. The editors, in wishing to hallow a memory and do their colleague intellectual justice, see both aims fused in this publication. As Beethoven inscribed above the score of one of his late string quartets: *Vom Herzen kommt es; zum Herzen gehe es*.

José M. Ruano de la Haza,
University of Ottawa.

Henry W. Sullivan,
University of Missouri

Preface

Compared with tragedy, comedy has received little attention from literary critics. Spanish Golden Age comedy, in particular, is a field which for long has suffered from undeserved neglect. In this book, I attempt to study a limited, but, perhaps, vital aspect of the comic art of Tirso de Molina, who is undoubtedly the best comic playwright of the Golden Age.

The field of research was suggested to me by Professor A. A. Parker, who has with long-suffering patience supervised this work through all its stages. I am indebted to him for criticism, at once tactful and illuminating, and innumerable suggestions as regards style and presentation of my arguments as well as the interpretation of the plays analysed and their relation to the wider context of Golden Age drama and literature. His criticism has at every stage forced me to re-consider my presentations and findings and modify them in the light of evidence which I had overlooked.

To Miss M. Crossland, who first introduced me, as an undergraduate, to Golden Age drama, I am equally indebted for criticism no less probing and valuable. Above all, it is due especially to her criticism that my arguments are more concise and more clearly formulated than they would otherwise have been.

I am also grateful to Professors J. E. Varey and A. D. Deyermond, who have read various chapters of this book, for their helpful and constructive suggestions. I must thank Dr. J. Lowe for having brought to my notice a point which I should otherwise have missed, and Mr. J. Sage for several valuable references.

Needless to say, none of the above is in any way responsible for the views put forward in this work. I shall doubtless soon regret not having considered their suggestions more carefully.

Finally, thanks are due to the Scottish Education Department for having awarded me a senior Scottish Studentship, which I held for the first two years of my period of study, and to the University of Edinburgh for the award of the Richard Brown Scholarship in 1965–1966.

Introduction

Two lacunae are immediately apparent in the study of the Spanish drama of the Golden Age. The first is the absence of any systematic study of the Golden Age comedy. The process of revaluation of the *comedia*, initiated by Professors A. A. Parker and E. M. Wilson, has tended to concern itself essentially with the tragedies. This, both within the tradition of literary criticism and also because of the natural preoccupation with the problems tragedy explores, is right and justifiable. However, as is the case with Elizabethan drama, an enormous number of the plays written in the Golden Age are comedies. While comedy has always been popular in the theatre, it has not been given much consideration by the critics, partly, no doubt, owing to the implicit traditional attitude that comedy does not merit serious consideration. Recently, however, there have been signs of a change in attitude among the critics.[1]

The second of these lacunae is the absence of any systematic study of Tirsian comedy. This, perhaps, is more puzzling. Tirso has been generally acknowledged as the best comic dramatist of the Golden Age. However, the criteria on which this judgment has been based are difficult to ascertain, for, apart from the vague generalizations, no serious study of his comic art has been undertaken. Two extensives studies of Tirso exist. The earlier, by Muñoz Peña, purports to be both biographical and critical. The criticism, however, is largely descriptive, not analytical. The second, E. Gijón's *El humor en Tirso de Molina*, is limited in scope.

It must be admitted, from the outset, that there exist, in the way of any critical evaluation of Tirso's comedies, and, indeed, of most of his plays, enormous difficulties of a textual, biographical, as well as a bibliographical nature. For the purpose of this book, I have used the three volumes of Tirso's plays edited by Doña Blanca de los Ríos.[2] The texts in these are not entirely satisfactory for several reasons. They contain, first, numerous printing errors. Secondly, they are not critical editions of the plays, but in the main reprints of Hartzenbusch's and Cotarelo's earlier editions. Their main advantages over these editions are those of availability and completeness. Thirdly, they preserve Hartzenbusch's scene divisions. These do not, of course, correspond to the English "scenes" or Spanish *cuadros* (which, in any case, are never indicated in the seventeenth-century editions), but to the French *scènes* or English "sub-scenes," which indicate the entrances or exits of characters. While I do not accept the validity or even desirability of such scene-divisions, all references in this book, for practical purposes and convenience, will be to Act, scene and page in Doña Blanca's edition. In the case of certain plays, I have consulted, where possible, other modern editions. Where these offer a correction of, or a more satisfactory reading than Doña Blanca's texts, I have followed them. Important deviations from Doña Blanca's texts have been recorded in the notes. I have occasionally altered the punctuation where this seemed desirable for easier comprehension, and have, of course, corrected obvious misprints. I have not attempted to compare the texts of existing modern editions with those of the seventeenth-century *partes* or *sueltas* or such manuscripts as exist. While I should have liked to do so, the limited time available to me has not allowed this. While some of my arguments, therefore, will almost inevitably be based, partly, if not wholly, on textual readings which may later turn out to be corrrupt, I do not think that my main argument will be affected thereby.

Bibliographical problems also make a fair evaluation of Tirso's works difficult. In the first place, only a fraction of his work survives.[3] Of the surviving works, almost the only ones which can with certainty be considered his are some sueltas and those contained in the *Primera, Tercera, Cuarta* and *Quinta partes*, and the *Cigarrales de Toledo*.

The *Segunda parte* is prefaced with an enigmatic statement. There are only two works in it, out of four which Tirso claims to be exclusively his own, which can be identified as his, since the closing lines affirm his authorship. These are: *Por el sótano y el torno* and *Amor y celos hacen discretos*. The authorship of *El condenado por desconfiado*, a play long believed to be a genuine work of Tirso's, seems to have been almost conclusively established by A. K. G. Paterson.[4] The suggestion by Doña Blanca that all the plays in this parte are either wholly by Tirso or written by him in collaboration with another author seems to have been refuted by the discovery that one of them, at least, is not by Tirso.[5] The question of authorship, therefore, is not solved with regard to a number of plays— including those found in *sueltas* or *partes* containing plays by or attributed to various authors.

Biographical data provide another and related, if slightly different, sort of difficulty. Such facts as are known about Tirso's life are few. This led, in the last century above all, to the creation of mythical stories about Tirso, most of them hardly contributing to a picture of a very normal man—at least not in his youth. These stories have now been largely discredited, thanks to recent research, but it is interesting to bear in mind that their justification was to be found mainly in the interpretation of Tirso's comedies, which many nineteenth-century critics considered immoral. While recent discoveries seem to have cleared Tirso of the charges of leading an immoral life, they have not simultaneously exonerated him from the charge of writing immoral plays, and they have also introduced fresh problems concerning both Tirso's life and the interpretation of his plays. While it is not my purpose to prove or disprove that Tirso was immoral or a hypocritical friar, my interpretation of some of his plays as satirical comedies would seem to weaken the charge that his comedies are immoral.

There is a traditional conflict of opinion with regard to Tirso's comedies. This has its origins in the views of Tirso's contemporaries and centres around two aspects of his plays: their technique and their morality. On both points we get not merely differing, but conflicting, even diametrically opposed views. Tirso's plays are both warmly praised and fiercely condemned for their technique and their morality. This conflict of opinion persists through the centuries and is, in some ways, still evident in recent criticism. Tirso and his plays undoubtedly constitute a topic which arouses strong passions. Leaving aside the clear element of polemical arguments *ad hominem* evident in so much of Tirsian criticism, there is still a fundamental ambiguity in Tirso's works which is reflected in these conflicting views. But, first, it would be convenient to review very briefly existing Tirsian criticism, paying special attention to these conflicting views.

In the seventeenth century, we find a curious situation. From Tirso's own statements, we learn that his plays were successful in the *corrales*.[6] His drama earned the approval of certain persons such as Calderón. Cervantes, at first an opponent of the Lopean *comedia*, seems to have praised Tirso equivocally as Cotarelo notes.[7]

There are a few other more or less favourable mentions of Tirso, none of them very important. What is more interesting is the fact that Tirso seems to have aroused enormous opposition to himself. He frequently refers in his works to the envy of others, their hostility towards him.[8] Such hostility even existed within his own Order.[9] A good indication of this is the attitude of Lope to Tirso, which R. L. Kennedy has been examining.[10]

While Tirso always acknowledges his debt to Lope, we have some indication that Lope gave grudging praise to Tirso, but this was interested praise. As Ruth Kennedy has argued, it was wrung from Lope by Tirso's defense of his *comedia* in the *Cigarrales*. But Lope's favourable attitude was short-lived, and seemed to have been confined to the period 1620–1622. Lope's attitude is normally at best equivocal,[11] more often hostile. As Dámaso Alonso has said, Lope is envious of Tirso's dramatic success.[12] Tirso seems to refer explicitly to this in the third act of *Antona García*:

> Pues véndese agora tanta
> envidia a ingenios diversos
> que hay hombre que haciendo versos
> a los demás se adelanta;
> y aunque más fama le des
> es tal (la verdad os digo),
> que niega el habla a su amigo
> cada vez que escribe bien.
>
> (III.iii p.439a.)

Lope's criticism of *Don Gil* seems to be on artistic grounds. But, as Dámaso Alonso points out, Tirso's play is not as technically faulty as Lope seems to imply.[13]

More serious were the criticisms levelled against the morality of Tirso's plays. These must be seen against the wider background of the moralists' criticism of the theatre.[14] As Ruth L. Kennedy has shown, most of his criticism was directed primarily against Lope, but it was, surprisingly, Tirso who, in 1625, was criticised by the Junta de Reformación for writing immoral plays.[15] The reasons for this ban are still obscure; modern critics have suggested that it was politically motivated. This seems probable. But what is important is that it completes the two-pronged attack which has traditionally been made on Tirso and which has persisted through the centuries.

Tirso was himself aware of this. In his defence of the Lopean *comedia* in the *Cigarrales de Toledo*, a passage which, according to Ruth L. Kennedy, may have been written in 1620–21, he attemps to deal with his critics.[16] The pasage has been regarded as one of the most brilliant defences of the *comedia*. I shall only draw attention to some of the main points Tirso makes.

This defence, as is well known, grows out of the critique of *El vergonzoso en palacio*. There are objections to the play on both moral and artistic grounds. As regards the former, the main criticism is directed against the characters of Serafina and Magdalena: "cuyas hijas pintó tan desenvueltas, que, contra las leyes de su honestidad, hicieron teatro de su poco recato la inmunidad de su jardín" (p. 141). This criticism is part of a larger point concerning the historical, factual accuracy of the history. Tirso answers the more general point, stressing the difference between history and poetry: "¡Como si la licencia de Apolo se estrechase a la recolección histórica, y no pudiere fabricar, sobre cimientos de personas verdaderas, arquitecturas del ingenio fingidas!" (p. 141). The argument here is that the story on stage is no more than a story. Tirso does not specifically answer the objection made to the characterisation of the women. He may have thought that it was not a point worth answering. But he probably regretted not having done so a few years later: for it was precisely that aspect of his plays which the Junta de Reformación singled out for criticism and which it used as a pretext for forbidding him to write any more plays. As I shall show, it is a form of criticism which has survived into the twentieth century.

But perhaps the main reason for Tirso's not having answered that specific charge was his eagerness to defend the artistic principles of the *comedia*. This is the main substance of the apology.

The criticisms of the *comedia* follow the well-known lines of the Neo-Aristotelian theorists. I shall not analyse closely Tirso's reply: what I am principally interested in is his full and conscious awareness of the difference between the "rules" of the *comedia* and those of the Neo-Classicists, his justification of the rules of the former, and his assertion that the classical form of drama is primitive and can—indeed, must—be improved by experimentation. That is to say, the *comedia* is a superior dramatic form. Even making allowances for the polemical aspect of this defence, we note Tirso's conscious attitude towards the *comedia*. His is no longer Lope's half-defensive, half-cynical view: "Que si él, en muchas partes de sus escritos, dice que el no guardar el arte antiguo lo hace por conformarse con el gusto de la plebe—que nunca consintió el freno de las leyes y preceptos—, dícelo por su natural modestia y porque no atribuya la malicia ignorante a arrogancia lo que es política perfección." (p. 145). Clearly, we must accept that Tirso's art is conscious, deliberate and artistic.

Almost no one, however, defended Tirso's art with the same passion that he defended the Lopean *comedia*. The decree of 1625 seems to have put a brake (perhaps not wholly complete) on Tirso's writing of plays. This did not prevent him and his nephew from publishing five *partes* of his *comedias*. In the introductions, we still get glimpses of the aggressive Tirso. Most of the *aprobaciones* seem mere formalities. A notable exception is that by Calderón to the *Quinta parte*. It is clear that Calderón admired Tirso: he praises him for his art and his morality. By the time of his death, however, Tirso seems to have been forgotten by the literary world.[17]

Much of the eighteenth century is characterized by a contempt for the seventeenth-century *comedia*, which, by the French Neo-Classical standards then prevailing in Spain, was regarded as a monument of bad taste. Through political circumstances, French chauvinism had imposed itself on Spanish taste. With the tide running against the Spanish *comedia*, Tirso falls into a period of virtual oblivion. The champions of the new francophile school direct their attacks mainly against Lope and Calderón. Luzán does not even deign to mention Tirso.

While the tide is running strongly against the *comedia* in the eighteenth century, there is an undercurrent which foreshadows its return to favour in the nineteenth century. This may be due in part to the less hostile attitude of the eighteenth-century German critics to Spanish and English drama of the sixteenth and seventeenth centuries, or, rather, to Lessing's acute critique of French Neo-Classical drama. In Spain, however, the revival of interest in Tirso among the reading public is due to book-sellers and printers rather than academics and literary critics. The explanation for this is not clear. The most important name, of course, is that of Doña Teresa de Guzmán, who between 1733 and 1736/7 published 33 *comedias* and one *auto* as *sueltas*.[18] This undoubtely helped to create a more favourable attitude towards the *comedia*. A product of the new atmosphere was Nipho, who was much less hostile to the *comedia*. However, as I. L. McClelland points out, he does not appear to have known Tirso.[19]

Towards the end of the eighteenth century, the revival of interest in Tirso is accelerated, and by the first quarter of the nineteenth century, Tirso is a firm favourite with theatre-goers and critics, as Bushee has shown. Because of the political climate, politically tendentious plays were not allowed to be performed (or, at least, such plays as could be regarded as tendentious—*La vida es sueño*, *La prudencia en la mujer*, etc).[20] The emphasis is therefore on comedy. Modern Tirsian criticism, then, begins with Spanish Romanticism. The critics of this period, of whom the most important is Hartzenbusch, display a great fondness for Tirso's comedies. They are particularly attracted by his wit (using this word in the modern sense).[21] They recognise Tirso's mastery of language, his gifts of characterisation. But they never tire of drawing attention to what they regard as the obscenities in his plays, the immoral behaviour of his characters, and his technical incompetence.[22] In other words, the two basic charges against Tirso are re-affirmed. Furthermore, these critics assumed that the immorality of his plays was a reflection of the immoral life Tirso himself led. The lack of biographical data on Tirso's life did not help the situation. The general attitude of the nineteenth-century critics towards Tirso is summed up in P. Muñoz Peña's lengthy study.[23] He has nothing to add to the existing views on Tirso the man. The critical section of his study repeats the views of earlier nineteenth-century critics: the lack of decorum in Tirso, the unsatisfactory nature of his dramatic technique. Furthermore, most of his criticism is descriptive rather than analytical. Where he does attempt an analytical evaluation of the plays, he adds nothing to the existing views: he merely elaborates on them.

The competition for which Muñoz Peña wrote his work is the starting point of contemporary criticism. Cotarelo y Mori produces valuable information about Tirso's life and works.[24] What really arouses interest is the claim made by Doña Blanca de los Ríos that Tirso was the illegitimate son of the Duke of Osuna.[25] Her theory has been disputed and is no longer very seriously considered, owing to the complete lack of supporting evidence.[26]

However, Doña Blanca has made other valuable contributions to Tirsian studies. Some of her findings help to refute conclusively the stories invented in the nineteenth century about Tirso's misspent youth. She has discovered various documents relating to Tirso's life and work. She has surveyed existing Tirsian criticism and added to it. Her views on Tirso's dramatic technique follow Hartzenbusch's closely. What is interesting is her division of Tirso's plays into various cycles or periods. The last one she calls the "teatro de oposición," because she sees a clear political intent in it. This point is being developed by other critics. She links this with the Junta de Reformación's condemnation of Tirso. Interesting, too, is her view that Tirso's late plays are "Calderonian."[27] She also explores the relationship between Tirso and other contemporary authors, such as Lope and Cervantes. Her theory that Tirso and Cervantes carry on a sustained polemic in their works does not seem completely convincing. On the other hand, her theory that Lope and Tirso, after a period of friendship, fall out is being developed by Ruth L. Kennedy, who sees the network of interrelationships between Tirso and other authors of the day as very important. Most of Doña Blanca's findings are incorporated into her edition, in three volumes, of Tirso's plays. There are, perhaps, two main drawbacks to her critical work. First, it is not methodically arranged. (Had she lived to revise her work, this fault would undoubtedly have been eliminated.) Secondly, she often relies on intuition and a vivid imagination to fill in gaps or to support her hypotheses, and then tends to present her theories as facts. As a result, it is very difficult to separate the grain from the chaff: to do so, indeed, would require many years' labour. However, it must be said that her intuition has not always led to wrong conclusions. At times, while we may disagree with the methods by which she is led to such conclusions, we are forced to admit that the conclusions themselves are not wholly erroneous.

This century has witnessed a spate of work by other critics. Most of it has been concerned with biographical and bibliographical aspects of Tirso, and much of it has been done in the United States. E. W. Hesse's bibliography is, of course, the fundamental tool of all comtemporary research.[28] Ruth L. Kennedy and G. E. Wade have done very valuable work. It appears, as a result, that Tirso moved among the upper classes, which lends support to the theory that his plays contain political and, perhaps, moral criticism of political leaders. G. E. Wade, for example, has followed up Nougué's theory that the *Cigarrales de Toledo* is a sort of *roman à clef* and that most, if not all, of the characters can be identified.[29] The same seems to be true of a number of Tirso's plays.

Some aspects of the relationship between Tirso's plays and the social, political, literary and moral climate of the time are being explored by Ruth L. Kennedy.[30] Using social and political events as a guide, she has been able to date a number of Tirso's plays.[31] Perhaps the only curious feature of her dating is the fact that so many plays can be assigned to the period 1620–1623. But Ruth L. Kennedy herself admits that these may be dates of revision rather than of composition.

Ruth L. Kennedy's examination of the political implications of Tirso's plays is of great importance. She has shown, in a fundamental study, the topical political import of *La prudencia en la mujer*, developing a suggestion first made by Doña Blanca.[32] In a later study, she has shown how Tirso's use of literary satire in a play is, ultimately, politically motivated.[33]

On the other hand, comparatively little literary criticism of Tirso's work is being done. Some valuable editions have been prepared, but these are mainly of Tirso's "serious" plays, i.e., tragedies and historical plays. Only very recently have critics turned seriously to his comedies. The general trend, however, is towards a revaluation of Tirso's dramatic art. A. Castro and, more recently, Casalduero have put forward the suggestion that the text of *El burlador* is by no means as corrupt nor the play itself as carelessly constructed as was once thought.[34] An examination of some other aspects of this play suggests that a considerable amount of care went into its composition.[35] *El condenado por desconfiado* has been shown to be an extremely subtle work dramatically.[36]

Some work has been done on Tirso's comedies. Casalduero's brilliant analysis of *El vergonzoso en palacio* reveals that it is a much more subtle play than had been thought. Some interesting work has been done on other comedies. What seems to me a difficulty gratuitously added to the analysis of Tirso's comic art has been the attempt by a number of critics to apply criteria of Baroque art to Tirso's plays. This is not undesirable in itself, of course. What does, however, lead to difficulties is the attempt to make Tirso's comedies conform to theories of Baroque art laid down *a priori*. An extreme example of this is H. A. Peyton's article, in which he argues that Tirso's art is Baroque because it deflates all idealistic values and because it stresses more earthly and earthy points.[37] This, I think, is an overstatement of the case. Tirso deflates falsely idealistic values; but nowhere can I discern a deflation of love or other genuine ideals such as Peyton asserts exists in Tirso. Rules of Baroque art are also applied to Tirso's *Don Gil de las calzas verdes*. But, as I point out in my analysis, this approach somewhat distorts the point of the play. On the other hand, Casalduero also regards Tirso's art as Baroque; but this epithet is not applied *a priori*, but *a posteriori*, and its meaning to a large extent defined from his analyses of specific plays.

The only work of any length devoted specifically to Tirso's comedies is E. Gijón's monograph: *El humor en Tirso de Molina*.[38] This contains a very valuable summary of various theories of comedy in the introduction. She is undoubtedly right in stating that there is no vindictive, bitter satire in Tirso. Although, as will be realized, her definition of satire is very restricted, she does at times imply that there is some satirical content in Tirso. This is seen, for example, in her very apt and witty description of Juana of *Don Gil* as an "Antitenorio." Her remarks on the "Antitenorio" in Tirso's plays are illuminating as regards Tirso's view of women, a view examined from another angle in her article "Concepto del honor y de la mujer en Tirso de Molina."[39]

In *El humor*, she also makes some other interesting observations. Her view of Antona Carcía, for example, is sympathetic: she points out that Tirso is deliberately uniting in Antona elements which are at first sight disparate. She also points out that *Mari-Hernández la gallega* contains a sub-plot which is a close and systematic parody of the main plot.

E. Gijón concludes that Tirso's view of life is sane and healthy. It is not her intention, of course, to present us with a coherent picture of Tirso's art. Her basic approach is descriptive and, to a certain extent, historical rather than analytical. Thus, although she does not attempt a systematic and thorough interpretation of the data collected, her book is a valuable register of certain very pertinent aspects of Tirso's plays.

All these approaches are valuable directly or indirectly. They point to a long-overdue revaluation of Tirso's comedy. They indicate that Tirso is not a slipshod artist, but a highly conscious craftsman.

However, some vestiges of the earlier view still survive. An interesting example is M. Penna's book.[40] He tries to defend Doña Blanca's thesis of Tirso's illegitimacy with a number of arguments, some plausible, others perhaps over-ingenious. When factual evidence is inconclusive, he tries to find support in what he regards as the twisted moral values in Tirso's plays, and especially in *Marta la piadosa*. I have argued that the values in this comedy are not twisted or perverted. Ultimately, Penna's argument is circular. Tirso was a resentful friar because of his illegitimacy which forced him into a monastery; therefore he wrote plays such as *Marta la piadosa*; therefore he was illegitimate. But it is interesting that Penna, granted a few points, can make a superficially plausible case. There would seem to be a conflict of values in Tirso's plays: on the one hand, he consigns offenders to hell-fire more often perhaps than any other Golden Age dramatist; on the other, he writes such "sacrilegious" plays as *Marta la piadosa*.

It is easy to see what a psychoanalytical critic would make of this. My contention, however, is that Tirso's plays do not call for such tortuous interpretations. They are straight-forward enough if we do not attempt to make them mean what we think they ought to mean. The main difficulty they offer, from the point of view of theme as well as of structure, is due to the subtlety of Tirso's art.

That is why I propose, in this book, to consider the structural function of social and literary satire in a number of Tirso's comedies. Thus, while incidental and largely topical satire will be considered where it seems to contribute towards an understanding of a play, my primary concern will be with the organic function of satire. Furthermore, my main interest is not in Tirso's satire of moral, social and literary foibles or trends *per se*, (an aspect of his comedies which has long been recognised), but rather in his satirical treatment of social and literary conventions for dramatic ends.

The hypothesis which I wish to test is this: that if we consider the satirical implications of Tirso's comedies, they present a sane, coherent view of the world, and that view is presented with consummate skill.

I should make it clear here that I propose to use the term "satire" in its widest sense. Tirso himself claims that he does not satirise individuals:

PORTUGUÉS 3º: ¿Satirizáis?
CASTELLANO 7º: No se hallará que presuma
                              de mí que muerda mi pluma

a nadie, antes si mirais
lo que he impreso y lo que he escrito
por modo y estilo nuevo
solemnizo a quien no debo
buenas obras.[41]

As Ruth L. Kennedy has observed, Tirso doubtless had in mind "formal" satires, i.e., long invectives against definite persons.[42] As I shall show, there are passages in some of his plays which seem to be directed against particular persons, but it is also true to say that none of his plays (and no Golden Age play until, perhaps, after Calderón) can be seen as sustained personal invective.[43] What is certain is that some of his best plays centre around the ridicule of a social or literary convention.

The ways in which such conventions are ridiculed are various. Formally Tirso concentrates on absurd situations which are produced by the adherence of certain individuals to these conventions. In this way, the absurdity of the conventions is made plain. Burlesque, wit, and at times the mere presentation of individuals in a bad light are frequently encountered in Tirso.

In so far as Tirso's plays centre around the ridicule of certain conventions, I shall consider them satiric. It will be clear also that in the social sphere the plays contain a "thesis" or a "point," namely that moral values should be man's guide in his relationships with others. But his point is never made with didactic seriousness or with moral indignation. In the literary sphere, Tirso's satire depends on an implicit contrast with conventional literary devices, figures, and structures.

It is often assumed that satire can be clearly distinguished from comedy. But, as has been pointed out, some of the basic theories of comedy which stress its corrective nature really refer to its satirical intent.[44] H. Bergson's theory of laughter as a social corrective implies that comedy which provokes such laughter is satiric.[45] As Sutherland has pointed out, satire can be regarded as a branch of rhetoric: its aim is to persuade people to accept the satirist's point of view. In so far as Tirso's ridicule of conventions is intended to convince his audience of the validity of his point of view, he is a satirist.

L. J. Potts has an interesting discussion on the differences between comedy and satire.[46] He stresses that the two have much in common, but that, ultimately, they are irreconcilable. This is so because the satirist's viewpoint is entirely subjective. He is a baffled idealist and his standpoint is the ideal. The standpoint of the comic writer is, on the other hand, the norm. The discrepancy between what is and what ought to be is much greater for the satirist who tends to present a deformed or exaggerated picture of the world he sees. This is, in general, an acceptable viewpoint, although it is perhaps too limited for the more subtle varieties of satire. In Tirso's late plays, he seems to have moved towards a more subtle, more complex view of the world, and his comedies are correspondingly more subtle and complex. It is fairly easy to see what or whom he ridicules in his earlier plays. In his later ones, the picture is not so clear. Everything is presented in the light of an irony which is ultimately turned on to the audience itself.

Finally, I should like to review a few theories of comedy which Tirso's plays at times illustrate. Bergson's theory of laughter and Meredith's essay on comedy are well known.[47] A. Nicoll has suggested that most comedies are constructed on situations which are based on one or both of these theories; namely, the mate-hunt situation, and the criticism of a mechanical approach to life.[48] The latter contains, generally, a social problem. These two situations will be found in the majority of the plays analysed.

R. O. Jones has proposed an interesting theory about Golden Age comedy, which I shall refer to as the cathartic theory.[49] His argument is that comedies present instances of social and moral disorder. By experiencing these vicariously, the audience is purged of the temptation to execute them in real life. Thus the existing moral and social order are re-affirmed and strengthened. This is an ingenious theory, and is ultimately based upon a view of drama as ritual. But I am not convinced that it can validly be applied to all Golden Age drama, and particularly to such plays of Tirso's as *Don Gil* and *Marta la piadosa*. Even if one were to accept the Aristotelian theory of tragic catharsis as valid, there is no necessary reason for supposing that the aim of comedy is the same.[50] The intellectual bias of comedy surely requires a more critical attitude on the part of the audience. But the validity of R. O. Jones' application of this theory to Tirso's comedies depends, ultimately, on the person or persons against whom the laughter of the audience is directed. R. O. Jones would see these as Juana and Marta. In my analyses, as will be seen, I argue that the butt of ridicule is really those members of society who, by following social conventions blindly, introduce moral and social chaos into the lives of men and the workings of society. We do not, I think, laugh at Juana and Marta so much as with them. If we are at first inclined to find Juana's male disguise and Marta's *beata* costume ridiculous and productive of chaos, our attitude soon changes when we consider that the chaos they produce is only an apparent chaos which, by the paradox of comedy, is really intended to restore order and sanity where conventional society has produced chaos and confusion. What is being upheld is an ideal order. As I point out, Tirso, like Shakespeare, does not normally ridicule women: in his plays, women uphold order and morality: they do not undermine them. In the context of seventeenth-century society (and even of society in general), the ideal moral order does not exist. The existing, prevailing order is unsatisfactory. The assertion of the ideal order, therefore, is not intended to reinforce the stability of the existing order but rather is a threat to it. Golden Age drama is, I suggest, more questioning, more problematic, more "subversive" (within limits) than is generally thought.[51] That Tirso's plays were seen as subversive seems to be borne out by the decree of the Junta de Reformación. They are directly critical of society. And Tirso had to pay the penalty which, as R. C. Elliott points out, awaits the satirist in society.[52]

A view of comedy which is supported to a large extent by Tirso's plays is that put forward by W. Kerr.[53] If tragedy, according to Kerr, is "an investigation of the possibilities of human *freedom*" (p. 121), comedy is the counter-weight which draws attention to man's limitations. Thus, tragedy is ultimately optimistic, whereas comedy is ultimately pessimistic. The paradoxical nature of Kerr's views seems, nevertheless, justified. We laugh in comedy because it is the only alternative to weeping. Tragedy and comedy between them, then, present a complete picture of human existence. Tragedy historically and existentially, as Kerr stresses, comes first: man is preoccupied with what he can do. Comedy comes afterwards to point out what man cannot do. It is thus, to certain extent, parasitic, depending on the view tragedy contains, but it is nevertheless, necessary.

Which brings me to a word on Golden Age comedy itself. Kerr's definition seems to provide a useful criterion for distinguishing between tragedy and comedy. But, as he points out, some forms of comedy approximate to tragedy, and to the extent that they do so they are "greater" and more serious forms of comedy. In such forms of comedy, the dividing line between tragedy and comedy is blurred. I do not suggest that all Golden Age comedy is great, but it is a fact that the *comedia* blurs the distinction between the tragic and the comic, just as Elizabethan drama does. This produces what I call the "ambiguous tonality" of the *comedia*, in which a delicate balance is maintained between the comic and the tragic. What ultimately determines whether the ending will be "happy" or not is whether there occurs an irreparable violation of the moral law.[54] The ending, then, is another factor which distinguishes comedy from tragedy. This is not so in all drama, but I shall use it as a rough guide in this book. Beyond that, there are no sure criteria. My selection of plays is therefore to a large extent empirical. I have avoided examining plays with "unhappy" endings, as well as, historical and religious or hagiographical plays. I have not considered *Antona García* a strictly historical play because of the freedom with which Tirso handles the historical facts about the heroine, and also because the theme of the play is, I think, neither historical nor political, but moral and social.

NOTES

1 See M. C. Bradbook, *The Growth and Structure of Elizabethan Comedy* (Peregrine Books, 1963. 1st published 1955), Chap. 1, p. 13. Professor K. Whinnom, in his inaugural lecture, *Spanish Literary Historiography* (Univ. of Exeter, 1967), stresses that neglect of the Comedies has "distorted the picture of the Golden Age Drama."

2 *Tirso de Molina. Obras dramáticas completas*, Vol. I (Madrid, 1946), Vol. II (2nd ed., Madrid, 1962), Vol. III (Madrid, 1958).

3 In the introduction to Tirso's *Parte tercera*, it is stated that he had written some 400 plays. E. Cotarelo y Mori draws attention to this on p. 79 of his book, *Tirso de Molina. Investigaciones biobibliográficas* (Madrid, 1893).

4 "Tirso de Molina: Two Bibliographical Studies," *HR*, XXXV (1967), 43–68.

5 See S. Montoto, "Una comedia de Tirso que no es de Tirso," *Archivo Hispalense* (2a época, VII 1946), 99–107.

6 Cf., e.g., his prologue to *El vergonzoso en palacio*. Quoted in A. Castro's ed. of the play in Clásicos Castellanos (7th ed., Madrid, 1963), p. 2.

7 *Investigaciones. . .* , p. 29.

8 Cf., e.g. *Ventura te dé Dios, hijo*: III.vi. p. 1673a.

9 See, e.g., Vol. III of Doña Blanca's ed. (p. 32 a–b), and Fr. G. Placer López's article "Biografía del Ilmo. Fr. Marcos Salmerón," *Estudios*, IV (1948), 554–60.

10 "A Re-appraisal of Tirso's Relations to Lope and his Theatre," *BC*, XVII (1965), no. 2, 23–34 and XVIII (1966), no. 1, 1–13.

11 Cotarelo notes this on p. 59 of *Investigaciones*.

12 *Poesía española*, (5th ed., Madrid, 1966), p. 214. See also *Epistolario de Lope de Vega*, ed. de Agustín G. de Amezúa, III, p. 206.

13 *Poesía española* (5th ed., Madrid, 1966), p. 214.

14 See E. Cotarelo, *Bibliografía de las controversias sobre la licitud del teatro en España*. (Madrid, 1904).

15 "Attacks on Lope and his Theatre, 1617–1621," in *Hispanic Studies in Honor of N. B. Adams*, eds. J. E. Keller and K. L. Selig, Univ. of North Carolina. Studies in Romance Languages and Literatures, no. 59, (Chapel Hill, 1966). See also: A. González Palencia: "Quevedo, Tirso y las comedias ante la Junta de Reformación," *BRAE*, XXV (1946), 43–84.

16 This valuable defence has been reprinted in A. Castro's ed. of *El vergonzoso en palacio*, in Clásicos Castellanos (7th ed., Madrid, 1963). My refs. will be to this ed. A survey of the main points of this defence has been made by J. H. Parker in his article "Tirso de Molina, defensor de la comedia nueva," *Revista Univ. de San Carlos*, XII (1948), 39–48.

17 See A. H. Bushee, *Three Centuries of Tirso de Molina* (Philadelphia, 1939).

18 For details, see A. H. Bushee, especially chap. V: "The Guzmán Edition of Tirso de Molina's *Comedias*."

19 *Tirso de Molina. Studies in Dramatic Realism* (Liverpool, 1948), especially the "Introduction."

20 Doña Blanca has drawn attention to this. See Vol. I of her ed. of Tirso (Madrid, 1946), pp. 13, 22.

21 Cf., e.g., Martínez de la Rosa's statement: "... mostróse superior a todos ellos en malicia y sal cómica." In *Obras literarias*, II (Paris, 1827), 449–50.

22 See the comments of Hartzenbusch in his two eds. of Tirso's plays: (1) *Teatro escogido de Fray Gabriel Téllez*, 12 vols. (Madrid, 1839–42); and (2) *Comedias escogidas de Fray Gabriel Téllez*, B.A.E., V (Madrid, 1848).

23 *El teatro del Maestro Tirso de Molina. Estudio crítico-literario* (Valladolid, 1889).

24 In his *Investigaciones*. Much of this information, with some modifications, is also to be found in the intro. to his ed. of Tirso's plays in N.B.A.E., IV, IX (Madrid, 1906–1907).

25 *El enigma biográfico de Tirso de Molina* (Madrid, 1928). Her arguments are reprinted in the introduction to Vol. I of her ed. of Tirso.

26 See, e.g., M. L. Ríos, "Tirso de Molina no es bastardo," *Estudios*, V (1949), 1–13; M. L. Ríos and J. Núñez Barbosa, "La hipótesis de doña Blanca de los Ríos de Lampérez sobre la fe de nacimiento de Tirso de Molina," *Atenea*, XC (1948), 299–314; M. Penedo Rey, "Ampliación al trabajo del Rev, P. Fr. Miguel L. Ríos 'Tirso de Molina no es bastardo,'" *Estudios*, V (1949), 14–18. A summing-up of the situation is made by A. Cioranescu in his article "La biographie de Tirso de Molina. Points de repère et points de vue," *BH*, LXIV (1962), 157–92, part of which is reprinted as an appendix to K. Vossler, *Lecciones sobre Tirso de Molina* (Madrid, 1965).

27 See, e.g., her introduction to *La celosa de sí misma* in Vol. II of her ed., and also various of her remarks in her introduction to Vol. I, e.g., pp. 39, 47–50, 63; see also her remark on the "Calderonian" monologue of D. Manrique in her introduction to *Cómo han de ser los amigos* in Vol. I, p. 267b.

28 "Catálogo bibliográfico de Tirso de Molina," *Estudios*, V (1949), 781–889. Supplements are in later numbers of *Estudios*.

29 "Tirso's *Cigarrales de Toledo*: Some Clarifications and Identifications," *HR*, XXXIII (1965), 246–72; "Tirso's Friends," *BC*, XIX (1967), no. 1, 1–6. A. Nougué's book is *L'Oeuvre en prose de Tirso de Molina: 'Los Cigarrales de Toledo' et 'Deleytar aprovechando'* (Paris, 1962).

30 See, e.g., "Certain Phases of the Sumptuary Decrees of 1623 and their Relation to Tirso's Theatre," *HR*, X (1942), 91–115; "The New Plaza Mayor of 1620 and the Reflection in the Literature of the Time," *HR*, XII (1944), 49–57; and "The Madrid of 1617–25. Certain Aspects of Social, Moral, and Educational Values," in *Estudios Hispánicos. Homenaje a Archer M. Huntington*, Vol. I (Wellesley, Mass., 1952), pp. 275–309.

31 See, e.g., "On the Date of Five Plays by Tirso de Molina," *HR*, X (1942), 183–214; and "Studies for the Chronology of Tirso's Theatre," *HR*, XI (1943), 17–46.

32 "*La prudencia en la mujer* and the Ambient that Brought it Forth," *PMLA*, LXIII (1948), 1131–90.

33 "Literary and Political Satire in Tirso's *La fingida Arcadia*," in *The Renaissance Reconsidered. Smith College Studies in History*, XLIV (Northampton, Mass., 1964), pp. 91–110.

34 A. Castro in his ed. of the play in Clás. Castellanos (Madrid, 7th ed., 1963), Casalduero in his articles "El desenlace de *El burlador de Sevilla*," in *Studia philologica et litteraria in honorem L. Spitzer* (Berne, 1958), and "Contribución al estudio del tema de Don Juan en el teatro español," *Smith College Studies in Modern Languages*, XIX (1938), nos. 3–4.

35 See D. Rogers, "Fearful Symmetry: The Ending of *El Burlador de Sevilla*," *BHS*, XLI (1964), 141–59; and a more idiosyncratic study by H. Bihler, "Más detalles sobre ironía, simetría y simbolismo en *El Burlador de Sevilla* de Tirso de Molina" in *Actas del primer congreso internacional de Hispanistas*, (Oxford, 1964), pp. 213–18.

36 See T. E. May, "El condenado por desconfiado," *BHS*, XXXV (1958), 138–56.

37 "Some Baroque Aspects of Tirso de Molina," *RR*, XXXVI (1945), 43–69.

38 (Madrid, 1959).

39 *Estudios*, V (1949), 479–655.

40 *Don Giovanni e il mistero di Tirso* (Turin, 1958).

41 *Antona García*, Act III, scene iii, p. 439b.

42 "A Reappraisal of Tirso's Relations to Lope and his Theatre," *BC*, XVIII (1966), 1–13.

43 Doña Blanca, of course, suggests that certain plays, notably *Marta la piadosa* and *El amor médico*, are sustained satires directed against Lope de Vega.

44 See J. Sutherland, *English Satire* (Cambridge, 1962).

45 *Le Rire* (Paris, 1900). See also E. Aubouin, *Technique et psychologie du Comique* (Paris, 1948).

46 *Comedy* (4th impression, London 1966; 1st published 1949), especially chap. 6: 'The boundaries of comedy.'

47 These two essays (Bergson's in an English translation) are reprinted in *Comedy*, with an introduction and appendix by W. Sypher (Doubleday Anchor Books, New York, 1956).

48 *The Theory of Drama* (London, 1931).

49 *"El perro del hortelano* y la visión de Lope," *Filología*, X (1964), 135–42. This theory has much in common with C. L. Barber's *Shakespeare's Festive comedy* (Princeton, 1959).

50 See, e.g., R. Piddington, *The Psychology of Laughter* (2nd ed., 1963; 1st ed., 1933).

51 E. Auerbach, in his brilliant work, *Mimesis*, has asserted that Golden Age literature is not problematic, it does not question the existing order in any way.

52 *The Power of Satire* (3rd printing, Princeton University Press, 1966; 1st published 1960).

53 *Tragedy and Comedy* (London, 1968).

54 This is, of course, one aspect of the principle of poetic justice which, as A. A. Parker has pointed out, is a characteristic feature of the *comedia*. See A. A. Parker, *The Approach to the Spanish Drama of the Golden Age* (London, 1957). B. W. Wardropper has pointed out the close resemblances between Golden Age comedy and tragedy. See B. W. Wardropper, "Calderón's Comedy and His Serious Sense of Life" in *Hispanic Studies in Honor of Nicholson B. Adams* (Chapel Hill, Univ. of North Carolina Press, 1966), pp. 179–93.

PART I

PERSONAL RELATIONSHIPS

CHAPTER I

Don Gil de las calzas verdes. The Reductio ad Absurdum of a Dramatic Device

The three plays which I propose to consider first are *Don Gil de las calzas verdes*, *La celosa de sí misma*, and *El amor médico*. They may be conveniently examined together for various reasons, notwithstanding the fact that *Don Gil* is separated from the other two by some seven years.

First, they all have in common the use of disguise as a central feature of the plot-structure. The convenience of disguise as a dramatic device has been discussed by V. O. Freeburg.[1] Basically, the assumption of disguise serves to complicate the plot; its abandonment unravels the complication. It has often been noted that disguise, and, in particular, male disguise, is one of Tirso's favourite dramatic devices. One might be inclined to draw the conclusion that Tirso tends to use convenient and elementary devices in the structuring of a plot, were it not for the fact that these plays show how he rings the changes on what is basically a naive dramatic device. Tirso's unconventional use of disguise, therefore, would indicate that he was interested in exploring its dramatic possibilites.

Disguise occurs in two forms in these plays; the woman disguised as a man (the so-called "female-page" figure) is central to *Don Gil*; the veiled woman, or *tapada*, to *La celosa*. In *El amor médico*, both figures occur. In these three plays, disguise cannot be regarded purely as a technical device; it is also a means by which Tirso explores the problem of identity and personality. Yet this philosophical and psychological exploration cannot be divorced from Tirso's exploration of the dramatic possibilities and implications on the technical level. The two levels are inter-related and complementary.

Closely associated with Tirso's unconventional use of disguise is the unorthodox construction of his plots. Again, these three plays provide us with fascinating examples of Tirso's experiments in dramatic form. I shall attempt to show that the traditional view that Tirso is indifferent to the niceties of dramatic technique is based on a failure to see the originality of his dramatic structures. These three plays offer different solutions, each satisfactory in itself, to problems in dramatic form.

These plays also allow us to identify some of the characteristics of Tirso's comedies. There is, first of all, his fondness for absurd situations. This is demonstrated especially in *La celosa de sí misma*, where the absurdity starts with the title. That the absurd situations are normally the result of a satirical handling of dramatic and social conventions is brought out by all three of the plays. In the satirical handling of his material, Tirso's ironic view of life plays a large part.

Another feature of Tirso's art is his development technique, by which he re-works or develops in some works situations, motifs, etc., found in other plays. It may be reasonably assumed that in a number of instances, at least, a play, A, which contains a more extensive development of a situation which exists in embryonic form in another, B, is probably later than B. While recognising the possibility that what may be taken as an embryo may in fact be a reference in short-hand to an earlier, more elaborately developed situation, we may admit the (limited) value of this technique as an aid to establishing the chronology (or, at least, the inter-relationship) of some of Tirso's plays. In any case, its importance for a study of his dramatic technique is self-evident.

Finally, the plays are interesting for the light they cast on certain theories of comedy. R. O. Jones has seen a number of Golden Age comedies, *Don Gil* and *El amor médico* among them, as "vacaciones morales."[2] The view that comedy aims at strengthening and reinforcing our sense of moral and social order by allowing us vicarious indulgence in disorderly behaviour owes much to the Aristotelian theory of the tragic catharsis. A closer look at the above-mentioned comedies, however, would seem to cast some doubt on the ultimate validity of his theory when applied indiscriminately to Golden Age comedy. On the other hand, W. Kerr's theory of comedy, which concentrates on comedy as an element in the tragedy-comedy complex and its function in philosophical terms seems to throw considerable light on *El amor médico*. As regards the basic situations on which these comedies are built, A. Nicoll's view still seems valid.[3] He sees two basic elements in comedy: the first, the mate-hunt; the second, the conflict between society and the individual. These two elements are related to the theories proposed by Meredith and Bergson. In many comedies, as Nicoll points out, these two elements may be found combined. This is true of the comedies which will be analysed in the first three chapters.

These three plays, then, provide a convenient introduction to my study of some of Tirso's comedies. They are among his best works and thus illustrate important aspects and problems of his dramatic art.

* * * * *

In an article which attempts to view *Don Gil de las calzas verdes* as an example of baroque dramatic art, E. W. Hesse and W. C. McCrary have claimed that there is an incompatibility between the ending of the play and the action which leads up to it: "La repentina admisión de verdadero amor de doña Juana por don Martín al final de la comedia es el resultado lógico de la acción, pero no especialmente de la acción en las tablas."[4] To explain this tension, they suggest that Tirso is here employing they term "forma interior," i.e., the dramatic objectification in opposite terms of inner feelings. Thus, Juana's vengeance is really an expression of her wounded love. A traditional, outer form is used to express a human, psychological problem. Their article is interesting in that it represents an attempt to interpret Tirsian comedy in the light of theories of baroque art applied to literature. It is valuable in that it draws attention to two very important aspects of the play: the ending and the structure. These are features of Tirso's dramatic art which have been traditionally singled out for severe criticism, but which, I hope to show, are crucial to the understanding of the Tirsian art form.

It is obvious, however, that much remains to be done, for it seems that the interpretation offered in this article is in some ways unsatisfactory. I do not propose to discuss whether Tirso's art-form is baroque or not, but I should like to examine the structure of the play more closely. This will make it clear that Juana's declaration of love is not—indeed, cannot—be the logical result of the action: the play does not set out to prove that Juana loves Martín. Her love for him is never called into question, and if this fact is taken into account, the interpretation of the play by these critics may need some modification. Nor is the nature of Juana's "vengeance" properly analysed.

Secondly, once it is seen that there is no tension between the stage action and the psychic action, the postulation of a consequent "forma interior" is invalidated. In fact, this term tells us very little about the real structure of this play. It does, indeed, draw attention to the presence of the so-called "third dimension," i.e., psychological analysis, in Tirso's play. Tirso's portrayal of feminine psychology is skilful and profound: Juana's

love has indeed suffered a severe blow. But we are not meant primarily
to think that the formal action of the play is to be seen as a translation of
Juana's offended love into apparent vindictiveness. Juana, significantly,
never allows her emotions to get the better of her in the play: the lesson
taught her by the events preceding the action proper has been well learnt.

There is, however, an unusual structural pattern in *Don Gil*, the identification of which would help us to understand the play itself as well as
the Tirsian dramatic structure more fully, for Tirso experiments constantly
with the art form which he receives from Lope. This pattern is hinted at in
a later article by E. W. Hesse, in which he analyses the complexity of the
play, clearly disentangling the various strands of action which form the
complex plot, and subtly analysing the motivations of the characters and
the themes around which the play is constructed.[5] He draws our attention
to the fact that there is a "play" (Doña Juana's machinations) within the
drama (Juana's pursuit of the unfaithful Martín). This is a vital point,
but its implications are not fully developed by Hesse. His article, moreover, follows too closely the approach employed in the previous one: the
vengeance-love opposition, for example, is taken too far.

Surprisingly, perhaps, a central feature of the structure of the play,
not considered in the articles mentioned, has not been properly analysed
yet: this is the conventional dramatic device of the female page. Carmen
Bravo-Villasante has drawn attention to the multiplication of the figure of
Don Gil in the play and notes that the various actions hinge on the use
of disguise. But her analysis does not go very far.[6] A. Valbuena Prat has
referred to the elements of parody contained in the play. He does not
develop his statement, but it is vital for a full appreciation of the comedy,
and we shall return to it later.[7]

Tirso's fondness for ringing the changes on conventional dramatic devices will become apparent as our study of his plays progresses. It will also
be noted that these changes usually contain an element of the grotesque,
which is itself often an indication of a satirical intention. The *mujer
vestida de hombre* is a figure who recurs over and over again in Tirso's
plays, and he hardly ever uses her in the conventional way.

Don Gil de las calzas verdes is a marvellous example of Tirso's unconventional use of "la disfrazada de hombre." Juana, to begin with, is not
strictly a female page. In fact, she stresses she is no page when she takes
Caramanchel into her service:

[JUANA:]   porque desde hoy te recibo
                  en mi servicio.
CARAMANCHEL: ¡Lenguaje

JUANA:
nuevo! ¿Quién ha visto paje
con lacayo?
          Yo no vivo
sino sólo de mi hacienda,
ni paje en mi vida fui:
vengo a pretender aquí
un hábito o encomienda;

(I.ii. p. 1718a)[8]

Her declaration provokes an incredulous reaction in Caramanchel, and
he counters with words which contain the germ of the situation to be
developed in the comedy:

CARAMANCHEL: Ninguno ha habido,
de los amos que he tenido
ni poeta ni capón;
parecéisme lo postrero,

(I.ii. p. 1718a)

There is, first, a hint of the tendency of the *comedia* to satirise its own conventions, which is further developed in the course of the play: no woman
disguised as a man, Tirso seems to be saying, can ever convincingly pass
herself off as one—especially if she does not pretend to be a page; thus
the attention of the audience is constantly drawn to the artificiality of the
situation on stage. Closely linked to this, is the note of ambiguous sexuality introduced at the very begining, a factor which is going to play an
important part in the comedy, and which is part of the grotesque effect
achieved by the multiplication of the Gil figure.

The effect on the structure of the play is evident. It has been said that
the plot is perhaps the most complex in the whole of Golden Age drama.
In spite of the apparent slips pointed out by G. E. Wade, one can only be
amazed by the complexity of the mind which produced the play.[9]

The basic outline, however, is simple enough. Juana disguises herself
as a man in order to pursue and win back her fickle lover. This she
succeeds in doing thanks to her machinations. Thus the basic situation
and its outcome are conventional.

The real complexity of the play, as Hesse has pointed out, lies in the
development of the plot, the means by which Juana brings Martín to heel,
or, as Hesse puts it, the "play" within the drama. This is where the
originality of the comedy lies. The underlying pattern of the play consists
of an initial split into three main strands of action (real or narrated) which
converge in the third act. An analysis of these strands of action has been

made by Hesse. It seems, however, that something more can be added to it. On closer analysis, the structure of the play appears strikingly original and the close connexion between form and content becomes evident. Secondly, it will be necessary to try and analyse the reasons for the complexity of the structure.

It seems to me that Hesse's statement that *Don Gil* is cast in the form of a play within a drama can be developed fruitfully. The structure of the play, in fact, can be accurately compared to a set of three Chinese boxes or a series of three concentric circles of diminishing radii whose focal point is to be found in that scene in the third act where we are presented with four Giles in succession.

The outer box or frame is provided by the Juana-Martín-Inés situation. Martín's morally irresponsible action is parodied in the second frame by the situation created by Juana in the Gil-Inés-Juan intrigue. The first link between the two frames is the ambiguous Gil figure who is Gil de Albornoz (Martín) in the first, and Gil de las calzas verdes (Juana) in the second. The second link is the fact that Juana-Gil is a parody of Martín-Gil, i.e., Juana is holding the mirror up to Martín. The travesty of Martín's actions is emphasised by the enlarging of the intrigue to include Clara. This is, so to speak, parody by augmentation. A third frame is provided by the Elvira-Miguel-Inés intrigue. The Gil figure provides a double link between this frame and the others: first, Miguel is impersonating the 'real' Don Gil, while the latter has been flirting with Elvira, who bears an amazing resemblance to him. The links and resemblances are not as extravagant as they may at first seem. Elvira is Juana herself in her wholly feminine aspect. Miguel is, likewise, Martín, but in his less flattering aspect, i.e., the fickle, unprincipled Martín who repudiated the obligations owed to Juana by the Martín who loved her. Secondly, the Gil figure seems to acquire somewhat greater individuality by being presented as someone who is neither Martín (who impersonates him) nor Juana-Elvira (whom he loves). But Gil's love for Elvira and his "almost" perfect resemblance to her make it clear that Gil and Elvira are only two different aspects of Juana.

The dramatic situation is thus quite extraordinary. We get, first, the tendency in the *comedia* to embody facets of character in dramatic figures (cf. the ghost in *El caballero de Olmedo*—part ghost, part Alonso's fears). But we also get a situation akin to one in modern drama which M. C. Bradbrook has referred to as different personalities trading under the same name.[10] In Tirso, we get different aspects of the one personality assuming different names as if they were individual and separate entities. The parallel, however, must not be pushed too far, although we shall meet similar situations again in Tirso. Tirso is aware of the conflicting aspects of an individual's character, but he does not, as M. A. Peyton would have us think, imply a disintegration of character.[11] The integrality of the character is not yet called into question, as it is in the literature of our times.

To recapitulate briefly, the structure of the play resembles a set of Chinese boxes with a definite focal point in the third act. There is a series of definite links, essentially psychological in nature, between the different boxes. But to understand the part this structure plays in the comedy, we must examine the actions of the characters.

Martín's abandonment of Juana, whom he had promised to marry, is the starting point of the play. His action betrays an attitude of callous irresponsibility: though conscious of his obligations towards Juana (who he has been told is pregnant), he finds the lure of the rich Inés too strong to resist:

> que el interés
> y beldad de doña Inés
> excusan la culpa mía.
>
> (II.ix. p. 1735a)

But this weakness is only one aspect of a spineless character. Martín is at first an unresisting puppet in the hands of his father, and it is perhaps for this reason that his punishment is not more severe.

In fact, it is on the shoulders of the fathers of Martín and Inés that the brunt of the moral responsibility falls. The part played by these parents is not fully recognised by Esmeralda Gijón in her analysis of the play.[12] Martín's father, from what we are told of his conduct (for he does not appear on stage), is a thoroughly despicable person. Driven by his lust for money, he encourages Martín to abandon Juana and go to Madrid as Don Gil de Albornoz in order to marry Doña Inés. Futhermore, he is deliberately deceiving his friend, Don Pedro, for the Don Gil he offers as a husband to Inés is none other than his son, Martín, who, he asserts, is pledged to marry Juana (I.iii. p. 1719a). Don Pedro, Inés's father, is also an unworthy parent. His greed and, more important, his acceptance of the social conventions of the time by which money and class are regarded as the normal criteria in arranged marriages blind him to the fact that it is wrong to marry off his daughter to a man he does not know, especially since he is aware that Inés already loves Juan. When Inés attempts to offer resistance, he adopts a tyrannical attitude. Ironically, folly is made to frustrate itself in this comedy. It is cupidity which leads Andrés to deceive Pedro, and greed and social conformity which make Pedro take Andrés at his word, and which fail to arouse Pedro's suspicion at the unlikely name of Gil or to the possibility that the second Gil may also be a humbug. Thus does Juana get the chance to prevent the marriage.

It is clear that the attitudes of Don Andrés and Don Pedro are unreasonable and immoral. Their plans, according to the conventions of the *comedia*, are thus doomed to frustration. Generally, it is the children themselves who circumvent unreasonable parental opposition in order to fulfil their love, but in this play, Martín passively accepts his father's suggestion, while Inés, after an initial show of rebellion, is soon head over heels in love with Don Gil—as she thinks.

So, while the ultimate moral responsibility lies with their parents, Martín and Inés are both guilty of irresponsibility in an immediate sense. Martín is a pathetic, passive, spineless and immature creature. He has no real understanding of the nature of love and its responsibilities. Nor is he free from a certain cynicism, as is seen in II.viii, when he agrees to fight a duel with Don Juan over Inés—a month after his marriage to the latter. This cynical attitude is extended to his treatment of Juana:

> pero entretendréla agora
> escribiéndola, y después
> que posea a doña Inés,
> puesto que mi ausencia llora,
> le diré que tome estado
> de religiosa.
>
> (II.x. p. 1736a)

He is to be punished for this as well as for failing to stand up to his father, and his pathetic attempt to shift the whole responsibility on to the shoulders of Don Andrés in III.i is of no avail. Inés, on the other hand, is to be punished for her fickleness. She, too, reveals her immaturity when she fails to show that she is fully aware of her obligations to Juan. As we shall see, it is essential to take into account this aspect of Inés's character if we are properly to understand the structure of the play.

Juana's counter-measures against Martín initiate the action of the play. She disguises herself as a man in order to pursue Martín and win him back because she loves him (II.i). This aim remains constant throughout the play. Juana reaffirms her intention later in the play:

> que he de perseguir, si puedo,
> Quintana, a mi engañador

con uno y con otro enredo,
hasta que cure su amor
con mi industria o con su miedo

(III.iv. p. 1747b)

This curing of Martín, which is bringing him back to his senses, is what
Juana refers to when she says immediately afterwards: "La mujer / venga
agravios desta suerte." (III.iv. p. 1747b). Thus it seems that Hesse and
McCrary interpret the word "vengeance" wrongly. Juana's *enredos* are
not examples principally of real or apparent vindictive revenge: they are
intended to foil Martín's plans and to awaken his conscience. Thus there
is no real conflict between the action of the play and the ending: the latter
is a logical and inevitable result of the former. Martín, at the end of the
play, is made to realise that he can no longer evade his responsibilities by
flight, disguise, or cynicism. All possible avenues of escape are blocked
to him: the only way out is by marring Juana. Let us see how Martín is
forced to marry the woman he abandoned.

While Juana's use of male disguise and her winning back Martín in the
end are conventional dramatic situations, an unconventional feature is the
multiplication of the Gil figure. This is the characteristic feature of the
play. Valbuena's statement, which I referred to earlier, hints at this:

En determinadas formas, Tirso juega con la intriga, y compone una especie de
"ballet" maravilloso, de gracia y malicia, pintoresco en las costumbres de ciudad
y de aldea, en que la trama inverosímil se combina con la parodia de motivos
usuales en el drama de honor o caracteres. Quizá el ejemplo más interesante sea
el de *Don Gil de las calzas verdes*.

In fact, it is the conventional use of male disguise by offended heroines
which is parodied in this play. Juana's assumption of male disguise—
perfectly motivated in her case (at least in terms of the dramatic conventions of the age)—leads to the assumption of her false personality by three
other characters in the play. The result is a ludicrous conglomeration of
four Giles in the final act.

The initial event which sets off this chain reaction is, of course, Juana's
disguising herself as Don Gil. However, we must not forget that Don Gil
de las calzas verdes is actually an usurper of the identity of the "real"
Don Gil de Albornoz (which is Martín's assumed personality). In other
words, Juana supplants Martín's deception with another deception (thus
parodying it): she usurps his assumed personality. Her immediate aim
is to forestall Martín and prevent him from courting Inés. However, so
successful is Juana's plan that not only does Martín find that his false

personality has been usurped and that he, the real Don Gil, is regarded as the spurious version, but he himself is led to assume the personality of the usuper of his assumed personality by wearing green breeches, i.e., he is forced to repudiate his own self. This is one aspect of the absurd position into which the spineless Martín is forced.

The destruction of the identity of the "real" Don Gil de Albornoz is carried a step further in the Elvira episode. Here he is presented as a usurper of the identity of Don Gil de las calzas verdes, who now claims to be the "real" Gil de Albornoz. This false Gil is Don Miguel, a false friend of a certain Don Martín. Don Miguel, as has been pointed out, is not entirely an invention: he is really the less flattering aspect of Martín. The immediate effect of Elvira's story is to alienate Martín even further from Inés, who now regards Don Miguel as a thoroughly unprincipled man, and, furthermore, one whom she cannot marry, since he is pledged to Elvira.

There are two further points which we need to note about this episode. The first has been referred to already: the Gil figure is here made more independent. But as it is only a shadow, a fiction, it may be identified with Juana (this is convenient for the perpetration of irresponsible actions which serve to frustrate Martín's plans), or with Martín (who must bear the consequences of those actions), or with anyone else (Clara, Juan), and *therefore*—with the help of wit—with no one at all! Secondly, there is a further change of sex in Juana's new *persona*, Elvira. The first change, which takes place in the second of these Chinese boxes, is from female to male (or pseudo-male), i.e., from Juana to Gil. The third box, which further complicates the situation, paradoxically provides a truer reflection of it, not only in the identities (real or feigned) of Juana, Martín and Gil, but also in the sexes of these characters. Gil, it is to be noted, who loves and resembled Elvira, is thus bi-sexual, hermaphroditic. We get therefore a dramatic situation in which one action is reflected, as in a mirror, in another, which is reflected in yet another, each successive reflection being a deformation revealing a different aspect of the problem. The Chinese boxes structure is the obvious vehicle for such a plan.

However, Juana realizes that Inés cannot be allowed to fall too deeply in love with Don Gil de las calzas verdes and the latter's promiscuous exploits coupled with the exploitation of the ambiguous nature of Inés's love (which we shall discuss shortly) are used to keep Inés at bay. At the same time, Juana foresees Martín's attempt to identify himself with Don Gil de las calzas verdes, and so she perpetrates a number of acts, the consequences of which will have to be borne by Martín. At the end of the play a number of persons are thirsting for Martín's blood: Fabio and Decio, who think Don Gil wounded Juan; Celio and Antonio, who intend to compel Don Gil to marry Clara; and, finally, Don Diego, who will be revenged on Martín for the murder of Juana. Martín, naturally, helps to condemn himself by wearing green breeches, and he finds himself unable to disclaim responsibility for Don Gil's actions. Juana, however, is in total control of the situation: her intention is not to place Martín's life in jeopardy. He is to be forced into a corner and made to realise his own folly. He cannot escape his responsibilities by assuming a false identity. Martín, in fact, as Hesse and E. Gijón have pointed out, is presented with a brilliant travesty of his own actions. His assumed identity is usurped and replaced by another identity (nominally the same), which is foisted upon him willy-nilly, and which he cannot disclaim. His trick has been turned against him and he becomes a victim of his own game. This is underlined by the fact that he, Don Gil de Albornoz, is frustrated by Don Gil de las calzas verdes, with whom, in the course of the play, he has identified himself.

Martín, moreover, is not the only character who repudiates his own identity to assume that of Don Gil. Juan and Clara also declare in the third act that they are Don Gil. One result of this multiplication of Gil is to reduce to absurdity the personality of Don Gil. Personality is of necessity something individual. Thus the multiplication of the Gil personality is a denial of its existence. The Gil figure is shown up for what it is—a deceitful mask. And a mask can be worn by anyone.

The result is that Martín is completely checkmated. Not only is his false personality usurped and shattered by being reduced to absurdity, but apparently he is also to be held to account for the irresponsibility of the usurper's actions. But though Martín's attitude has been an irresponsible one, he has been prevented in spite of himself—thanks to Juana—from actually infringing the moral law, i.e. from marrying Inés. So Juana's machinations have not only served to ridicule and chasten Martín, but also to save him from himself and from his unprincipled father. Therefore, after being taught a lesson, he is saved from more severe punishment. Juana's revelation of her identity ends the confusion, and order is restored by the marriages at the end.

The secondary implications of the unusual use of the device of the disguised woman still remain to be examined. Esmeralda Gijón has very neatly described Juana as the Antitenorio. This description is apt as far as it goes, but one may add that Juana could with equal fitness be described as an Antitenoria.

The play is not only an attack on the moral irresponsibility of men in their relations with women. We have already seen that the unprincipled behaviour of Don Andrés and Don Pedro serves as the moral background to the play's action. This lack of moral standards is reflected in the children, and the comedy thus deals with the irresponsible and frivolous attitudes of women as well. In fact, the question of responsibility in personal relations is the general moral theme of the play.

Along with Martín, both Inés and Clara are ridiculed for their fickleness in *Don Gil de las calzas verdes*. Inés abandons Juan to turn to Don Gil, and Clara falls in love with Gil at first sight. The portrayal of Inés in particular is highly ironical. When her father insists that she leave Juan and marry Don Gil, she, unlike Martín, grows rebellious. She warns her father that he would be wrong to marry her off for financial considerations. Her contempt for Don Gil is unbounded:

> ¿Don Gil?
> ¿Marido de villancico?
> ¡Gil! ¡Jesus! no me lo nombres;
> ponle un cayado y pellico.
>
> (I.v. p. 1721b)

In the *huerta del Duque*, however, Inés performs a volte-face. She falls in love with Don Gil even before knowing his name, and when she discovers she is in love with the only lately-despised Don Gil, she no longer looks with contempt upon the pastoral name: "Ya por el don Gil me muero, / que es un brinquillo el don Gil." (I.viii. p. 1724b) When Juan accuses her of fickleness, she finds it to her glory to proclaim that *la donna è mobile*:

> La hermosura
> del mundo tanto es mayor
> cuanto es la naturaleza
> mas varia en él; y así quiero
> ser mudable, porque espero
> tener ansí más belleza.[13]
>
> (II.ii. p. 1730a)

This impudent rationalisation of fickleness betrays moral irresponsibility and emotional immaturity. This last is stressed when in Act III she is courted by four Giles in succession (one of them is actually Juan). She is perplexed and cannot tell in her blindness (symbolised by the night) which of them is the Gil she loves.[14] She is obsessed by the figure of Don Gil, but is no longer sure who exactly Don Gil is. She does not know whom she loves precisely because the Don Gil she loves is neither a man nor, in fact, a real person.

Nor does it seem as if we are meant to excuse Inés on the grounds that she is young and inexperienced. Young she may be, but she is certainly not naive. She carries on a secret affair with Juan and when her father overhears her promising to marry him, she can brazen it out. She, like Martín, is not without cynicism: she exploits Juan's love for her in order to try and rid herself of the odious Gil de Albornoz and also to protect at the same time her beloved Gil de las calzas verdes (II.ii. p. 1730a.b.). It is only Martín's own cynicism (as has been pointed out) which saves him. Inés's request to Juan also reveals in her a streak of wanton cruelty. It is not only evident in her heartless jilting of Juan and her cynical exploitation of his love for her, but also in her desire to have the bearded Gil murdered and her willingness to expose Juan to being killed. And, in Act III when she learns that Don Gil de las calzas verdes has been "unfaithful" to her, she has no scruples in thinking of repeating her offer to Juan, on condition that he murder the other Gil this time (III.iii. p. 1746b). Inés's portrait is, on the whole, an unflattering one.

The multiplication of the Gil figure proves that Don Gil is really a chimaera. Inés is ridiculed for pursuing a will-o'-the-wisp, and the disintegration of Don Gil is meant to punish her by leaving her frustrated. She has to return to Juan chastened and punished for her fickleness. She, too, has to be made aware of the responsibilities which love and a personal relationship entail.

There is another element which we must take into account in the analysis of the characters of Inés and Clara. The nature of Inés's love for Don Gil and of her friendship for Elvira is ambiguous. When Gil-Martín is introduced to Inés, she reacts violently: he cannot be her Don Gil:

> ¿Don Gil tan lleno de barbas?
> Es el Don Gil que yo adoro
> un Gilito de esmeraldas.

> (I.x. p. 1726b)

This does not seem to be merely, as Hesse puts it, an expression of her aesthetic scorn. There is a hint of a lesbian element in Inés's character. This is emphasised by the ambiguous nature of her friendship for Elvira. As Juana explains to Quintana, Inés is a great friend of Elvira's:

> Porque afirma quiere bien
> a un galán de quien retrato
> soy vivo, y que en mi presencia
> la aflige menos la ausencia

de su proceder ingrato.

(II.i. p. 1728b)

Elvira is thus a Gil-substitute for Inés who affirms this shortly afterwards:

que aunque no puedo negar
que te amo, porque pareces
a quien adoro, mereces
por ti sola enamorar
a un Adonis, a un Narciso
y al sol que tus ojos viere.

(II.v. p. 1731a)

These words, to say the least, appear ambiguous. They are hardly words one would expect one woman to address to another. More significant is the use of "Narciso." Since Narcissus can only love himself, it is thus a female Narcissus, i.e., a woman, who Inés thinks may fall in love with Elvira. But if the use of "Adonis" and three nouns in the masculine mean anything, this woman must be a manly one, i.e., a lesbian. There is also the further complexity that there is such a Narcissus, viz., Don Gil, who is Elvira. But here we enter the realm of absurdity, where the Neo-Platonic concept of like loving like can lead us.

In the third act, too, Juana makes use of her knowledge of Inés's psychology to get out of an uncomfortable situation. For a moment, Juana seems to have overreached herself. Inés sees Gil courting Clara just after she learns from Caramanchel of his affair with Elvira. In her jealousy, she threatens to ruin Juana's game completely. Juana sees the danger which might arise of her actually forcing a marriage between Inés and Martín, but she manages to keep her wits. She finds it easy to persuade Inés that she is not Gil but Elvira, and Inés's speech is a revealing one:

Ansí se ha de hacer.
Vestirte con tu traje puedes;
que con él podremos ver
cómo te entalla y te inclina.
Ven, y pondráste un vestido
de los míos; que imagina
mi amor en ese fingido
que eres hombre, y no vecina.
. . . .
. . . (Aparte) ¡Qué varonil
mujer! Por más que repara
mi amor, dice que es Don Gil

en la voz, presencia y cara.
                    (III.vii. p. 1751a)

Doña Clara also seems to share Inés's "aesthetic" appreciation of Don Gil:

Un ángel de cristal es
el rapaz: cual sombra sigo
su talle airoso y gentil.
                    (I.viii. p. 1724b)

She is a rival of Inés's for the attentions of Don Gil who plays off the two women against each other. In the third act, we see that Clara is so obsessed with her love for Don Gil that she assumes the identity and dress of the man with whom she is in love—a further *reductio ad absurdum* of Neo-Platonic theory. The case of Serafina in *El vergonzoso en palacio* immediately comes to mind. These two women reveal not only narcissism but also lesbianism in their behaviour, for it is clear that what they find attractive in Don Gil is precisely what is obvious to Caramanchel from the start—his effeminacy. These psychological irregularities in both Inés and Clara are ridiculed when the man they are pursuing turns out to be a real woman. Underlying their frivolity (and, in the case of Inés, her moral irresponsibility) is a psychological abnormality. They are made aware of this and "cured" by being forced to recognise the absurdity of their attitudes.

To sum up, then, we may say that the play satirises a frivolous, irresponsible, unprincipled and, ultimately, immoral attitude toward life. The ultimate blame for the social and moral chaos in the play lies with the unprincipled parents, Don Andrés and Don Pedro, who are willing victims of their own cupidity and selfishness and of social conventions. The tyrannical, unreasonable attitude on the part of the parents is wrong; therefore their plans are frustrated.

But Tirso does not use the parents' guilt to absolve the children of all blame. For Tirso, the moral law is the ultimate guide of the individual, and when it comes into conflict with parental authority or social conventions, the latter must be defied so that the moral law can be upheld. In Martín and Inés, the same problem is put from two different angles: Martín acquiesces in his father's immoral plan; Inés, at first rebellious, also submits to her father's wishes, but for a different reason. Tirso insists that both are wrong. Therefore both have to endure frustration and ridicule.

The above analysis now makes the structure of the play more understandable. The situations which provide the dramatic conflict of the com-

edy are themselves basic to the *comedia* as a whole. Juana's pursuit and
recapture of the fickle Martín is a typical variation of the traditional mate-
hunt in which the woman outwits the man. This provides material for
the action. The problem it illustrates is a variation of the traditional clash
between the individual and society, between what is naturally right and
what is conventionally stipulated. Juana has to overcome Don Andrés's
opposition as well as to save Martín from becoming the victim of social
conventions owing to his own moral inertia.

She achieves her aim in two main stages. In the first, she presents
a parody of Martín's action. This gives us the two inner boxes of the
play's structure. In the second step, Martín is made to realize what the
possible consequences of his irresponsible acts could be. This necessi-
tates the identification of Don Gil with Martín, which is effected by the
disintegration of the false Gil figure at the climax of the play.

This comes late in the third act where we are presented with four
Giles. If the test of a true personality is its uniqueness, Don Gil cannot
pass this test. There are a number of points which can be noted here. The
appearance of four Giles—all of them spurious, for the "real" Gil, Gil de
Albornoz, has renounced his identity in favour of that of the usurping Gil
de las calzas verdes—is a *reductio ad absurdum* of the device of the female
page, for three of the characters are using this conventional device quite
gratuitously. What underlines the grotesque absurdity of the situation is
the fact that two of these Giles, Juan and Martín, without realizing it, are
pretending to be a woman pretending to be a man—and to do this Martín
has had to repudiate himself twice over!

With this collision of Giles, the figure is shattered. The various false
Giles disperse—Juana, Juan and Clara—and Martín, the original Gil, now
in green breeches, is left as the scapegoat for the sins of all the Giles,
only, however, to be rescued by Juana when he finds himself unable to
disclaim responsibility. Once he accepts responsibility for his actions as
Martín, harmony is restored.

The long opening speech by Caramanchel in I.ii, traditionally seen as
serving at best only to inject additional humour into the play, is now
revealed as a brilliant, wittily satirical introduction to the comedy. The
satirical note is sounded at the beginning and is developed in the course
of the play. The moral failings of Caramanchel's masters are a prelude to
the moral failings of Martín, Inés and their respective fathers. But there
is not only a betrayal of responsibility in Caramanchel's masters. Con-
comitant with it is their hypocrisy: they are all humbugs, seeming to be
what they are not, profiting from the advantages which they derive from

their masks, their *personae*. Caramanchel cannot tolerate them. Juana, too, unmasks Martín, the sordid motivations of Andrés and Pedro, the emotional immaturity and callousness of Inés. There is one further point: Caramanchel wants a master whom he can serve; the master's moral integrity and physical presence are as important to him as his food and pay. But, like Lazarillo, he is fated to go from bad to worse. He finds a master who provides him with food and money; but the master's moral integrity is doubtful, although Caramanchel never stops wondering whether Gil's integrity can indeed be doubtful. Worse, Caramanchel's master is a non-master: he is invisible most of the time, and, at the end, turns out to be neither a man nor a hermaphrodite, but a woman. The connexion with the central situation in the play *via* the problem of identity is obvious.

Thus a conventional dramatic device is ridiculed, and this ridicule also embraces a social convention which is both unnatural and immoral. Social and literary satire, then, are linked in this play, as in so many others by Tirso.

While it is clear that the theme of the play (social responsibility) is at bottom a serious one, it is not treated in a grave way. The comic aspect is provided by the literary satire. It is the lightness and subtlety with which Tirso handles his theme which allows us to laugh when Martín says: "La muerte tuve tragada" (III.xxii. p. 1761b). In fact, the makings of tragedy are contained in the subject of the play. Juana herself very nearly pushes Inés into Martín's arms in III.vii. More seriously, Inés, on two occasions, tries to have Martín and then Juana killed, inciting the violently jealous Juan to murder them. It is no surprise that the irresponsibility of the kind displayed by Martín, when raised to a power so high that it becomes a disintegrating force which seriously threatens the whole moral and social order leads to tragedy in *El burlador de Sevilla*. The preoccupations of Spanish comedy are akin to those of Spanish tragedy. Hence the ambiguous tonality of the *comedia*. It is the moral element in human behaviour which ultimately tips the scales in favour of a tragic or comic ending. *Don Gil* is a comedy because in it irresponsibility is prevented from turning into immorality.

The above analysis, it is hoped, has brought out the relationship between form and content by showing that the play combines satire of a social convention with satire of a dramatic one. The analysis would be incomplete, however, without a brief reference to some stylistic features, for language is one of the most important aspects of comedy. There are two stylistic aspects which interest us in particular, as they are concerned with vital aspects of the play: the first is the witty exploration of the green symbolism in the play; the second is Tirso's clever use of language to underline certain traits of character, We shall examine the latter phenomenon first.

The basic situation of the play arises from an attempt by Andrés and Pedro to marry Martín to Inés on the grounds that the match is a sound one financially. Marriage, a holy sacrament, is thus converted into a purely business transaction which ignores human emotions and individual responsibilities: Inés does not want to leave the man she loves, Juan, to marry an unknown person; Martín is pledged to marry Juana. The latter, in the following speech, reveals the sordid financial basis for the arranged marriage in her metaphors:

> Enamoróse de oídas
> don Miguel de ti: al poder
> de tu dote lo atribuye,
> que ya amor es mercader;
> y atropellando amistades,
> obligaciones, deudo y fe
> de don Gil, le hurtó las cartas
> y el nombre, porque con él
> disfrazándose, a esta corte
> vino, pienso que no ha un mes,
> vendiéndose por don Gil,
> te ha pedido por mujer.
> Yo, que sigo como sombra
> sus pasos vine tras él,
> sembrando por los caminos
> quejas, que vendré a coger
> colmadas de desengaños,
> que es caudal del bien querer.
>
> (II.v. p. 1732a)

Martín's love is directed towards money. His credit is ensured by his father's "cartas de favor":

> [JUANA:]   y el interés
> de tu dote apetecible
> alas le puso a los pies.
> Diole cartas de favor
> el viejo, y quiso con él
> partirse al punto a esta corte,
> nueva imagen de Babel.
>
> (II.v. p. 1732a)

In these passages, the stylistic equation of love and money is obvious and serves to establish the correspondence between the two. Thus a more subtle use of equation is possible in passages where the characters use the financial terms to express their emotions. The criteria of their scale of values are thus cleverly exposed. A good example is the scene in which Pedro eagerly welcomes Martín-Gil:

> Seáis, señor, mil veces bienvenido
> para alegrar aquesta casa vuestra;
> que para comprobar lo que he leído
> cobra el valor que vuestro talle muestra.
>
> (I.iii. p. 1719a)

Gil's "valor" is, of course, the "diez mil ducados de renta" which Andrés refers to in his letter to Pedro.

The word play is intensified to an impudent level immediately afterwards, as both Martín and Pedro, waxing eloquent, shower on each other hypocritical compliments. The heightening of emotion leads to an effort on the part of both to find the most exalted and accurate terms to express their feelings, their hopes, their values. The terms they hit upon eloquently reveal their real motivations and thoughts:

MARTÍN:
> Comenzáis de manera a aventajaros
> en hacerme merced, que, temeroso,
> señor don Pedro, de poder pagaros
> aun en palabras (que en el generoso
> son prendas de valor), para envidiaros,
> en obras y en palabras victorioso,
> agradezco callando . . .
>
> . . . .
>
> aunque si os informáis, de los cabellos
> quedará mi esperanza, que codicia
> lograr abrazos y cumplir deseos,
> abreviando noticias y rodeos.
>
> . . . .

PEDRO:
> No tengo yo en tan poco de mi amigo
> el crédito y estima, que no sobre
> su firma sola, sin buscar testigo
> por quien vuestro valor alientos cobre.
> Negociado tenéis para conmigo;
> y aunque un hidalgo fuérades tan pobre
> como el que más, a doña Inés os diera,

> si don Andrés por vos intercediera.
>
> (I.iii. pp. 1719–1720a)

Pedro, not chastened by the discovery that the first Gil de Albornoz was a fraud, extends an equally warm welcome to Juana-Gil, and the latter takes up the word-play:

PEDRO: Aquí otra vez me encomienda
              don Andrés la conclusión
              de vuestra boda, y que entienda
              la mucha satisfacción
              de vuestra sangre y hacienda
                   . . . .
              mucho gano en conoceros
                   . . . .
INÉS: Y yo deshago
              sospechas, porque me inclina
              vuestro amor.
JUANA: Con ese os pago.

> (II.xiv. p. 1740b.)

This word-play pervades the comedy and accounts for a large part of the comic effect. Inés's defence of Juan is a subtle appeal to her father's scale of values:

> Y no pierdes siendo así,
> nada en que don Juan pretenda
> ser tu yerno, si el valor
> sabes que ilustra su hacienda.
>
> (I.v. p. 1721a.)

Money in the play is all-powerful, and, with typical Tirsian humour, is shown to have the power of faith and religion to perform miracles. Juana, with the help of money, finds out all she needs to know when she first arrives in Madrid, and has suborned one of the servants:

> En casa de mi opuesta he ya obligado
> a quien me avise siempre; darle quiero
> gracias destos milagros al dinero.
>
> (I.vi. p. 1722a.)

Money, too, secures Pedro's acceptance of Gil: the "milagros" are, of course, his money:

> Milagros, don Gil, han sido
> desa presencia bizarra.

> Negociado habéis por vos;
>   (I.x. p. 1726a.)

And money can even resurrect the dead:

JUANA:	Habéisme vuelto
	el alma al cuerpo.
INÉS:	¡Interés
	dichoso!
	(II.xv. p. 1741a.)

The above quotations exemplify what we shall see as one of Tirso's typical tricks, namely, the use of language to underline or point up a ridiculous situation. A factual absurdity is reflected in a stylistic absurdity. Take, for example, the name of Gil. It is absolutely inconceivable (at least within the dramatic tradition) that a genuine *hidalgo* should bear the name of Gil: Inés points this out to her father, who, however, brushes her objection aside; there are other ways of tellings a man's worth apart from his name: "No repares en los nombres / cuando el dueño es noble y rico." (I.v. p. 1721b.) And yet Inés is right. Soon afterwards she repeats her point of view to Juana-Gil, before being told that she is speaking to Gil. Caramanchel drives the point home: Gil, after all, is an adjunct, a suffix, to things rustic or feminine: *peregil, torongil, cenogil* (I.viii. pp. 1723b– 1724a).[15] Thus is Inés made all the more ridiculous when she straightaway falls in love with Don Gil de las calzas verdes. Just as cupidity had blinded her father, her passion blinds her, too, to points which she had seen and which are emphasised by Caramanchel.

A similar, but more obvious, use of metaphor, occurs in the third act when Inés, in the throes of her love for Gil, seems to discover that he is unfaithful to her. Not merely does Caramanchel suggest that she is an *asno*, but the sensual nature of her love is made obvious when, under the stress of overpowering emotion, she, too, reveals in telling metaphor that her love is appetite, i.e., desire:

	. . . .
INÉS:	¡Que regalado papel!
	A su dueño se parece,
	tan infame que apetece
	las sobras de don Miguel.
	¡Doña Inés le da disgusto!
	¡Valgame Dios! ¿Ya empalago?
	¿Manjar soy que satisfago
	antes que me pruebe el gusto?

	¿Tan bueno es el de su Elvira
	que su apetito provoca?
CARAM.:	No es la miel para la boca
	del . . . *et caetera*.[16]

(III.ii. p. 1746a–b.)

But it is in the play on the symbolic connotations of the word *verde* that we find the fullest development of the above two points, viz., the fact that Don Gil is a contradiction in terms and can refer to no man and the fact that Inés's love is base, sensual desire.

From the structural point of view, *verde* is a recurrent *leitmotif* which serves to reinforce the play's unity. Juana, by transferring her "calzas verdes" to Martín, simultaneously transfers to him the responsibility for his actions from which he cannot escape. But it will appear obvious that the green breeches symbolise more than one thing in this comedy.

Traditionally, in the Golden Age, green is the colour of hope.[17] In the play, it is expressly associated with hope. Inés's and Pedro's hopes are fulfilled with the appearance of Don Gil:

PEDRO:	¿No vería
	yo al don Gil de las calzas, Inés, verdes?
	. . . .
[INÉS:]	Pero, ¿no es éste, cielos? Haga alarde
	con su presencia la esperanza mía.

(II.xiii. p. 1739b.)

This symbolism is consistent with Juana's aim: she hopes to win back Martín: to do this, she disguises herself as a man, and the colour of her disguise symbolises the hope she has in the success of her plan.

But Clara, as well, sees the "calzas verdes" as symbolising her hope of marrying Don Gil. Her love, however, is a blind passion, and she tells us that she is by no means unpopular with the city gallants. She issues an invitation to Gil to visit her, and, in her speech, the spring-fertility-sex connotations are evident:

¿No? Pues sabed que mi casa
es la Red de San Luis;
mis galanes, más de mil;
mas quien en mi gusto alcanza
el premio por más gentil,
es verde cual mi esperanza,
y es en el nombre don Gil.

(III.v. p. 1748a.)

In fact, green symbolises hope because it is the colour of spring; and spring is lusty. So, too, is Don Gil:

INÉS: ¿Uno de unas calzas verdes?
JUANA: Y tan verdes como él,
              que es abril de la hermosura,
              y del donaire, Aranjuez.
                        (II.v. p. 1732b)

The *Diccionario de Autoridades* gives this definition of verde: "Metaphoricamente se llama el mozo, que está en el vigor, y fuerza de su edad, y lo dá a entender en las acciónes." There is no doubt that this epithet, in both its senses (lusty, and by extension, lustful), is eminently fitting for Don Gil de las calzas verdes.[18] Inés, Clara and Elvira are all the objects of his attention. But such behaviour is, like Martín's, far from being moral, and Caramanchel suggests as much:

                  Es arador
             que de vista se me pierde;
             por más que le busco y llamo,
             nunca quiere mi verde amo
             que en sus calzas me dé un verde.
             Aquí le vi no ha dos credos,
             y aunque estaba en mi presencia,
             cual dinero de Valencia,
             se me perdió entre los dedos;
             mas tal anda el motolito
             por una vuestra vecina,
             que es hija de Celestina,
             y le gazmió en el garlito[19]
                  (III.ii. p. 1745b.)

Inés, in her anger, declares the same thing: "Este es don Gil, el que engaña / de tres en tres las mujeres." (III.vii. p. 1750a.)

But such behaviour seems as impossible as the combination of "Don" and "Gil." Caramanchel points out the puzzling contradiction: "que aunque es lampiño el don Gil / en obras y en nombre es verde." (III.ii. p. 1745b.) But there is, in fact, no contradiction. To return to the *Diccionario de Autoridades*, *Verde* "se aplica también a las cosas, que están a los principios, y que les falta mucho para llegar a perfecionarse." In fact, Don Gil is an immature man: emotionally, in that his affections are fickle (and in this Gil is a parody of Martín), and sexually, in that Gil is no man—as Inés unwittingly points out:

> Padre de mis ojos,
> don Gil no es honra, es la gracia,
> la sal, el donaire, el gusto,
> que amor en sus cielos guarda:
>
> (I.x. p. 1726a.)

Thus the wit of the paradox emerges: the man whose emotions are unstable, who tries to be a Don Juan, is in reality a sexually, because emotionally, immature person.

The immature Inés, therefore, without realising it, is engaging in word-play, of the full import of which she is not aware:

MARTÍN: ¿Qué don Gil o maldición
             es éste?
PEDRO: Don Gil el verde.
INÉS: Y el blanco de mi afición.

(II.xviii. p. 1742b)

Verde symbolises the object (*blanco*) on which Inés's hopes are centred; but her love is to be a "chaste" (i.e., nonsexual) one since *blanco* symbolises chastity. The paradox is confirmed in Juan's speech, the first line of which would make little sense unless its full symbolical implications were grasped:

> Don Gil, el blanco o el verde,
> ya se ha llegado la hora
> tan deseada en mí,
> y tan rehusada de vos.
>
> (III.xiv. p. 1755b.)

Thus, when Clara appears in green breeches towards the end of the play, an amazing complexity of meaning is revealed in the following two lines: "Don Gil de las calzas soy / verdes, como mi esperanza" (III.xvi. p. 1757a.) Here, *verdes* has all three meanings: of hope—Clara's hope; lusty—Clara, by identifying herself with the immoral Gil condemns herself; and emotionally and sexually immature—her hopes are going to turn into *uvas verdes*.

We may note that Juana is the only one who comes out of the whole intrigue unscathed. Her hopes are fulfilled, her object attained, and thus the equation *verde* = hope is proved correct in her case. But this is because her intrigue was justifiable, and her disguise equally so. The equation *verde* = hope proves false in the case of Inés, Clara and Martín, since it is in these that the equations *verde* = lusty, immoral, and *verde* = immature prove correct. Their hopes are frustrated because their fulfilment would mean the triumph of immorality and/or immaturity.

The demonstration that Don Gil is an immoral figure ought also to be seen in the light of contemporary views on the *mujer vestida de hombre*. This figure existed in real life and was not wholly confined to the stage. Transvestism, of course, has traditionally been regarded as sinful, as it obviously symbolises a confusion of the sexes. The ambiguous sexuality of Gil-Elvira scandalises the puritanical Caramanchel (II.ix. p. 1752b.). And he tells us of the punishment accorded to such persons:

> Azotes dan en España
> por menos que eso. ¿Quién vió
> un hembri-macho, que afrenta
> a su linaje?

The implications of such a state are further developed and the Church's disapproval re-affirmed—"no es aprobado":

> No quiero señor con saya
> y calzas, hombre y mujer;
> que querréis en mí tener
> juntos lacayo y lacaya.
> No más amo hermafrodita,
> de comer carne y pescado
> a un tiempo, no es aprobado.
>
> (III.ix. p. 1752b.)

This is an excellent opportunity for Tirso to deflate the Neo-Platonic conception of love. With the help of wit, Tirso can carry the Neo-Platonic premises to their logical conclusions: such a love is narcissistic (Gil and Elvira are exact replicas of each other) and potentially homosexual (like the original Platonic love)—Elvira, like Inés and Clara, must love the effeminate aspect of Gil and be loved by him:

> [JUANA:]   ¿Pensáis que vuestro señor
> sin causa me tiene amor?
> Por parecérseme tanto
> emplea en mí su esperanza.
> Díselo tú, doña Inés.
> INÉS: Causa suelen decir que es
> del amor la semejanza.
>
> (III.ix. pp. 1752b–1753a.)

This is one justification for the exploding of the Gil figure.

Secondly, the dramatic device of male disguise was condemned by the moralists of the seventeenth century. The position of Tirso, the friar, is curious: he does not seem to have shared the opinion of the moralists. But it is his keen irony which justifies his stand. Juana's disguise is justifiable: it is not only a convenient dramatic device (which allows Tirso to give full rein to his sense of the absurd), but also sociologically justifiable: to regain her honour, Juana has to invade a masculine sphere of action (revenge for honour) and her wearing breeches symbolises this.[20] Clara's use of male disguise, however, is quite unjustifiable (a woman does not win a man's love by being masculine), and therefore immoral—in the real-life as well as the theatrical situation—, and the destroying of the Gil figure (which achieves Juana's aim and leaves the others frustrated) frustrates this gratuitous use of the device.

To end, it is clear that in *Don Gil de las calzas verdes* an attack is made, on the one hand, on conventional social and moral behaviour, and, on the other, on a literary convention. The social satire stresses the need for a sense of social and moral responsibility, and this is achieved through the *reductio ad absurdum* of a dramatic device. These two aspects are thus united and reinforce the basic unity of the play. The satire itself is underlined by the brilliant use of wit and symbolism, stylistic features which are characteristic of Tirsian comedy. Finally, I have tried to show that the structure of the play is a distinctive one, being based on the Chinese boxes pattern. Tirso thus moves away from the mature Lopean structure and in this respect does not serve to link Lope to Calderón. The structure of this early play reappears in *Amar por arte mayor*, a late play of Tirso's, which Calderón must have admired.[21] In this play, Tirso's style is much more Calderonian than Lopean. It is therefore stylistically that Tirso serves as a bridge between Lope and Calderón. Symbol, conceit, image, all play a vital and increasingly important part in Tirso's plays. This is not to suggest that Tirso is to be seen merely as a bridge figure. The asyndetic structure of his plays (a structure which Lope rejects as he develops) allows him much greater freedom to experiment with, and exploit the structural possibilities of, wit and symbol. This makes for an amazingly subtle form of playwriting, which produces some of the best comedies written in the Golden Age.

NOTES

1 *Disguise Plots in Elizabethan Drama* (New York, 1915).

2 *"El perro del hortelano* y la visión de Lope," *Filología*, X (1964), 135–42.

3 *The Theory of Drama* (London, 1931).

4 "La balanza subjetiva-objetiva en el teatro de Tirso: ensayo sobre contenido y forma barrocos," *Hispanófila*, no. 3 (1958), 1–11.

5 "The Nature of the Complexity in Tirso's *Don Gil*," *Hispania*, XLV (1962), 389–94.

6 *La mujer vestida de hombre en el teatro español* (Madrid, 1955), 114–15.

7 *Historia de la literatura española*, II (5th ed., Barcelona, 1957), p. 413.

8 All quotations are taken from Tirso de Molina, *Obras dramáticas completas* I, ed. B. de los Ríos, Madrid, 1946. The references are to act, scene and page.

9 "On Tirso's *Don Gil*," *MLN*, LXXIV (1958), 609–12.

10 *English Dramatic Form* (London, 1965), especially chap. X.

11 "Some Baroque Aspects of Tirso de Molina," *RR*, XXXVI (1945), 43–69.

12 *El humor en Tirso de Molina* (Madrid, 1959).

13 For the irrationality of courtly love see, e.g., R. O. Jones, "Ariosto and Garcilaso," *BHS*, XXXIX (1962), 152–64; A. Solé-Leris, "The Theory of Love in the Two *Dianas*: A Contrast," *BHS*, XXXVI (1959), 65–79; *et. al.*

14 For the symbolic use of night scenes, see E. H. Templin, "Night Scenes in Tirso de Molina," *RR*, XLI (1950), 261–73.

15 J. B. Nomland draws our attention to this passage in his article, "A Laughter Analysis of Three *Comedias* of Tirso de Molina," *MLF*, XXXI (1946), 38. In his article "Tirso's *Cigarrales de Toledo*: Some Clarifications and Identifications," *HR*, XXXIII (1965), 246–72, G. E. Wade has drawn attention to the name "Don Gil de Albornoz." There is, first, the Cardinal Gil de Álvarez Albornoz, Archbishop of Toledo, buried in the chapel of San Ildefonso in Toledo. The *banda* of the Albornoz coat-of-arms, Wade notes, was green in colour. (See the allusion to this Don Gil in the "Cántica de los clérigos de Talavera" in the *Libro de buen amor*). A more immediate reference, according to Wade, would probably have been to the Cardinal Gil de Albornoz, *Inquisidor de la Suprema* in 1627. Wade comments: "It appears that Tirso was making fun of a clerical friend . . . We feel quite sure that it was this don Gil de Albornoz whose name Tirso gave to the protagonist of *Don Gil de las calzas verdes*, with its *mujer disfrazada de hombre* and its malicious homosexual implications."

16 The same image recurs, for example, in *La venganza de Tamar*, II. xii; III. iv.

17 See, e.g., S. G. Morley, "Color Symbolism in Tirso de Molina," *RR*, VIII (1917), 77–81; H. A. Kenyon, "Color Symbolism in Early Spanish Ballads," *RR*, VI (1915), 327–40; and W. L. Fichter, "Color Symbolism in Lope de Vega," *RR*, XVIII (1927), 220–31. For Calderón, too, green symbolises hope (See E. M. Wilson and J. Sage, *Poesías líricas en las obras dramáticas de Calderón* [London, 1964], p. 45, No. 59: "EL JUEGO es de las colores . . .").

It is bright green, of course, which symbolises hope; dark green may suggest its frustration. This distinction is clearly seen in Alonso de Ledesma's "El juego de las colores" (In *Juegos de Noches Buenas a lo divino* [Barcelona, 1605]. In B.A.E., XXXV [Madrid, 1885], p. 179b).

18 In the *Enciclopedia del idioma*, III, ed. M. Alonso (Madrid, 1958), we find the following (12th) meaning given to *verde*: "fig. s. XVI al XX. Libre, indecente, obsceno. Apl. a cuentos, comedias, poesías, etc. Góngora: *Obr.* II–102." The ref. to Góngora is also to be found in B. Alemany y Selfa, *Vocabulario de las obras de Don Luis de Góngora y Argote* (Madrid, 1930).

19 Some of the words in this passage perhaps call for brief comment. "motolito": "Fácil de ser engañado o vencido, por ser poco avisado, o falto de experiencia y manejo en lo que se trata" (*Dicc. de Autoridades*). "gazmió": Gazmiar= "Quitar y andar comiendo golosinas." "Se toma también por quejarse y resentirse. Es voz burlesca, y en este sentido verbo neutro." (*Aut.*) Here it seems to mean "seduce" or "catch." The latter sense is reinforced by "garlito": "Especie de nassa à modo de orinál de vidro, y en lo mas estrecho de él se hace la red de unos lazos, que en entrando el pez no puede salir, porque se enreda en ellos." "Metaphoricamente significa celada, lazo ò assechanza, que se arma a alguno para molestarle y hacerle daño." (*Aut.*), i.e., a trap. More interesting, perhaps, is "arador": it is , of course, a ploughman and also the ring-worm: "Piojuélo o gusanillo casi imperceptible, que se cria lo mas ordinariamente en las palmas de las manos, que sacado y puesto al Sol, se vé mover: y con ser tan pequeño, tiene una manchita negra que paréce cabéza. Díxose Aradór, porque paréce vá formando surcos, como hace el arádo" (*Aut.*). Caramanchel may be comparing Don Gil to this almost invisible mite; but, in the context of the passage, the word seems to have sexual overtones, by a metaphorical extension of the basic meaning.

20 This sociological dimension, arising out of a social structure in which the male and female roles are clearly defined, is discussed more fully in J. G. Peristiany (ed.): *Honour and Shame* (London, 1965), pp. 70–71.

21 G. E. Wade in "Notes on Two of Tirso's plays," *BC*, XII (1960), no. 2, 1–6, has suggested that *Don Gil* was written between 21st January and 25th June, 1615. It was produced by Valdés in Toledo in July, 1615. Wade does not agree with the date of composition (1614) which Doña Blanca assigns to the play in her introduction to it in her ed. The date of *Amar por arte mayor* is discussed in a later chapter, where it is suggested that internal evidence seems to point to the years 1627–29 as the period of composition.

CHAPTER II

La celosa de sí misma.
The Frustration of the *Tapada*

La celosa de sí misma is without doubt one of Tirso's most remarkable plays. It is Hartzenbusch himself, who, in his analysis of this play remarks that: "El plan . . . es el mejor de los que trazó la pluma de Fray Gabriel Téllez."[1] The structure, indeed, is, as we shall see, elegantly simply and economically planned. There are not superfluous characters: each is strictly functional. The style is witty and humorous, as is to be expected. The characters—and especially the heroine—are interestingly portrayed. At the same time, there are some features which at first sight seem to provide further proof of Tirso's reputed indifference to dramatic technique. The use of disguise is obviously unsuccessful in the play: one might argue that Tirso had yet again got himself into a sticky situation from which he extricated himself in his usual impudent manner. The final revelation of identity, too, would seem to be a needlessly long drawn-out process. However, a closer analysis of the play reveals that these features, far from being flaws, are the consequence of Tirso's studied manipulation of his material.

This play, like *Por el sótano y el torno*, with which it has a number of features in common, is set in Madrid. This is crucial, for, not merely does it ensure the Neo-Classical unity of place (a consideration which bothers the great *comedia* writers not in the least), but also provides the vastly more important unity of atmosphere. The exploitation of atmosphere in a definite setting is, when it occurs, of considerable dramatic significance in Tirso. The confusion of Madrid life in this play is very much like the Midsummer madness in Shakespeare's comedy.[2] Melchor's opening words establish this atmosphere of confusion from the very beginning: "Bello lugar es Madrid / ¡Qué agradable confusión!" (I.i. p. 1441a.).[3] This motif is taken up by Ventura in his satirical description of the rapidity with which the faces of Madrid and of women, and the fortunes of men,

change (I.i. p. 1441a–b.). This confused aspect of things is attributed to
the rapid pace of life in Madrid. Sebastián's accounts of life in the Plaza
Mayor, in I.ii. p. 1443b, reinforces this view: there is no communication
between members of society, perhaps the various stages of existence—
birth, marriage, death—have been telescoped into simultaneous events.

To this confusion is added, as a matter of course, corruption. Innocent
husbands have to be imported into Madrid from the provinces:

JERÓNIMO: Esperamos de León
                  un deudo con quien procura
                  casar mi madre a mi hermana,
                  que maridos cortesanos
                  son traviesos y livianos.
                                          (I.ii. p. 1444a.)

Madrid has corrupted the values of its inhabitants; it is not a city, but a
dangerous sea in which merchants, seeking *interés*, venture:

VENTURA: ¿Mar dices? Llámale así,
                  que ese apellido le da
                  quien se atreve a navegalle
                  y advierte que es esta calle
                  la canal de Bahamá.
                  Cada tienda es la Bermuda;
                  cada mercader inglés
                  pechelingue[4] u holandés,
                  que a todo bajel desnuda.
                  Cada manto es un escollo.
                  Dios te libre de que encalle
                  la bolsa por esta calle.
                                          (I.i. p. 1442a.)

Into this setting of corruption (which will be illustrated by Sebastián's—
and, to a lesser extent, Angela's—intrigues in the secondary action) and
confusion (which the heroine, Magdalena, will provide) is thrown the
naive, idealistic provincial, Melchor. And the resultant confusion in the
plot will be worthy of the capital city.

At the same time, we must bear in mind that all this confusion stems
from apparent changes in things, and it is money and cosmetics which
produce these optical illusions. There is thus an intermediate agent which
changes the aspect of things, without, however, changing the nature of
those things themselves. The art of producing such changes in appearances
is called *tropelía*. This is going to be the dominant theme in the play.

The word itself is first mentioned by Ventura when he discusses the fast-changing appearances of things and persons in Madrid: "tan presto que es tropelía" (I.i. p. 1441b). Its first recorded appearance, as J. Corominas informs us, is in *La pícara Justina*, and in the early seventeenth century it alternates between the meanings of legerdemain and the magical art which changes the appearance of things.[5] It is in this latter sense, as Corominas reminds us, that Cervantes uses it in his *Coloquio de los perros*:

> sé que eres persona racional, y te veo en semejanza de perro, si ya no es que esto se hace con aquella ciencia que llaman tropelía, que hace parecer una cosa por otra.[6]

In *La celosa* Tirso seems to combine both meanings in his exploration of the concept. I shall now analyse the structure of the play to show how the *tropelía* theme is worked out in it.

As we have seen in *Don Gil*, the gratuitous use of disguise ends in failure in the case of Clara. Where it has a valid dramatic function, however, as in the case of the heroine, Juana, it succeeds. The female-page device, therefore, is partly successful and partly unsuccessful in *Don Gil*. In *La celosa de sí misma*, on the other hand, disguise (the *manto* of the *mujer tapada*) is employed gratuitously by the heroine, Magdalena, and fails. Its more orthodox use by Magdalena's rival, Ángela, also ends in failure. It is on this central failure of the device that Tirso constructs his play.

There are two strands of action in *La celosa de sí misma*, the development of each being governed by the principle of causality. The main one deals with the fortunes of Melchor and Magdalena. The secondary action deals with the ambitions and schemes of Sebastián and his coy sister, Ángela. The two intrigues form a neat contrast to each other, for, while the main action wanders among the absurdities of love created by the imagination, the secondary action finds its feet trailing in the mud of *interés*, from which it is lifted only by the exercise of Ángela's imagination, itself fired by love. But, at the same time, the situations and their developments in both strands of the action are largely interdependent. So closely linked are the actions that their trajectories converge inevitably and clash in Act III, and it is the impinging of the secondary action on the principal which leads to a solution of the apparently insoluble problem posed in the latter. The implications to be drawn from this structural pattern are of considerable interest for the study of Tirsian comedy.

The main intrigue, which exemplifies the unconventional use of the devise of the *mujer tapada* is undoubtedly the more complex. As if to harmonise with the prevailing atmosphere of confusion and corrupted values, it contains a parody of the two basic comic situations, viz., the individual-society conflict and the hunt for a mate. The inversion of these conventional situations is brought about by *tropelía*.

There exists—or seems to exist—for Melchor a clash between the individual's wishes and the dictates of society. His father has sent him to Madrid ". . . a casar / con sesenta mil ducados" (I.i. p. 1442a.). But he himself declares:

> que aunque el dinero es hermoso,
> yo no tengo de casarme,
> si no fuera con belleza
> y virtud: esto es notorio.
>
> (I.i. pp. 1442b–1443a.)

So, no sooner does he arrive in Madrid, than, while attending Mass, he falls in love—ironically—with a hand!

From the psychological point of view, this is more realistic than any idealistic spontaneous combustion of souls. Ventura's comment stresses the physical nature of this love: "La primera vez es ésta / que entró el amor por grosura" (I.iii. p. 1447a.). M. A. Peyton sees Melchor's description of the hand as a manifestation of sensuality, and, therefore, as evidence of the typically baroque disintegration of traditional idealistic love values.[7] It would perhaps be more accurate to say that Tirso's treatment of love implies a disintegration of traditional literary conceits engendered by the courtly and Neo-Platonic traditions, since it would be extremely hazardous to suppose that the baroque age, more than any other, was characterised by a preponderance of sensuality over love (if, indeed, such a distinction can be validly made).

What is evident, however, is the fact that there is an element of morbidity in Melchor's love. He loves, not a woman, but a hand.

> [MELCHOR:]   ¡Ay qué mano! ¡Qué belleza!
>   ¡Qué blancura! ¡Qué donaire!
>   ¡Qué hoyuelos! ¡Qué tez, qué venas!
>   ¡Ay qué dedos tan hermosos!
>
>   (I.iii. p. 1445b.)

This is a case not of love, then, but almost of a perversion: the hand seems to have been converted into a fetish, and Melchor's description of it arouses our sense of ridicule by its very absurdity. The description, perfectly apt if it referred to a face, is absurd when it is applied to a hand. Ventura stressed the absurdity in his immediate burlesque of Melchor's description:

> ¡Ay qué uñas aguileñas!
> ¡Ay qué bello *rapio, rapis*!
> ¡Ay qué garras monederas!
>
> (I.iii. p. 1445b.)

Melchor argues that the beauty of the hand must indicate beauty of countenance (an argument *a priori*, not devoid of Neo-Platonic overtones) (I.iii. p. 1447a). This is immediately defeated by Ventura's empirically based anecdote about the negress in the same scene, which further stresses the absurdity of Melchor's position.

This absurdity reaches its height in I.x, when Melchor fails to recognise Magdalena's hand as the object of his heart's desire, notwithstanding Ventura's arguments and protestations:

> [MELCHOR:]   Esta [mano de Magdalena] es asco, es un carbón,
> es en su comparación
> el yeso junto al cristal.
> A sus divinos despojos
> no hay igualdad.
>
> (I.x. p. 1457a.)

Doña Blanca de los Ríos describes the situation perfectly:

Y era lo grande que, cuando en su prometida encontró a su amada, empeñóse en separarlas a las dos y en desdeñar a la verdadera por la imaginada. ¡Qué hermoso es y cuánta poesía contiene este deleitoso error! La Quimera interpuesta entre un alma y la realidad. El goce de oponerse a lo corriente de lo previsto, de lo ordinario, lo vulgar y mejor aún a lo impuesto.[8]

Melchor has, in fact, actually succeeded in converting into a reality a possible clash between himself and society (which, though expected, never materialises) by creating an obstacle in his own imagination. (One might almost say that by refusing to identify Magdalena—the bride chosen for him—with his beloved *tapada* he insists on making himself the victim of a traditional dramatic—and social—convention). The clash is thus partly between Melchor and himself. The situation is not merely romantic, but absurd: a chimaera stands in the way of Melchor's happiness, and it is in part a chimaera of his own creation.

The difficulties created by Melchor's attitude are regarded by Doña Blanca as the central core of the play. However, one fact leads me to shift the emphasis slightly, and that is the fact that the chimaera is not entirely of Melchor's own creating, and is also more material than Doña

Blanca supposes. Melchor fails to recognise his beloved hand because, as he explains to Ventura:

> La mano que a mí me ha muerto
> de una vuelta se adornaba
> de red,
>
> (I.x. p. 1457a)

Leaving aside Ventura's puns, which have a comic value of their own, we realise that this net stands between the hand Melchor loves and Magdalena's hand as he sees it. Similarly, a *manto* stands between Magdalena and the mysterious owner of the hand with which Melchor fell in love at first sight. The *tropelía* motif thus stands at the centre of the complication of the main action.

The confusion is raised to a still higher power later on when we see that the *manto* stands between Magdalena and her own self. She, too, has created an obstacle which is going to lead her into self-conflict. This clash, more intense than Melchor's, stems from feminine coquetry in the first place, and, in the second, from a woman's inevitable desire to satisfy herself of her lover's constancy. A closer look at the heroine would be rewarding.

Magdalena's manipulation of her glove and veil is at first sheer feminine coquetry. As Melchor confesses in I.iii, it was the repeated actions of withdrawing the hand from the glove and again concealing it that first attracted his attention in church. It is a psychological commonplace that interest in the female body is increased by semi-disclosure, a partial revelation, the point of maximum interest being the frontier between the concealed and the revealed. The effect of the sight of Magdalena's hand on Melchor, therefore, can be compared to the effect produced in less sophisticated times by a glimpse of the female ankle. Furthermore, we are given to understand that the display and concealment of the hand were possibly calculated. Magdalena seems to have been aware of Melchor's not uninterested presence:

> [MELCHOR:] Tenía hasta el pecho el manto
> y santiguóse cubierta:
> pudo ser de verse ansí
> transformado en su belleza.
>
> (I.iii. p. 1446a.)

Our suspicions are confirmed when the gambit is repeated:

> MELCHOR: Dadme una seña

MAGDALENA:	Esta mano.
MELCHOR:	¡Ay aurora hermosa!
MAGDALENA:	Adiós.

(I.iv. p. 1450a.)

Magdalena, then, is carrying on a mild flirtation with an unknown stranger, who is, of course, her betrothed. As we learn, she is more than mildly attracted to him:

[MAGDALENA:]	Luego . . . ¿tu piensas que ignoro
	que no fue él el robador
	del usurpado favor
	que me restituyó en oro?
QUIÑONES:	Para mí no hay dudar deso.
MAGDALENA:	Pues de tanta eficacia es
	conmigo, no el interés,
	la acción sí, que te confieso
	que hechizo para mí ha sido.

(I.viii. p. 1455a–b.)

What her initial surprise is when she sees her betrothed we can only guess at. There is little doubt, however, that she realises that she has had a lucky escape, as the following half-teasing speech to Melchor demonstrates, by revealing her own relief—and sense of 'guilt':

[MAGDALENA:]	Si como os mostré una mano
	ayer, menos advertida,
	os permitiera cebar
	en mi rostro vuestra vista,
	¡qué burlada que quedara,
	siendo después conocida,
	y ocasionando en mi ofensa
	pesados motes y risas!
	Bien haya quien hizo mantos.

(II.iv. p. 1463b.)

Melchor's turning out to be the attractive stranger not only increases Magdalena's love for him, but, unfortunately for her, raises doubts in her mind:

> Mi amor es ya desatino,
> pues sin él, morir espero.
> Mas ¿con qué seguridad
> rendiré mi voluntad
> a quien, con tan fácil fe,

> la primer mujer que ve
> triunfa de su voluntad?
> Hombre que a darme la mano
> viene aquí desde León,
> y es tan mudable y liviano
> que a la primera ocasión,
> liberal y cortesano,
> a un manto rinde despojos
> y a una mano el alma ofrece,
> ¿no quieres que me dé enojos?
>
> (II.i. p. 1459b.)

The irony of this speech is not to be missed, however, for Magdalena is herself guilty of losing her heart to the (then) unknown stranger. It is perhaps this unacknowledged feeling of guilt which forces her to try and test Melchor's constancy by assuming a dual identity. So, the *tapada* device, first used as an instrument of coquetry, is now to be employed by Magdalena to reassure herself. In II.iv,v, Magdalena realises that Melchor will remain true to his *tapada*, and is determined to give Magdalena up for her. As a result, she rewards him by revealing to him one eye after the other. This is surely the earliest representation on stage of an embryonic strip-tease![9] But there are unfortunate complications.

The first stems from Magdalena's discovery that Melchor is to remain faithful, but to his unknown *tapada* and not to her. She makes him promise to give up Magdalena and come to her house to live. This is in itself absurd, since we know that Magdalena and the *tapada* are the same person. But, on reflection, we realize what is happening: Magdalena is not merely playing a practical joke on him; she is actually becoming "celosa de sí misma," i.e., her own rival. On the psychological level we get a personality split: this is confirmed when she rewards Melchor for loving her and hating Magdalena: she has identified one aspect of herself with the *tapada*. But this is not all.

In II.v, we get an amusing case of mutual deception. Santillana invents an identity for the *tapada* in order to deceive Ventura (II.v. p. 1465a–b). Santillana's ingenuity goes unrewarded, of course, but here the deception remains on the level of farce. What is more intriguing is that out of this farcical episode a new complication is built. Magdalena allows herself to be carried away in her confused state of mind and accepts—at least tacitly—the identity offered to her shadow self. Her double becomes more concrete. And yet Magdalena continues her reckless game.

In II.ix, she analyses the situation. She is the object of a love-hate relationship. A veil has actually managed to make her appear to be two persons. The tragedy of it is that the veil is what controls Melchor's emotional reaction. She loves Melchor and wants him to love her. He, however, can only love her when she is veiled, and, consequently, she can only communicate on an emotional level with him when she is the Condesa (II.ix. p. 1470b). She reacts to this situation by developing a split in her personality. She is forced to play a dual role when her emotional needs would compel her to maintain her integrity as a personality. This dual role is going to influence her relationship with Melchor:

[MAGDALENA:] Premiaréle porque intenta
pagar firme mi esperanza,
y entonces daré venganza
a su injurioso rigor,
porque el desdén y el favor
paguen firmeza y mudanza.
Yo le querré eternamente,
y eternamente también
se vengará mi desden
de lo que en el suyo siente.
(II.ix. p. 1471a–b.)

Thus the situation is an ambiguous one for Magdalena, too, who simultaneously loves and hates Melchor. The two emotional forces play a tug-of-war game at which neither can win—to the pain and frustration of both lovers.

When Melchor arrives to take leave of Don Alonso, he finds that his sacrifice of Magdalena is to no purpose, for he is to lose both the Countess and Magdalena (II.xii). In III.ii, however, Santillana's arrival lifts him from the bottom of despair, into which he again falls in III.xii. The same curve is traced once more in III.xviii. It is clear that Magdalena has miscalculated. She has completely lost control of the situation. Driven on by her curiosity to see if Melchor can at all be trapped into revealing signs of "infidelity" (a morbid preoccupation, which is virtually the manifestation of the "death-wish" of love), she devises a game which becomes an emotional trap for herself. Her own strength is inadequate to secure her release. In a psychological and human sense, this is, in a way, tragic: it is surely Magdalena's feelings of guilt which make her desire to establish Melchor's guilt, i.e., his infidelity. His constancy to the *tapada* makes it impossible for Magdalena to abandon her disguise. But Melchor cannot marry the *tapada*, for not only is the Condesa de Chirinola non-existent, but even when Melchor agrees to marry Magdalena in order to please his

Condesa, the latter, curiously enough, will not have it. As we shall see, Magdalena's problem will not be resolved until the *tapada* is proved to be another person, i.e., until her feelings of "guilt" which divide her against herself are swamped by an outside threat to her love. But the situation is, at the same time, ridiculous. Not only is it absurd (for how can any normal woman be "celosa de sí misma"?), but it also has been created by Magdalena's own folly. It is the ridiculous aspect of this situation which Tirso is going to develop in order to bring about a *dénouement*.

Thus it would be wrong to see Magdalena as another "typical" Tirsian heroine who manages to trap a husband. Just as Tirso inverts the normal society-individual clash in the case of the arranged marriage which turns out to be suitable (though a number of the characters on stage do not realise it), he likewise inverts the normal mate-hunt situation in this play. There is no need for Magdalena to resort (as she does) to any stratagems in order to win a husband. There is no husband to be trapped: he has already been caught. The only difficulty is that he does not know that the woman by whom he has been trapped is the one he is meant to marry. This is partly his own fault, but largely Magdalena's doing. The *manto* is at the source of the whole problem.

In addition, the Tirsian heroine is generally mistress of the situation she creates, as we saw in *Don Gil*. Jerónima, too, in *El amor médico*, controls the whole game and every move of hers is merely another step towards the final checkmate. The heroines in those plays are typical comic wits. Magdalena, however, soon loses control of the game she starts. She thinks she is a wit, but only proves that she is her own gull. She is virtually a parody of the "typical" Tirsian heroine.

The secondary action, which, as I have stated, is essential to a resolution of the problem, is built around the intrigues of Sebastián and Angela. These, as a convention of the *comedia* seems to demand, are rivals of Melchor and Magdalena. As a result, their machinations, which are the means they employ to fulfil their ambitions, are conditioned to a certain extent by the situations developed in the main action. Conventional rivals though they be, they are made to serve a vital purpose in the structure of the play.

The genesis of the secondary action (which introduces the corruption motif into the play) is to be found in I.ii. pp. 1443b–1444a, where Sebastián cleverly manages to extract from the relatively inexperienced Jerónimo the fact that he is rich and has a rich sister. Sebastián's greed is immediately aroused and he at once seeks to establish a friendly relationship between the two families. He tells Jerónimo of his *melindrosa* sister, beautiful but immensely proud, at whose *extremos* he invites Jerónimo to laugh:

SEBASTIÁN: Sí, pero es nunca acabar
si os cuento en lo que se estima.
De todos hace desprecio;
el más Salomón es necio,
si a pretenderla se anima;
Tersites el más galan,
Lázaro pobre el más Creso,
y el más noble, hombre sin seso.
No quiere venir de Adán,
porque dice que no pudo
progenitor suyo ser
quien delante su mujer
se atrevía a andar desnudo.

(I.ii. p. 1444b.)

In I.ix, we realise that his desire to cement the friendship between his house and Jerónimo's has not grown cold. He is obviously eager that Magdalena should see him before she sees Melchor. Thus both the principal and the secondary actions have a common source in the existence of the rich nubile Magdalena.

In II.vi, Sebastián's plans take shape. He is interested in marrying Doña Magdalena, and thinks of ways of preventing her marriage to Melchor. His first thought is to kill Melchor, but he renounces this in favour of an easier (and cheaper) ruse. In the following scene, however, Ángela discovers that Melchor loves the Condesa: this puts a valuable weapon into her hands, and at the end of the act she has the satisfaction of seeing the engagement between Melchor and Magdalena broken off. This situation is, for a start, equally satisfactory to Sebastián as to Ángela, while Sebastián loses no time in suggesting himself and his sister to Don Alonso as a suitable son and daughter-in-law (II.x. p. 1472b).

At this point, control of the action passes into Ángela's hands, with the unhappy result that Sebastián's plan to marry Magdalena is thwarted, and his attempt to marry his sister to Jerónimo very nearly fails. Sebastián's failure is morally justified. His desire to marry Magdalena and his attempt to foil the plans for her marriage to Melchor were motivated by greed, by *interés*. Marriage is more than a profitable merger of partners, and Sebastián's failure has the weight of the traditional *comedia* attitude (which favours love) behind it.

The case of Doña Ángela, however, is more complex. She is by far the more important of the two rivals. Sebastián in his initial remarks to Jerónimo painted her as a *melindrosa* creature. Her first appearance on stage gives further proof of the nicety of her scruples:

ÁNGELA:	¡Jesús! Delante de un cura
	(por más que el Cielo dispuso
	que se desposen así),
	y tanta gente, ¿ha de haber
	tan atrevida mujer
	que le diga a un hombre "sí"?
SEBASTIÁN:	Pues ¿qué escrúpulo hay en eso?
ÁNGELA:	¡Jesús! Quien hace tal cosa,
	o es muy libre y animosa
	o no tiene mucho seso.

(I.ix. p. 1456a–b.)

But we soon see that even the staid, sensible Ángela is completely transformed by love.

When Ángela first sees Melchor her remarks give an ambiguous twist to her character: "El leonés es por extremo / como no oliera a marido" (I.x. p. 1458a). We are puzzled, until, in the next act, we realise that we had been witnessing the beginning of a change in Ángela's character. In II.vi, she frankly confesses her love for Melchor to Sebastián, whose phlegmatic, matter-of-fact acceptance of the news is, to say the least, surprising. However, love and initiative appear simultaneously in Ángela, and by the end of the act, she and Sebastián have denounced Melchor to Don Alonso and Don Jerónimo.

In Act III, Doña Ángela comes to the fore. A rift now begins to appear between herself and her brother. The latter's plan includes the marriage of his sister to Jerónimo; but Ángela herself is in love with Melchor and she plans her strategy with marriage to Melchor as her aim. Love, in fact, has effected a complete change in Ángela's character. All her former scruples are thrown overboard and she launches out upon a daring plan which consists in no less than usurping the personality of her real rival (as she has discovered), the *Condesa tapada*, in order to trick Melchor into marrying her. This act of Ángela's links the two actions of the plot.

So far, the presentation of Ángela has been fairly conventional. We have, first, the traditional ridicule of the beautiful but cruel woman who is "punished" for rebelling against nature by being made to fall hopelessly in love. Secondly, the device Ángela resorts to is also a conventional one—though at the same time it emphasises the extremes to which the once haughty and very proper Ángela has been forced.

What is novel, however, is the way this situation is developed in the context of the play. Our analysis of the main action revealed that an impasse had been reached owing to Magdalena's psychological problem. There is thus a psychological as well as a dramatic need for a solution. Now, dramatically, the complication produced in a plot by the use of disguise is normally resolved by the revelation of the identity of the disguised person. It is clear that the situation created in La *celosa de sí misma* can only be resolved by the discovery of the Condesa's identity. Self-revelation is the obvious way out, but we have seen that Magdalena is unable to renounce her shadow self. Therefore the revelation of identity must be forced by external factors. One way of forcing this revelation is to confront the genuine shadow figure with a false one. Basically, this is the device Tirso employs, but his use of it is remarkably subtle.

Ángela's resorting to disguise is precisely the catalyst that produces the final *dénouement*, and is a further variation on the *tropelía* theme. Her disguise leads to the clash of the two actions, and it is this impinging of the secondary action on the principal which forces Magdalena to reveal her identity. III.xi, then, is the crucial point of the play, for it is here that the trajectories of the two actions clash, with a consequent shattering of the false personality around which the action of the play has been constructed. It deserves a closer examination.

In III.viii, we see that the Condesa has materialised, and confronts Magdalena in the following scene. The appearance of a flesh-and-blood Condesa saves Magdalena from the sterile, self-destructive conflict with herself by giving her a real rival. However, a show-down is prevented by the appearance of Jerónimo and Sebastián (producing, one is tempted to say, an interrupted cadence), and the revelation of identity is postponed. The evidence, though abundant, is inconclusive. The two veiled women are virtually carbon copies of the Condesa, whose right to identity is being challenged. The confrontation ends with an apparent discomfiture of Magdalena. Ángela, however, is too timid to follow up the advantages of her victory, and the outcome of the battle is to be decided later that night.

The "interrupted cadence" (if we may call it thus) is puzzling. There is no dramatic reason why the *dénouement* should not have been effected in this scene. True, the postponement of the discovery scene prolongs Melchor's mental torture. But this in itself, though comic, does not seem to be the reason for Tirso's unusual procedure. An explanation is to be sought, first, in Magdalena's subsequent behaviour, now that she is confronted with a concrete *tapada* who is not herself, and then, in its implications.

The fact is that while the *tapadas* retain their incognito, for Magdalena, Ángela is still the Countess and, therefore, her second self (albeit a *second* second-self):

QUIÑONES: Ya de otra dama ofendida,
               no tendrás de ti recelo.
MAGDALENA: Con ese mismo desvelo
               quejas de mí misma doy;
               pues si la condesa soy
               que él ama, y mi opositora
               finge ser la misma agora,
               mal conmigo misma estoy.
               Como a Condesa, ¿no me ama
               don Melchor?
QUIÑONES: Por ti se enciende.
MAGDALENA: ¿Ser condesa no pretende
               mi enemiga?
QUIÑONES: Así se llama.
MAGDALENA: Luego si una misma llama
               causa aqueste frenesí
               y yo quien le abrasó fui,
               aunque esotra lo enamore;
               mientras en ella me adore,
               celosa estaré de mí.
               Dame tú que ella dijera
               ser Magdalena fingida,
               y vieras que aborrecida
               della como de mí huyera.
               Mira qué extraña quimera
               causa este ciego interés,
               que en tres dividirme ves,
               y aunque una sola en tres soy,
               amada en cuanto una, estoy
               celosa de todas tres.
                              (III.xvi. p. 1486a.)

Magdalena obviously prefers the identity of the Condesa to her own, since it is the Condesa whom Melchor loves. But these two figures must somehow be reconciled. In the final interview with Melchor in III.xviii, Magdalena makes a last attempt to fuse the identities of the Countess and herself. However, although she gets Melchor to promise, albeit unwillingly, to marry Magdalena, we see that she has not been entirely cured;

for in a fit of jealousy and anger, she slams the window in Melchor's face. It is now Magdalena's preference of the false Countess to her own self which is the obstacle to her marriage with Melchor. To solve this problem, her second self has to be shown to be someone else, a person who threatens the happiness of both Magdalena-Condesa and Magdalena-Magdalena. Ángela's claim to be the Countess provides precisely such a threat when she declares that she, Ángela, is the Countess. Magdalena, no longer eager for Melchor to remain faithful to his Countess, refutes this claim with her hand as conclusive proof, and all ends happily.

Or perhaps not as happily as may appear at first sight. There is no doubt that Ángela's plans have failed. First, her attempt to thwart Sebastián's plan to marry her to Jerónimo fails. She also fails in her attempt to help Sebastián to marry Magdalena, for the very steps she takes to prevent Magdalena's marriage to Melchor actually precipitated it. Her own attempt to marry Melchor is also frustrated, for the tricks she resorts to, i.e., impersonating the Condesa, actually provides a way out of the impasse created in the main plot. In other words, the device of the *mujer tapada*, resorted to by Ángela as a conventional way of capturing a husband, is a failure. It has been utterly useless, for it defeats its own purpose.

Nor are we to think that Magdalena's employment of the device has been more successful. The fact that any such device was unnecessary from the start has been pointed out already. It has only succeeded in creating unnecessary confusion. The game which Magdalena initiates out of sheer thoughtlessness eventually gets out of hand, and, in fact, it is only Ángela's intervention in III.xx, which prevents Melchor from coming to grief. Magdalena discovers that the more she clings to her assumed personality (which in a conventional situation would get her her man), the less chance she has of winning Melchor. So she is at the end forced to reveal her true identity in order to avoid losing Melchor. We must conclude that the use of the device of the *mujer tapada* in this play ends in complete failure.

How is this to be explained? In the first place, we note that the plans of the main characters deserve to fail. Sebastián has been motivated by greed. Ángela is punished for her earlier haughtiness. Melchor is ridiculed for his folly, which consists in being constant "a lo ridículo," and Magdalena for hers. On the psychoanalytic plane, too, Magdalena's "cure" depends upon the failure of the device which has divided her against herself. All these characters betray a frivolous attitude to life. Important human emotions, actions and relations have been reduced, in the confused Madrid setting, to the level of a frivolous game. Thus the interior moral logic of the play demands that the use of the device in question (the concrete illustration of such frivolity) should fail.[10]

But the condemnation of this frivolity is also turned into a comment on existing dramatic conventions, which are, by implication, no less frivolous. The structure of the play, we recall, consists, in skeleton form, of two converging actions, the clash of which produces the disintegration of the *tapadas*, Magdalena's dramatically unconventional (because gratuitous) use of the *manto* produces the complication of the plot, but cannot bring about its unravelling. The *dénouement* is achieved by Ángela's conventional use of the *manto*, which fails to achieve its purpose, but, because of its failure, solves Magdalena's problem, the two failures, so to speak, cancelling each other out. Two would-be wits turn out to be unwitting gulls of their own bungled games. But the irony of comedy converts their failure into a success of sorts. The structure of the play is thus itself satirical of dramatic conventions. The comedy is a perfect example of Tirsian "anti-drama."

There is a further explanation for the ridicule of the device if we consider the social context in which the play first appeared. The *manto* was widely used in sixteenth- and seventeenth-century Spain, but it clearly was no longer a sign of feminine modesty by the seventeenth century. It lent itself to abuses not only on the part of women, but also on the part of men, as the following extract from the *Cartas de jesuitas* illustrates with a real-life version of *tropelía*:

No sé sobre qué andaba la justicia estos días buscando á un religioso de grave religión; supo que estaba en una casa, buscóla, y al fin vió en el estrado con la señora á una tapada; alzaron el manto y hallaron al santo religioso con su cerquillo y en hábito de mujer.[11]

The *manto*, by preserving the anonymity of the wearer provided women with considerable moral freedom (which finds a reflection in Tirso's *El amor médico*). *Premáticas* in the years 1586, 1594, 1610 and 1639 prohibited the use of the *manto* as a result.[12] Quevedo himself wrote a poem on the occasion of one of these *premáticas*.[13] Of course, the fact that the *premáticas* had to be repeated suggests that the women paid little heed to them. But that the *mantos* were regarded as morally dangerous is obvious, and is a further explanation for Tirso's ridicule of the custom in this play.

The final dimension to our exploration of the play's meaning emerges from an examination of its style. Here, too, the *tropelía* theme dominates. There is little doubt that Tirso was deliberately satirising Gongorism.[14] And Gongorism, of course, is a form of *tropelía*. There is an overt reference to the *Soledades* at the beginning of the play:

VENTURA: A la puerta
desta devota capilla
de la Soledad, y en ella
a un fraile, que, esgrimidor,
juntó el pomo a la contera.
(I.iii. p. 1445a.)

As if to ensure that the point was grasped, the allusion returns a few lines later:

[MELCHOR:] ¡Ay si de la Soledad
esta hermosa imagen fuera,
y no de la compañía,
porque ninguna tuviera!
(I.iii. p. 1445b.)

The implications of the religious terminology will be discussed later, but Tirso manages another reference to Góngora later on the same scene:

[VENTURA:] Mas ven acá; si esta mano
viene a ser, cuando la veas,
de algun rostro polifemo,
o alguna cara juaneta,
¿qué has de hacer?
(I.iii. p. 1447a.)

Melchor persists throughout the play in interposing a Gongoristic style between reality and his perception of it, and this is mercilessly satirised by Ventura from the start:

MELCHOR: ¿De qué suerte pude verla,
si me embarazó los ojos
aquella blancura tierna,
aquel cristal animado
aquel . . .
VENTURA: Di candor, si intentas
jerigonzar critiquicios;
di que brillaba en estrellas,
que emulaba resplandores,
que circulaba en esferas,
que atesoraba diamantes,
que bostezaba azucenas.
(I.iii. p. 1446a.)

Tirso manages to include most of the obvious features of Gongorism in
the course of the play. Melchor refers to the whiteness of the hand he
adores thus:

> Cúpome, al oír la misa
> su lado; y cuando la empiezan,
> quitó la funda al cristal,
> y en la distancia pequeña
> que hay desde el guante a la frente,
> vi jazmines, vi mosquetas,
> vi alabastros, vi diamantes,
> vi, al fin, nieve en fuego envuelta.
>
> (I.iii. p. 1446a.)

Some of Góngora's favourite images appear in the following passages:

> [MELCHOR:]   y salgo a aguardarla aquí,
> deseando que amanezca
> el alba de aquella mano,
> cuando, cisne puro, vuelva
> a bañarse en la agua santa
> que en esta pila desean
> mis esperanzas gozar,
> después que no la vean, secas.
>
> (I.iii. p. 1447a.)

> [MAGDALENA:]   Pidióme que de su parte
> me despidiese a lo fino,
> y enjugó a los soles perlas
> con aquel marfil bruñido,
> en cuya comparación
> es yeso, es carbón el mío,
> y es, en fin, una Etiopía.
>
> (II.xii. p. 1473b.)

Syntactical tricks are not omitted:

> MELCHOR: Ya sale; apártate, y mira
> la hermosa mano que llega
> a transformar gotas de agua
> si no en diamantes, en perlas.
>
> (I.iii. p. 1447b.)

And the light-darkness opposition is developed at length in the following
speech:

MELCHOR: Deslutalde al sol la noche,
                    dejad su luz descubierta,
                    pues no es bien cuando despierta
                    deseos en que me abraso,
                    señora, que al mismo paso
                    que la adoro, me atormente
                    y apenas goce su oriente,
                    cuando me aflija su ocaso.
                    Crepúsculos tiene el día,
                    como al nacer, al ponerse
                    que ven antes de esconderse,
                    los que adoran su alegría.
                    Sol hermoso, mano mía,
                    si al nacer me os habéis puesto
                    en el ocaso molesto
                    que mis esperanzas ciega,
                    sol parecéis de Noruega,
                    pues os escondéis tan presto [;]
                    agua traéis; no me espanto,
                    mi amor llamas multiplica,
                    porque llover pronostica
                    el sol, cuando abrasa tanto.
                    Basta que el avaro manto
                    sirva de nube sagrada
                    a esa gloria idolatrada;
                    descubríos, blanca aurora,
                    que dirán que sois traidora,
                    pues dais muerte, disfrazada.

                                          (I.iv. p. 1448a.)

Examples could be quoted at length, but there is no need to stress the point further: reality is made to appear other than it really is. Ventura sums up the confusion in which the process ends:

VENTURA: Quitad la encella a esa nata
                    si es que hay natas con encellas;
                    que yendo a decir "cuajada,"
                    andan, desde que hablan cultos,
                    las metáforas bastardas.

                                          (III.viii. p. 1481a.)

The connexion with the chaotic Madrid is evident, for, as A. Valbuena Prat puts it:

El culteranismo se convirtió en una moda de Corte. El lenguaje culto se hizo típico de los galanes y lindos del Madrid de los últimos Felipes.[15]

However, this is not all. The love-affair between Melchor and the *tapada* begins in the Church. This play, as Valbuena states on p. 238 of the same work, suggests that the Victoria was one of the focal points of Madrid:

La *Iglesia de la Victoria*, que se hallaba en la Puerta del Sol, era el templo cortesano por excelencia donde acudían a Misa magnates, galanes y grandes señoras, lo que diríamos hoy *la iglesia de moda*, como se desprende de un pintoresco texto de Tirso en su animada comedia *La celosa de sí misma*."

The suggestion is repeated in *Por el sotano y el torno*. Thus it is only natural that religious terminology should mingle with the words of love. Much of the comic effect of the language springs from this subtle allusion to Biblical or religious contexts. A number of the characters' names have religious associations: Magdalena, Ángela, Jerónimo, Sebastián. The following two quotations have obvious Biblical overtones:

MELCHOR: ¿Soy yo, señora, el llamado?
VENTURA: ¿Sois vos, decid, la escogida?
                                              (II.iv. p. 1463a.)

[QUIÑONES:] A alargar la dilacion
             de mi ama voy agora,
             porque su competidora
             le gane la bendición.
                                              (III.vi. p. 1479b.)[16]

References to the Inquisition are not missing:

[QUIÑONES:] Nuestra doña Magdalena
             (que para decir verdad
             tiene extraña voluntad
             a don Melchor), con la pena
             y celos de quien adora,
             en fe que por él se abrasa
             para saber lo que pasa
             me ha hecho su inquisidora.
                                              (III.v. p.1478a.)

And there is a humorous comment on Magdalena's display of her eyes: "VENTURA: ¿Son reliquias / de una en una?" (II.v. p. 1466b.) Ventura realises that his jokes are a bit outrageous:

¡Oh que mano, más celebrada. . . ! (*Aparte*)
Iba a decir que una misa
nueva y de aldea; mas no,
que es descompuesta osadía.
                    (II.v. p. 1467a.)

Cleverly, Gongorism and the amorous-religious terminology are fused:

[MELCHOR:]   Volvió en ocasos de ámbar
                segunda vez a esconderla,
                hasta que en pie al Evangelio,
                amaneció aurora fresca.
                Santiguóse al comenzarle
                y al darle fin la encarcela
                hasta el *Sanctus*, que desnuda
                da aldabadas a la puerta
                del pecho, llamando al alma
                que deseosa de vella,
                debió penetrar cartones,
                pues corazones penetra.
                Duró esta vez el gozarla
                sin la prisión avarienta,
                hasta consumir el cáliz.
                ¡Ay Dios, si mil siglos fueran!
                Volvió a ponérseme el sol,
                hasta que, acabando, empieza
                el Evangelio postrero,
                siendo también la postrera
                liberalidad feliz
                que hizo a mi vista, ciega
                con la oscura privación
                de su cándida pureza.
                    (I.iii. p. 1446a–b.)

But Melchor's words make it clear that we have to do with the religion of love:

            ¡Ojalá fuera
divina mi devoción,
y la imagen causa della!
Devoto salgo, Ventura;
pero a lo humano, ¡Ay, qué bella
imagen vi! Si es imagen
quien a sí se representa.
                    (I.iii. p. 1445a–b.)

Melchor, as he has declared, is a "devoto . . . a lo humano," and his language faithfully reflects this:

> Verdadera información
> habéis hecho, y tan cumplida
> como la fe con que os amo;
> mas creed, tapada mía,
> que obligado a diligencias
> tan amorosas y dignas
> de la eterna estimación;
> si como el alma imagina,
> sois hermosa (que sí sois,
> pues por más que el manto impida
> milagros que reverencio,
> es mi amor lince en la vista);
> ni el oro, ni la belleza,
> ni imposibles de la envidia,
> tienen de ser poderosos
> a que no os adore y sirva.
>
> (II.iv. p. 1464a.)

This has been led up to by the earlier insertion of religious terms into an as yet ordinary, secular love:

[MELCHOR:]   Cesó el no oído oficio,
               que me holgara yo que fuera
               de Pasión.

                                        (I.iii. p. 1447a.)

And there is an implicit condemnation of the blasphemous overtones by Ventura:

MELCHOR: Si vieras tú aquella mano
               y aquel talle, no dijeras
               blasfemias a su hermosura.
VENTURA: A tu amor digo blasfemias.

                                        (I.iii. p. 1447b.)

Valbuena has rightly draw attention to the frivolous nature of this situation:

Al ir describiendo la dama que le enamoró, y sus actitudes durante la misa, hay un juego encantador entre lo devoto del tema y la frivolidad amorosa en torno a él. Todas las observaciones de la blanca mano de la dama al santiguarse, al darse golpes de pecho, están expresadas con toques culteranos de refinada poesía y delicada malicia típica del ingenio de Tirso. (p. 239)

We may add that the ambivalence inherent in the language of the religion of love is a stylistic version of the *tropelía* motif. The religion of love is and is not a religion at all. But human love, by being clothed in the garb of religious terminology, is made to appear to be what it is not. That is why the goddess Melchor worships, i.e., the Condesa de Chirinola, is proved to be a non-existent, false deity.

The Condesa is a product of *tropelía*. Magdalena's use of the *manto* as a disguise, a mask behind which she can carry on a frivolous and pointless flirtation, sets up an opposition between what she poses as and what she is. But the distinction is not as clear-cut as we might at first think. The Condesa is and at the same time is not Magdalena. The hand is and simultaneously is not Magdalena's. The Condesa and her hand are illusions created by the *manto* and the *red*. And not merely is it that Melchor, ignorant of this *tropelía*, refuses to accept that Magdalena is the Condesa, but Magdalena herself thinks she can change while yet remaining the same (the sexual overtones implying that the Condesa-Melchor relationship is at bottom human):

MAGDALENA: Iguálame ese vestido,
                que con el otro que dejo,
                los pensamientos desnudo
                que aquel extranjero pudo
                engendrar.
                                (I.viii. p. 1454b.)

There would seem to be a contradiction or confusion here. A thing clearly cannot be both itself and simultaneously something else. And yet the *tapada* is simultaneously Magdalena and the Condesa, who, even to Magdalena herself, are almost distinct persons. The situation is absurd, like the complex relationships in the plot. But this absurdity has a respectable justification—Neo-Platonic philosophy.

Neo-Platonism is a complex phenomenon and has a considerable influence on various aspects of life, religion, philosophy and culture in the sixteenth and seventeenth centuries. Not surprisingly, its influence on literature is marked. It is the literary conventions which derive from Neo-Platonic premises and which serve as the bases for so many works of literature that Tirso sets out to satirise in this play. The ensuing remarks, then, refer essentially to these literary conventions and not to the philosophy itself as a whole.

The principal conventions for the purpose of this analysis are as follows. Human love is idealised and regarded as something spiritual, and, consequently, non-sexual. It is born of a spiritual affinity which springs from a recognition of spiritual and moral beauty. Such beauty, however, in a world of shadows and imperfections is indicated by and reflected in physical beauty (hence the assumption of the period that physical imperfections reflect inherent moral ones). This physical beauty is loved not for its own sake but because it is a symbolical representation or indication of spiritual beauty. The whole process is one of abstraction from reality, the ultimate stress being on the abstract of the ideal of feminine beauty which is the object of a non-physical love.

These literary conventions are for Tirso, in some of his satirical comedies, absurd affectations, not based on a sound, realistic appraisal of human love. Thus we can appreciate the full force of Ventura's humorous remark, quoted earlier: "La primera vez es ésta / que entró el amor por grosura." (I.iii. p. 1447a) This is not to imply that Tirso denies the spiritual aspect of love. He is merely asserting that love between man and woman is not and cannot be the basis for a satisfactory marriage. I shall try to show how these ideas are worked out in the play.

Melchor's language makes it plain that he is a Neo-platonist and the *tapada*, his platonic ideal of beauty. This is why the Condesa de Chirinola is hidden from human eyes by a veil,[17] for the Idea is perceived, not by gross human eyes, but by the intellect. The beauty of the *tapada* has to be imagined. But from glimpses of her hand and eyes,[18] Melchor deduces that her beauty must exceed that of any other woman. If Neo-Platonic philosophy is true, the beauty of the net-covered hand promises a countenance which it is implied must be much more beauteous than Magdalena's ((II.iii. p. 1461b.)

Melchor has insisted from the beginning that the hand must indicate the face's beauty (I.iii. p. 1447b.). But if we are to be consistent as Neo-Platonists, the beauty of the face must be Absolute Beauty, the perfect Form which exists only in the Platonic heaven—and Melchor's imagination. Magdalena is fully aware of this inherent danger in the Neo-Platonic outlook:

> Pero, no,
> que vuestro deseo me pinta
> más bella de lo que soy,
> y temo perder la estima
> en que estoy, imaginada,
> cuando no la iguale, vista.
>
> (II.iv. p. 1464a.)

What is more, since we know the Platonic reality only by recreating it in our minds from the evidence of its reflection on earth, how are we to know this real reality when and if we see it? Melchor, on seeing Ángela's eye, is sure, notwithstanding Ventura's protest, that Ángela is his love (III.viii. p. 1481b.). But when another *tapada* enters, Melchor is faced with another philosophical dilemma, and, for its solution, would revert to the prime, material cause of his love:

> ¡Problemática cuestión!
> Dos sendas hallo encontradas
> y yo indiferente entre ellas,
> ignoro por cuál me vaya.
> Pero la mano, que fue
> de mi amor primera causa,
> tengo dentro el alma impresa,
> y la memoria la guarda;
> mostradme, señoras mías,
> cada cual la suya, y salga
> victoriosa la que oblique
> que mi amor llegue a besarla.
>
> (III.ix. p. 1483b.)

He is still not enlightened when, towards the end of the play, he is prepared to accept Ángela, now unveiled, as his wife:

> ¡Ay señora de mis ojos!
> No en balde el alma discreta,
> sin veros, hizo elección
> de tan celestial presencia.
> Vos sois mi querida esposa.
>
> (III.xxi. p. 1491b.)

Suddenly we realise what Tirso has done. The distinction between Magdalena and the Condesa, while only an apparent one to us (being the product of *tropelía*), is half-real to Magdalena herself and fully valid for Melchor, to whom his beloved *tapada* is the Neo-Platonic ideal of beauty. But human love desires the unveiling of this ideal beauty. This, as any Neo-Platonist knows, is rash: human eyes cannot look upon the *sun*—and here, certainly, is where Neo-Platonism and Gongorism join hands![19] Yet the sun *is* unveiled, and Melchor can look it straight in the eye—and see a woman's face. The Neo-Platonic reality behind the veil seems to be, after all, only another Platonic "shadow." The explanation for this lies in the fact that this so-called "reality" takes the earthly "shadow" as its

starting point and model, and, in fact, *is* a "shadow" which is transformed
into "reality" by the imagination and reason. Neo-Platonic "reality" is the
Platonic "shadow" which, of course, is the reality we all know.

But there is a further complication. The Platonic "reality," being an
abstraction, a concept, has no such thing as identity. Therefore, when it is
unveiled—and here the wit of the situation emerges—we can get only the
equivalent of the Platonic "shadow," i.e., *any* beautiful woman—Ángela,
Magdalena (or any other). The true Condesa has no identity on this earth:
she is non-existent, a mere figment of the imagination. Tirso has wittily
equated the Neo-Platonic reality with an unsubstantial shadow, a mere
abstraction from the Platonic "shadow," which is the real reality.

The structure of the play exposes the limitations and ultimate absurdity
of the literary Neo-Platonic view. It is because the Condesa is the ideal
woman that Melchor loves her, and this, in turn, is why Magdalena wants
to be the Condesa and is angry in III.xviii when Melchor agrees to marry
Magdalena. But Magdalena's identification with the Condesa is only possible for so long as the latter remains the abstract Platonic ideal, without
an identity. A man cannot marry an abstract concept of beauty, however,
and that is why Melchor's marriage to the Condesa is an impossiblity.

For similar reasons Ángela also seeks to identify herself with the Condesa. The situation is virtually the same as in Magdalena's case, but, as we
have seen, the effect on the plot is crucial. Magdalena is perversely content to pretend to be the Condesa, hoping to fuse their identities somehow,
and encouraging Melchor to marry the Condesa. But once the Condesa
materialises and presents a threat to Magdalena's happiness by declaring
she is Ángela, Magdalena is glad to put an end to her game. For Ángela's
claims are as valid as Magdalena's. It is only on the coarse, earthly level
that such trivial distinctions as the colour of the eyes have any importance
or validity. But, also, it is only on the same coarse, earthly level that
human love and marriage are possible. To the Neo-Platonic Melchor, one
woman would make just as good a wife as another. This is a view no
sane and moral woman—and Magdalena *is* a woman—would share.

The *manto*, the *red*, Gongorism, the religion of love and Neo-Platonism
are thus all shown as variations of *tropelía*. Neo-Platonism converts objects, the reality we know, into shadows, the "unreal" reflections of ideal
forms. Similarly, the religion of love converts love into an apparent religion and woman into an apparent goddess. Gongorism, too, converts a
hand into *cristal*, a veil into a cloud, a face into the sun. But these are
all apparent changes, for we know that a face remains a face, a woman, a
woman, and love, love. Magdalena must remain Magdalena, and Ángela,

Ángela. This is something the main characters discover. Melchor cannot marry the Condesa, who is a non-existent abstraction. Therefore she must be destroyed so that human beings can carry on with the business of living. *La celosa de sí misma* is a systematic and witty satire of all forms of *tropelía*: Gongorism, the religion of love, dramatic devices, morally perverse customs, and, the most absurd of them all, the literary derivations of Neo-Platonism.

NOTES

1 In vol. II of his *Teatro escogido de Fray Gabriel Telléz* (Madrid, 1839–42).

2 See E. Schancer's article, "A Midsummer-Night's Dream" in *Shakespeare. The Comedies*, ed. K. Muir (3rd printing, Prentice Hall, Englewood Cliffs, New Jersey, 1965). The structural function of setting in Shakespeare and other Elizabethan dramatists is examined by M. Doran in *Endeavors of Art* (Madison, Univ. of Wisconsin Press, 1954), chap. X. This analytic method owes much to the "Lexicon Rhetoricae" of K. Burke's stimulating *Counter-Statement* (2nd ed., Los Altos, California, 1953).

3 Quotations are by Act, scene and page. The ed. used is Doña Blanca de los Ríos in *Tirso de Molina. Obras dramáticas completas*, vol. II (Madrid, 1962).

4 "Pechelingue." Doña Blanca suggests that here the word means "pirate," and at other times "heretic." However, in the intro. to *Amar por arte mayor* (vol. III of her ed., p. 1166b) she gives what appears to be a more acceptable meaning, viz., that the word is a phonetic transcription of "speech English." I have been unable to find the word in such dictionaries of the period as I have consulted. It seems to be one of Tirso's inventions. The fact that it occurs in *Amar por arte mayor* may suggest a chronological proximity with *La celosa*, although the former appears to be considerable later than *La celosa*, (1627–29 as opposed to 1622).

5 Vol. IV of the *Dicc. crítico etimológico de la lengua castellana* (Berne, 1957), pp. 604–5.

6 The function of the *tropelía* motif in Cervantes' *Novela ejemplar* has been brilliantly analysed by L. J. Woodward in *"El casamiento engañoso y El coloquio de los perros,"* BHS, XXXVI (1959), 80–87.

7 "Some Baroque Aspects of Tirso de Molina," RR, XXXVI (1945), 43–69.

8 In her intro. to the play, *op. cit.*, p. 1436b.

9 S. E. Leavitt has analysed examples of "strip-tease" in Golden Age drama in his article 'Strip-tease in Golden Age Drama,' *Homenaje a Rodríguez-Moñino*, I (Madrid, 1966), pp. 305–310. He does not, however, refer to this scene which is much more delicate, and, perhaps, even more suggestive than the ones he discusses.

10 We note that almost all the characters contribute in some way towards the failure of the device. This process (but on a different level and in a different key) bears some resemblance to the working of what A. A. Parker has aptly termed "diffused responsibility" in Calderón's tragedies (in "Towards a Definition of Calderonian Tragedy," *BHS*, XXXIX [1962], 222–37).

11 *Cartas de jesuitas*, vol. I (Madrid, 1861) p. 45. Letter dated Madrid, 6th May, 1634, from Francisco de Vilches to P. Rafael Pereyra.

12 See, e.g., P. W. Bomli, *La Femme dans l'Espagne du siècle d'or* (La Haye, 1950), p. 115. Bomli confirms that all foreigners spoke of the liberty of the *mujer tapada*.

13 "Confisión que hacen los mantos de sus culpas en la premática de no taparse las mujeres." No. LXX in *Obras completas. Verso*, ed. Astrana Marín (3rd ed., Madrid, 1952), pp. 361–64.

14 This is pointed out by Cotarelo in *Tirso de Molina: Investigaciones bio-bibliográficas* (Madrid, 1893) and by Ruth L. Kennedy in "On the Date of Five Plays by Tirso de Molina," *HR*, X (1942), 183–214.

15 *La vida española en la edad de oro* (Barcelona, 1943), p. 251.

16 The first passage is obviously an echo of the parable of the marriage feast (Matthew, chap. 22, vv. 1–14, and, in particular, v. 14: "For many are called, but few are chosen"). The second passage is a ref. to the story of Esau and Jacob (Genesis, chap. 27).

17 So, too, is God. Thus the parallel of the religion of love is valid here too; the goddess of this religion is also a hidden one.

18 On the level of the religion of love, these are the "revelations" granted to the "worshipper" in Church. Melchor, in fact, had asked for such a "revelation:"

> En fin: ¿mi amor no os obliga
> a que lo que por fe adoro
> vea?
>
> (II.v., p. 1466a.)

19 Here, too, there are religious overtones. Human eyes cannot look upon the Godhead. Also, it is clear that this play wittily establishes a relationship on the stylistic level between Gongorism and Neo-Platonism. R. O. Jones, in various studies, see, e.g., "The Poetic Unity of the *Soledades* of Góngora," *BHS*, XXXI (1954), 189–204; "Neo-Platonism and the *Soledades*," *BHS*, XL (1963), 1–16; "Góngora and Neo-Platonism Again," *BHS*, XLIII (1966), 117–20, has, on the other hand, sought to establish a serious, ideological connexion between the two, which is suggestive.

CHAPTER III

El amor médico.
Feminism versus Femininity

Two almost contradictory features make *El amor médico* a curiously intriguing play. On the one hand, the comedy is characterised by a brilliant play of wit which effects a reconciliation of apparent opposites by showing them to be, at bottom, one and the same thing. On the other, the play seems to be marred by a certain lack of structural coherence and dramatic economy, faults which are all the more surprising in view of the brilliance of its wit, the technical excellence of some aspects of its construction, and its probable chronological position in Tirso's dramatic production.

First, it may be helpful to try and place this comedy—if only very roughly—in its chronological context. Internal evidence indicates that the play was written after the highly complex *Don Gil de las calzas verdes* (1615). This is based not on the fact that the *disfrazada de hombre* is common to both plays (a factor which proves nothing, inasmuch as the figure constantly recurs in Tirso's production), but on the clear evidence that the play was written after Tirso's return from the Indies (1618). Reflexions on the experience which is born of travel and reminiscences of Tirso's sojourn overseas provide concrete proof of this, as Doña Blanca de los Ríos has pointed out.[1] Doña Blanca herself suggests 1619–1621 as the period during which it was written, especially as the play would seem to allude to the outbreak of the plague in Lisbon in 1619. This suggestion seems reasonable. The most obvious link between the play and historical fact is the 1617 *premática* concerning doctors to which G. E. Wade has drawn attention.[2] Medical satire is, of course, a commonplace of comedy of the period, but, while Tirso satirises the medical profession as early as 1615 (the date of *Don Gil*), the virulence of his attacks increases after 1618 (when he returns to Spain). The question of appointing doctors to the royal household remains a burning one and finds echoes in La *prudencia en la mujer* (1622).[3] Medical satire is also present in *La fingida Arcadia*

(1622–3).[4] But it is in *El amor médico* that this satire is seen at its most sustained. In fact, a modern doctor wonders whether Tirso was not being grossly unfair to members of the medical profession of his time, since he attacks them,

> insistiendo machaconamente en la ineptitud de nuestros colegas, la ineficacia de la medicina de la época, y lo que es peor, en la calidad moral de los galenos contemporáneos; no es posible recoger en la obra del mercedario una crítica más apasionada y corrosiva, si exceptuamos las privanzas cortesanas.[5]

Be that as it may (and Tirso's intimate knowledge of medical jargon would make us hesitate before we accuse him of injustice born of ignorance), the satire of doctors is an integral part of the play's theme.

Some other features also help us to establish *El amor médico* as a sort of mid-way house between *Don Gil* and *La celosa de sí misma*. As will become evident in the course of this book, some of Tirso's earlier plays appear to contain the germs of future development in his dramatic technique.[6] *El amor médico* illustrates this developing technique in a number of ways. First, disguise: this takes two forms in this play: the well-known female-page which is a common factor in *Don Gil* and *El amor médico*, and the *mujer tapada*, which serves as a link between this play and *La celosa de sí misma*, which was probably written in 1621–22. Whereas Tirso's treatment of the *tapada* is satiric in the much better constructed *La celosa*, his use of the figure conforms to a fairly conventional pattern in *El amor médico*. His more subtle handling of the *tapada* in *La celosa* would seem to indicate that *El amor médico* was a preliminary exercise in the use of this figure.

Furthermore, certain stylistic features in *El amor médico* (which I shall discuss later in greater detail) seem to point towards *La celosa*, where they are developed more extensively: these are, in particular, the use of Gongoristic devices and the humorous use of religious imagery. The latter feature, it may also be noted, finds an important structural function in *Por el sótano y el torno* (1622),[7] and, if the developing technique is accepted as valid, this argues for the prior composition of *El amor médico*. No less important is the fact that the use of Portuguese as an element of disguise is a common factor in *El amor médico* and *Por el sótano*, which seems to reinforce both their technical and chronological proximity, without, however, establishing the chronological priority of either.

Finally, the episode in II.xiii, where Gaspar's passion is aroused when Jerónima, *tapada*, reveals her uncovered hand to him would seem to confirm the relationship suggested between *El amor médico* and *La celosa*.

The motif recurs in the penultimate scene of *El amor médico*, where Gaspar's scepticism as to the real identity of Barbosa-Marta is overcome in part by his recognition of Marta's hand as the one which fired his love. In this play, the motif, appearing only at two almost isolated moments, lacks any systematic development within the play. But the motif of the hand (if we may call it thus) is extensively exploited in *La celosa*, where it is intimately connected with the dominant motifs and thus the structure of the play. Here again, it seems licit to argue that Tirso saw the potentialities of the "hand-motif" as he wrote *El amor médico* and developed them in the later play.[8]

El amor médico may thus reasonably be placed approximately midway between two high points of Tirso's dramatic art: *Don Gil* on the one hand, and *La celosa* on the other. In view of this, its apparently clumsy technique comes as a surprise, for it would suggest that Tirso's experience in the composition of *Don Gil* was of little use to him in the writing of *El amor médico*. An analysis of the latter can thus cast some light on certain aspects of Tirso's dramatic art. We may be led to conclude, among other things, either that the play is more subtly constructed than it would seem at first sight, or that Tirso's dramatic production is of a consistently uneven standard.

The initial impression produced by the play is certainly not a satisfactory one. Bruerton has stated unequivocally that the play is not one of Tirso's best.[9] Hartzenbusch, whose comments on Tirso's plays are normally lucid, seems to respond in a rather uncertain way to the play, giving it enthusiastic but at the same time qualified approval.[10] As we shall see, some of his comments on the heroine are rather ambiguous, reflecting an uncertain frame of mind, which is not surprising when we consider that the presentation of Jerónima is itself ambiguous. This seems to have been an effect deliberately aimed at by Tirso. But there is no denying the existence of flaws in the play. Some of them are real enough; others, as will become clear, are, to some extent, only apparent flaws which must cease to be regarded as such if the play's structure is examined more closely.

First, the play suffers from a repetitiousness (which one is tempted to equate with long-windedness) into which Tirso seems rather prone to fall: his plays, it may be remembered, are considerably longer than the average *comedia*. This repetitiousness seems to mar the dramatic economy of the comedy. The superb exposition of the opening scene, for example, is to a great extent repeated in I.vii. The only new detail is the knowledge that Jerónima has carried out her plan to rifle Gaspar's papers. What she has found out we know already from Gaspar himself in scene ii.

Jerónima's long speech in scene vii, then, from the technical point of view, unnecessarily slows down the action, nor is there any justification for this delay on the grounds of pure stage business. This is a curious fact, and its significance will emerge later on.

This double exposition is not the only violation of dramatic economy. There are frequent reviews of the situation: an example is Jerónima's opening speech in II.xii.: this tells us little that is new—the action has been clear enough—, and the review seems even more tautological after Gaspar's jealous speech in the immediately preceding scene. The repetitions, admittedly, are more obvious to a reader than they would be to an audience, but, as I shall suggest, Tirso probably intended that his audience should be aware of them.

The violation of economy is not confined to the verbal level. The unity of place is not observed. This is understandable enough within the contex of the conventions of the *comedia*, but the case seems to be more complex than usual in this play. The violation seems to have been quite deliberate, especially as the Castilian-Portuguese opposition is stressed throughout. Worse, the shift in setting from Seville to Coimbra occurs between Acts I and II. As the last two acts take place in Coimbra, they constitute, in one sense at least, a self-contained unity.

More striking is the fact that Acts II and III, taken together, can also be seen as a self-contained action. In other words, Act I, from the point of view of the action, appears to be almost a superfluity. What happens in the first act could have been narrated with only a minimum of additions in Act II. The latter can almost be said to start a new action in a new setting. The introduction of Rodrigo and Estefanía (with her family) to form the other two angles in a new triangular love-affair involving Gaspar, around which the main part of the rest of the plot turns, strengthens our impression that Act II virtually begins the play afresh and that Act I is little more than introductory background material to the play proper.

Tirso's management of his characters seems to be no less contributory to the prevailing impression of a self-indulgent indifference to technique. Gonzalo is introduced at the beginning of the play, indirectly in the opening scene and then directly in the following one. He promises to play an important part in the plot—he is, after all, the main obstacle between Jerónima and her Gaspar—, but he disappears permanently at the end of the play. His function is thus to serve as confidant to Gaspar in the last scene of Act I.

Gonzalo and Machado, his servant (who speaks but one line in the entire play—a feeble joke in I.ii.) are replaced in Act II by much more important characters, Rodrigo and Estefanía, along with Íñigo and Martín. Of these, Martín is a pretty useless figure and does little more than occasionally mumble the correct words at the appropriate moment. Even the appearance of the King himself seems almost a burlesque of the dramatic convention whereby the monarch intervenes at the end of a play (not, as here, at the opening of Act III) to bring justice to the wronged and restore order to a chaotic situation, for the vindication of the persecuted Barbosa is turned into an occasion for satirical innuendo about the position and privileges of palace doctors. The scene with the King marks the summit of Jerónima's feminist achievements and undoubtedly adds a dash of colour and excitement to the opening of the last act, but its main functional purpose is to be seen in the context of the medical satire in the play.

There are also some curious features concerning the characterisation. From about the end of the second act, a partial dissolution of Jerónima's personality into a stock farcical figure becomes evident. While this transformation is not absolute, in the third act especially, what seems to have begun as a comedy of character turns into a comedy of situation and wit. There are ambiguities in Gaspar's character, too, as we shall see, and we may infer that they stem, in part at least, from the demands of the action: if Gaspar is seen largely in a functional role, these ambiguities can be considered as responses, controlled by the author, to the momentary demands of external plot situations and not emerging from inner motivations of a coherent personality integrated into the plot. Such an explanation would fit in with the fact that the other secondary characters are also conceived as largely functional.

It is possible, of course, that the play may have been hastily written as a *pièce d'occasion*. Doña Blanca suggests that it may have arisen out of one of Tirso's visits to Portugal. If so, that would explain the use of Portuguese, which would be a natural way of acknowledging the presence of a largely Portuguese-speaking audience. Apart from this, however, the profusion of small, seemingly unimportant roles should be seen in the context of the theatrical conventions of the time. The play was probably written for a specific *autor* (actor-manager), and parts therefore had to be provided for all the actors in his company. Later in the century, companies would no longer be able to dictate dramatic requirements in such a way. But the conventions of the period in which Tirso wrote most of his plays were not the same as those under which Calderón was to work. Yet, it does not seem that external factors can account for all the apparent weaknesses in the play, and perhaps not at all for what appear to be its major flaws.

I suggest that the structure may be more subtle than it appears to be at first sight. Out of its apparent incongruities (which make *El amor médico* seem to be two plays arbitrarily combined to form one), there seems to emerge a binary pattern, based on the theme of the comedy, which makes for a brilliant play of wit in and through the action and characters. The play, in fact, may almost be seen as an enormous dialectic on stage, which would help to explain some of its unusual features. Tirso, in other words, seems to be experimenting here with a novel dramatic structure. In view of this, an attempt will be made to examine the witty thematic development in the play in the hope that this will lead up to a fuller understanding of its structure.

The view of comedy put forward by W. Kerr in his book, *Tragedy and Comedy*, seems to be fully supported by Tirso's *El amor médico*. Here we see the so-called "parasitic" aspect of comedy: the humorous treatment of potentially noble aspirations in man—and woman. Here, too, we detect the incongruity between these aspirations and human limitations, between an intellectual and emotive approach to life. This basic incongruity has other ramifications in the comedy which I shall presently explore.

What feminism is and whether it can be reconciled with femininity are the intriguing questions Tirso asks in this delightful play. Feminism is generally thought of as an attempt to secure the *rapprochement* of the sexes: women want to have the same rights as men; they want to practise the same professions as men; they almost seem to want to be men. This, on the surface, may appear a ludicrous impossibility (although Tirso shows how it may be possible in one sense), but the problem is perhaps a more serious one. Feminism may be regarded as a manifestation of woman's self-assertion as a free being. Such an assertion of freedom, if carried far enough, i.e., to the point where her nature was in danger of being altered, could bring her into conflict with social and natural laws—and the stage would be set for tragedy.

A woman can refuse to love, or, at least, reject marriage as a humiliating form of servitude. In so doing, she denies herself a deep emotional and physiological fulfilment which is a fundamental need of her femininity. But not only does she thus reject nature: her stance is anti-social and anti-vital, inasmuch as it tends to undermine the existence of the basic social unit, the family, the existence of which is essential for the continuation of the human race.

A further justification for this anti-vital and anti-social attitude is often sought in an alleged incompatibility between love and intellectual pursuits. This view is a recurrent one in literature. The pursuit of learning is a basic intellectual freedom: studies in themselves constitute an attempt on man's part to extend the frontiers of human knowledge. The extension of these frontiers widens the individual's sphere of action by increasing his ability to act and multiplying the opportunities for him to intervene in increasingly numerous events.

The consequences of education in a woman are easy to envisage. The range of her possible careers being widened, her functions in society changes, and so does her hierarchical position in any social structure. Thus education allows her to extend her sphere of action; but, in a social set-up in which a woman's sphere of action is rigorously defined, any such extension of her capacity to act leads her to encroach upon territory regarded as the preserve of the male. If we accept that a thing is defined not merely by virtue of what it is, but also by virtue of what it is not, we can understand more readily the view of so many persons who regard a breakdown of the male-female polarity as something verging on the absurd, if not on the horrific. Such a reaction would be much stronger in the seventeenth century, when the roles of men and women were more clearly defined and the spheres of their activities more rigidly limited. For a woman to want to usurp the functions of a man would be unfeminine, anti-social, and immoral, because unnatural. By it, the male's function in society is threatened—and perhaps his very existence. In fact, the corollary of female emancipation would seem to be an almost Shavian reduction of man's role to a secondary sexual one. And if the feminist aversion to love and marriage were erected into a norm, man would become a superfluous appendage in a feminine world.

The absurdity inherent in such a world, however, becomes immediately apparent. An exclusively feminine (like an exclusively masculine) world could exist for no longer than a single generation. The view that intellectual activity tends to be anti-vital and sterile, an assertion made through the ages and repeated by modern writers such as Ionesco and Unamuno, is not an entirely pointless one. There is thus a profound irony, which comedy exploits to the full, in the theme of the woman, the giver and propagator of life *par excellence*, who rejects her femininity in order to embrace sterile learning. This is done in the name of the pursuit of freedom, and here the irony runs even deeper. For we are faced with the paradox that the pursuit of freedom to extremes is self-defeating, since it leads to a situation where the possible field for its exercise, i.e., human existence, is destroyed, and, along with it, freedom itself.

There is another consideration to be borne in mind, however. This is the question of whether a woman is in fact capable of rejecting her femininity.

A woman's femininity is a fact of life rooted in nature, and nature is a force which few can resist and even fewer deny without peril to themselves. A woman's femininity is an essential part of her make-up, and she is thus to a certain extent controlled by it. In other words, on the emotional level, woman is susceptible to love. Its fulfilment brings into play her biological role as mother, and this is exercised in the social context of the marriage relationship. Femininity, by being an integral and, therefore, inescapable part of woman's make-up, tends, when it comes to the fore, to restrict her sphere of action. There is thus an inherent limitation in woman's very being which is at odds with the feminist desire for intellectual and social freedom. The feminist seeks to overcome this limitation by suppressing any dangerous manifestations of her femininity and by giving full rein to the instinct of curiosity which characterises the pure pursuit of knowledge for its own sake.

The feminism-femininity opposition is the basic motif in the comedy under examination. This opposition can be seen in terms of an opposition between freedom—man's desire to enlarge his sphere of action, whether it be physical or intellectual—and the limitations which militate against the exercise of such potential freedom.[11] The clash is a potentially serious one. But in this light-hearted play, there are only echoes of seriousness here and there, and these lie deep below the surface. In any case, Tirso eschews any metaphysical seriousness in *El amor médico*, and, by a brilliant *tour de force* of wit, suggests that feminism and femininity are, at bottom, one and the same thing. A potentially serious conflict is dissolved by wit.

Such a startling reconciliation of the feminism-femininity opposition is already foreshadowed in the play's title: *El amor médico*. The basic meaning is clear enough: love, to find fulfilment, becomes a doctor. This is on the level of the fable. But the symbolic level is more complex. Love symbolises all that is alive and self-renewing. It is associated with the motif of femininity. The doctor, on the other hand, symbolises learning. Traditionally in comedy, he stands for all that learning ought not to be— pedantry, pompous and dressed-up ignorance, a mechanical (as Bergson would say) attitude towards life, etc.—and is therefore a satiric figure. In comedy, he starts off as a university professor, but then turns into a physician. This adds a grotesque element to the implications of the comic figure, for to the seventeenth century especially, the doctor was virtually the emissary of death,[12] and the implied equation *médico* = *muerto* must account for a lot of the black humour implicit in such a play as Calderón's *El médico de su honra*. Tirso, in this comedy, gives us a heroine who is both physician and university professor, thus combining the original with the later version of the comic figure. Furthermore, the portrayal of the doctor is ambiguous: Jerónima is both a satirical and a satiric figure, by being both a model doctor and a parody of a quack one. The implications of this will be discussed latter.

We are presented, therefore, with a title which in itself contains a violent paradox: in it, life and death, love and learning are innocently combined, even though such a combination is, at first sight, an impossibility, and even an absurdity.[13] The reconciliation of these virtual opposites is achieved through their reconciliation in the heroine. It is interesting to try and discover the key which would reveal to us the means by which the paradox in the theme can be made intelligible. We shall see, for example, that love is, contrary to expectation, presented as a form of illness, instead of a state of health. Medicine, therefore, is the means by which this illness can be cured. But, as the play goes on, it becomes clear that the cure for this particular illness is really tantamount to spreading the contagion, not eliminating it. The doctor's skill, therefore, lies in his incompetence. This, of course, is one reason for the emergence of the "quack" element in Jerónima's portrayal: her competence in the treatment of ordinary illnesses is of no use in the case of the illness of love. But, in the end, it is only sterile learning which is killed. The illness of love is necessary for the existence of the human race. By a process of comic inversion an illness is shown to be health, and medicine, incredibly, effects a cure.

The basic thematic opposition between feminism and femininity is manifested psychologically in the inner conflict in Jerónima between learning and love. This carries on the binary pattern referred to, and the way in which the structure of the opening scene presents this conflict will be analysed later on. Before I examine Jerónima's character in greater detail, however, it would be convenient initially to trace the main stages in the development of the thematic conflict.

The learning motif can be broken into the following elements. We are presented at first with Jerónima's obsessive passion for study, which has incurred her brother's displeasure. This passion is intimately linked with her feminist aspirations to freedom, liberty, and the assertion of her individuality. But her aspirations are not all selfish: she is not only striking a blow on behalf of herself and womankind, but also dedicating her life to study for the benefit of human beings at large. That is why her particular field of study is medicine. But the practice of medicine is in the seventeenth century virtually an exclusively masculine sphere of activity. Jerónima's own competence in this skill is thus a direct challenge to existing masculine incompetence and, consequently, a challenge to men themselves (this is an extension of the feminist element in her character). Jerónima, furthermore, is not content only to invade a masculine sphere of activity, but, with the help of disguise, "becomes" a man. Meeting men fully on their own ground, she can give rein, directly and indirectly, to the criticism of doctors and existing medical practices. While the medical satire in the play will be discussed more fully later on, it is convenient to note its two basic aspects at this point. There is, first, the social element in this satire: not only is it highly topical, as has been stated, but the play offers serious, constructive criticism concerning the medical profession. Secondly, there is the traditional comic aspect associated with the quack doctor (already mentioned) which comes to the fore in the later stages of the play. A fuller possible explanation for this shift from the serious to the farcical will be offered later on.

The love motif has a simpler but equally logical development. Jerónima's intellectual curiosity (allied to a more normal curiosity) starts the process:[14]

> [JERÓNIMA:]   Causó en mí este sentimiento
> una curiosa impaciencia
> y deseo de inquirir
> si vivían hombres de piedra;
>
> (I.vii. p. 980a.)

The last line, of course, reveals that the curiosity is not wholly intellectual: Gaspar's attitude has wounded Jerónima's female vanity and aroused her anger—and jealousy. His continued apparent indifference turns her indignation and jealousy into love, which, as we discover at the end, is the prime motivating element in the plot. At first, however, love stands in frank opposition to Jerónima's intellectual aspirations—a physical limitation in the way of her desire for freedom. A resolution to this conflict is found when we discover how love turns Jerónima's pursuit for knowledge into a weapon in her hunt for a mate; her intellectual activity is made subservient to love, and used as an instrument for the furtherance of love's designs.

The development of these two motifs finds a common link in disguise: it is not only Jerónima's feminist aspirations which lead her to disguise herself as a man, but also her love for an indifferent Gaspar which turns her into a "female-page" figure. Thus, in this play also, the two basic comic situations appear linked together. There is the hunt for a mate— Jerónima's pursuit of Gaspar—, and there is the satire of doctors, which is intimately bound up with the question of feminism. The incompatibility between these two activities creates a tension which moves along the plot until a reconciliation is effected between love and learning.

Since Jerónima is the central pivot of the plot, not only is the main thematic conflict embodied within her, but she virtually controls the whole action of the play. If the characters in comedy may be said *grosso modo* to fall into two categories, the butts and the wits, the separation is very clear in this play in one sense. On the level of the action, the wit is Jerónima, for she controls the action, using almost all the other characters as her puppets. But, as we shall see presently, the ironical development of the play on the level of wit exposes Jerónima as a puppet of her own nature by showing her to be a puppet of love. Thus two main antagonists can be identified in the comedy: Gaspar, first of all, and, secondly, Jerónima herself. This latter factor introduces into the comedy a structural complexity which is lacking in the earlier *Marta la piadosa*, where we have a clear separation of the characters into wits (Marta and her accomplices) and butts. In *El amor médico*, then, Jerónima is both wit and butt. What is more, being very self-conscious, she is aware of the grotesque, paradoxical inconsistency in her character. Paul Goodman has stressed the dual aspect of many characters in comedy:[15] a character, on the one hand, may possess certain traits which we consider "normal"; on the other hand, the character also possesses a certain specifically comic trait which the overall action of the comedy aims at deflating. The comic trait classes the character as one of the "humours." Now, Jerónima, as a machinating woman in love, is a wit and a normal character. Her femininity is not a deflatable trait (or, at least, not regarded as such in the social and literary context of the seventeenth century). As a feminist, however, Jerónima is a humour and a butt. She must be purged of her feminism, which, presumably, is "unnatural." The play is thus both a comedy of intrigue in which Jerónima is wit and a comedy of character in which Jerónima is butt.

For analytical purposes, certain clear advantages are gained from look-ing at the play in the light of that statement. The plot of the comedy is seen to possess two strands of action, one of which is overt, while the other is more or less latent. The former is motivated by Jerónima, the feminist, the latter by Jerónima as the wit. Unity is achieved in the overall structure of the plot when we are made to realise that Jerónima's erstwhile fault is cleverly transformed into a positive virtue, thus converting Jerónima the butt into Jerónima the wit. With this, the two strands converge to a single end. Let us proceed to examine the feminist aspect of Jerónima's character first.

As has been said, Jerónima's feminism is an "unnatural" and deflatable trait of which she must be purged. Yet the particular form which her obsession takes is not an ignoble or inherently ridiculous one. From the beginning we learn of Jerónima's dedication to study. Although this found favour in her father's eyes, it has led to an estrangement between herself and her brother, who is now head of the household as their father is dead:

[JERÓNIMA:]	que como muestra disgusto
	porque no me determino
	en admitir persuasiones
	casamenteras, pasiones
	de hermano, a que no me inclino,
	le ocasionan a no hablarme
	dos meses ha.
QUITERIA:	No me espanto:
	haste embebecido tanto
	en latines, que a cansarme
	llego yo, sin que me importe,
	cuanto y más quien se encargó
	de ti desde que murió
	tu padre.

(I.i. p. 971a–b.)

This bothers Jerónima not a wit, as she is determined to have her own way. Her assertion of independence is reinforced by her feminist desire to widen the sphere of female activity. Her resolve is at one with the actions of Isabel la Católica:

JERÓNIMA:	Yo sigo el norte
	de mi inclinación; ¿qué quieres?
	Mi señor se recreaba
	de oírme, cuando estudiaba.
	¿Siempre han de estar las mujeres
	sin pasar la raya estrecha
	de la aguja y la almohadilla?
	Celebre alguna Sevilla
	que en las ciencias aprovecha.
	De ordinario los vasallos
	suelen imitar su rey
	en las costumbres y ley:
	si da en armas y en caballos,
	soldados y caballeros
	son el sabio y ignorante;
	enamorados, si amante;
	si ambicioso, lisonjeros.

Dicen que en Indias hay gente
que porque a un cacique vieron
sin un diente, todos dieron
luego en sacarse otro diente.
La reina doña Isabel,
que a tanta hazaña dio fin,
empieza a estudiar latín,
y es su preceptora en él
otra que, por peregrina,
no hay ingenio que no asombre;
tanto, que olvidan su nombre
y la llaman "la Latina."
Por esto quiero imitalla.

(I.i. p. 971b.)

There is a fine irony in this speech which should not go unremarked. It
begins with a bold assertion of individual freedom: "Yo sigo el norte / de
mi inclinación." But this is obviously a freedom which is not absolutely
free. Her dedication to study is clearly motivated in part by a desire to
please her father: "Mi señor se recreaba / de oírme, cuando estudiaba."
Then she tries to justify her attitude by an appeal to authority: the Queen
"empieza a estudiar latín," and is taught by "La Latina." (We may note,
en passant, the political overtones of this section of the speech). Whereas,
judging from the bold initial assertion, we should have expected Jerónima
to be anything but a conformist tribal Indian, that is what she ironically
declares herself to be: "Por esto quiero imitalla." Although the Queen
and her tutor may be regarded as exceptional rather than run-of-the-mill
individuals, Jerónima's desire to imitate them is only the first stage in
a long process which culminates in the undermining of her desire for
autonomy.

At the same time, Jerónima is not yet a complete conformist. Unlike
Isabel, she will not marry, since marriage, she argues, is incompatible
with the freedom which the pursuit of learning demands:

[JERÓNIMA:]   El matrimonio es Argel,
la mujer cautiva en él,
las artes son liberales
porque hacen que libre viva
a quien en ellas se emplea:
¿cómo querrás tú que sea
a un tiempo libre y cautiva?

(I.i. pp. 971b–972a.)

The opposition between freedom and captivity takes up the basic theme
of the play, and is a traditional assertion. But Tirso's sharp irony is
transparent here also: "las artes son liberales / porque hacen que libre
viva / a quien en ellas se emplea." Jerónima's decision to opt for the
freedom of the liberal arts has obvious moral implications, as is indicated
by the phrase, "libre viva." The education of women leads to a slackening
of moral rules. This is as yet only a vague innuendo, but, as the play
progresses, the implication grows stronger.

All the same, Jerónima's refusal to marry has a wholesome side to it:
the independence of mind it reveals finds a reflection in her unorthodox
choice of subject:

[QUITERIA:]	Pero ¿por qué ha de estudiar
	medicina una mujer?
JERÓNIMA:	Porque estimo la salud,
	que anda en poder de ignorantes.
	¿Piensas tú que seda y guantes
	de curar tienen virtud?
	Engáñaste si lo piensas;
	desvelos y naturales
	son las partes principales
	que con vigilias inmensas
	hacen al médico sabio.
	Por ver si a mi patria puedo
	aprovechar, contra el miedo
	que a la salud hace agravio.

                                        (I.i. p. 972a.)

A strong idealistic trait can be discerned in Jerónima. There is her concern
for health—a concern not devoid of some altruism. More, there is her
concern for the dignity of learning: it is something to be taken seriously.
There is, enveloping both of these, her more idealistic patriotism, which, as
the continuation fo the speech indicates, would find some satisfaction in the
reform of medical teaching and practice in the country. Her disinterested
study of medicine is re-affirmed later on in the play. (Although the latent
irony in her words is very strong here, we may grant that her *initial* interest
was largely disinterested.) The study and pratice of medicine have been
prostituted for base, selfish ends, asserts Jerónima, but:

[JERÓNIMA:]	Yo estudié la medicina
	por inclinación no más.
	sin que intentase jamás
	que facultad tan divina

fuese de "pane lucrando."
(III.viii. p. 1008b.)

Jerónima herself is a more than competent physician: though largely self-educated (there is no evidence of her having received any formal education in medicine), she becomes professor of medicine at Coimbra, physician to the King and Queen, and earns the envious hatred of her less successful colleagues:

[QUITERIA:]   Das en querer catedrar
de vísperas o maitines,
con que médicos rüines
no te acaban de envidiar,
sin que haya en ellos quien hable
en favor de tus recetas;
que en médicos y en poetas,
la envidia es sarna incurable.
(II.xii. p. 997a.)

(One wonders if there is a veiled reference to Lope in the last two lines, incidentally.)

There are two sides to this achievement. The first is the fact that it constitutes a devastating victory in the feminist war against men. Dr. Barbosa is not only more competent than "his" colleagues, but is also very young, and, what is more, really a woman, as the audience knows.

The second side to Jerónima's achievement consists in the reflection it casts on the medical profession of the time. Impelled, as we have seen, by a combination of feminist, altruistic, and idealistic motivations, Jerónima devotes herself to the study—and then practice—of medicine. This was, in the seventeenth century, traditionally a masculine occupation, but one in which masculine incompetence was notorious. Jerónima is a woman, virtually self-educated, and young enough to arouse the hatred of her fellow-doctors, the misgivings of Gaspar,—and the admiration of the King. The stage is thus set for the satire of the medical profession.

Hartzenbusch does not admit that the play satirises the medical profession. Arguing against an earlier view that Lope's *El acero de Madrid* and Tirso's *El amor médico* are satirical in intent, he is at pains to point out that our reaction is a purely comic or hilarious one to what is basically an unusual situation:

. . . lo cómico del personage de doña Gerónima no nace de que haga el papel de médico por su gusto, ni de que emplee la fraseología técnica, sino de la novedad que causa una muger tomando pulsos y ordenando recetas, de la extrañeza del disfraz á que ha recurrido para colocarse entre don Gaspar y doña Estefanía. No creemos nosotros que Téllez al idear su doctor con faldas quiso ridiculizar a los médicos de su tiempo con la intención profunda que Molière en varias de sus *comedias*: doña Gerónima, aunque dirije algunas pullas a los médicos, no nos parece la sátira personificada de la medicina: doña Gerónima estudia el arte de curar para aventajarse en ella, para saber más que sabían los doctores de su época, y porque estudia y sabe, le dan el grado. Si sus argumentos y citas nos hacen reir, es porque en una obra dramática mueve a risa a todo lenguaje afectado o simplemente facultativo; y es muy de creer que si Tellez hubiera introducido en alguna *comedia* la persona del mismo Hipócrates con ánimo de ensalzar su ciencia, le hubiera hecho hablar casi lo mismo que la Marisabidilla sevillana.[16]

The play is, of course, not primarily a sustained invective against doctors. As we have seen, its scope is much broader; but the medical satire in it consists of considerably more than "algunas pullas." Hartzenbusch, apparently expecting to find a traditional burlesque figure, seems to have missed the ambiguity in Jerónima's portrayal. For it is important to remember that Jerónima is not primarily or always a satiric figure within the play. Tirso is at pains to modify the conventional approach, principally because of the varied implications of the theme. The satire in the play is both positive, i.e., constructive, and negative.

Constructive criticism of the medical profession occurs principally in the first section of the play, and, more specifically, in the first act. This straighforward approach is consistent with Jerónima's high and passionate seriousness. She is indignant that human lives should be placed in the hands of ignorant, unskilled tyros, and decides to become a model doctor herself and remedy current abuses. But it is not enough to expect doctors to be as honest and as diligent in their studies and dedication to their profession as they ought to be. The vital role played by doctors calls for something more. Jerónima laments the fact that the practice of medicine is not subject to supervision and control:

JERÓNIMA: ¡Cosa extraña, que en cualquiera
                        arte, por poco que valga,
                        hay aprendiz que no salga
                        con ella, echándole fuera,
                        y que en esta no ha de haber
                        médico que deshechar,
                        Quiteria!

                                                (I.i. p. 972b.)

Strict and proper training of doctors is necessary:

[JERÓNIMA:]

¿No es lástima que examinen
a un albéitar herrador,
a un peraile, a un tundidor,
y que antes que determinen
que practiquen su ejercicio,
aprueben su suficiencia:
y la medicina, ciencia
que no tiene por oficio
menos que el dar o quitar
la vida, que tanto importa,
con una asistencia corta
de escuelas, un platicar
dos años, a la gualdrapa
de un dotor en ella experto
porque más hombres ha muerto,
prolijo de barba y capa,
en habiendo para mula,
luego queda graduado,
antes de ser licenciado
de dotor? Quien no regula
estos peligros, ¿no es necio?

(I.i. p. 972a.)

The last two lines are a clear enough call for legislation. The matter is urgent, for, as Quiteria humorously points out, the reputation of doctors is at an absolute low (I.i. p. 972b).

In II.viii, we see that Jerónima has taken a further step along the feminist and medical road. She physically invades the medical profession, disguising herself as a (male) doctor. She can now put into practice her ideas about medicine. Her opening speech, well-ordered and rigorously logical in its argument (which is virtually irrefutable if we accept the medical premises underlying it), confirms that her intellectual training leaves little to be desired. Nor is she lacking in learning, as we are forced to admit on hearing her long speech towards the end of this important scene, when she defends her youth against Gaspar's accusations of ignorance. The sheer weight of authorities she summons to back up her arguments is overwhelming. She finds similar support for her constructive advice on dress and appearance, while the psychological value of her argument (which has its source in Hippocrates, as Zamora-Vicente points out in note on pp. 76–77 of his edition) is supported by San Román in his booklet already referred to. In the following scene, Íñigo's favourable report on the doctor confirms that the latter is both skilful and respected in Coimbra:

the city owes its health to Dr. Barbosa.

At the same time, if we return to scene viii, which is one of the central scenes in the play and a *pièce de résistance*, so to speak, we must acknowledge that Tirso's treatment of the doctor is not wholly serious. The Latin quotations are an inevitable adjunct of the traditional comic doctor and Estefanía says as much:

ESTEFANÍA: No gastéis, señor dotor,
                  de aforismos tanta copia;
                  que es almacén ordinario
                  de todo médico broma.
                  Ved si tengo calentura.

                            (II.viii. p. 990b.)

The examination of the patient, Estefanía, is also not without its burlesque aspects. The clearest example is perhaps to be found in the patent absurdities of the diet which is prescribed for Estefanía, and the effect of which is to be enhanced by "unos jarabes" and "cinco píldoras solas." Similarly, the medico-philosophical explanation to Rodrigo of love at first sight is an amusing piece of sophistry. F. Halstead has noted its debt to a philosophical theory and also questioned the soundness of the argument in the speech.[17] But the excessive length of the speech, together with the implications at the end, makes it obvious that Tirso does not intend to be serious here. He is aiming rather at producing a comic effect with a display of spurious logic and apparent learning. It is clear that an element of ambivalence has been deliberately introduced into the portrayal of Jerónima. She is no longer to be seen solely as the serious feminist-doctor, but also as a comic figure, and this is confirmed by her farcical encounters with Tello in II.iv and III.iv. Part of the explanation, of course, lies in the fact that the satire is now also being effected by means of parody and burlesque.

The introduction of a tone of greater levity provides ample opportunity for the introduction of innuendo and indirect attacks on doctors and their moral standards. When Jerónima first appears on stage as a doctor (II.viii), her opening words are "Dios sea en aquesta casa." On one level, it is grotesque that a doctor should utter such a salutation on visiting a patient— much as if he were a priest. The invocation is, to say the least, hardly a heartening one, especially since we read in *Por el sótano y el torno* that a certain doctor's nickname is "Extreme Unction!"[18] On a more subtle level, however, one can see a further implication. The doctor's pious words seem to be an echo of Fabia's in Lope's *El caballero de Olmedo*: "Paz sea en aquesta casa!" (Act II, line 1407), which, of course, hark back directly to Celestina's "¡Paz sea en aquesta casa!" (*La Celestina*, Act IV). The insinuation from the very start seems to be that the doctor is an *alcahuete*. This, in fact, finds confirmation in the subsequent development of the intrigue. We are told that the doctor has free entry into his patients' house:

ESTEFANÍA: Entre y advierta
que al dotor nunca la puerta
se le cierra.

(II.vii. p. 989b.)

This presupposes a necessary confidence in his professional and moral integrity. But it is hinted that the latter are qualities not always possessed by doctors. Rodrigo, conveniently for Jerónima, is smitten with love for Estefanía. Jerónima, as Dr. Barbosa, has forbidden Gaspar to talk to Estefanía. This move is aimed at isolating Gaspar and preventing a marriage between him and Estefanía, while preserving him as a future husband for Jerónima herself. But as the other characters are ignorant of Jerónima's true intentions, her action is interpreted in various ways. To Rodrigo, the doctor presents himself as a sympathetic third party, explaining why he has forbidden Gaspar to speak to Estefanía: he will intercede on Rodrigo's behalf and is sure of success (III.v. p. 1006a.). Immediately afterwards, Rodrigo unequivocally states that some doctors are intermediaries, the implication being that Dr. Barbosa is such a person:

[RODRIGO:]   ¿No es mujer? ¿No me apercibe
a amarla un dotor tercero?
Pues él vencera imposibles;
que hay médicos "in utroque,"
criminales y civiles,
con billetes por recetas,
que a amor y a Galeno sirven.

(III.vi. p. 1006a.)

Furthermore, the doctor also emerges as a *tercero de sí mismo*. In III.xiii, Doña Marta reveals to Estefanía that her brother is carrying on an intrigue with Leonor, Estefanía's cousin. But just before Marta leaves in the following scene, she hints that the doctor is not uninterested in Estefanía either ". . . porque o doutor / ou tem ser de Leonor, / ou de vossa senhoria" (III.xiv. p. 1013b). Estefanía is very naturally angry, and refuses to let the doctor feel her pulse when he next visits her:

ESTEFANÍA: No le fío

de médicos licenciados
(licenciosos, dotor, digo)
que su facultad profanan,
y donde son admitidos,
las doncellas enamoran.
(III.xviii. p. 1015a.)

Not a minor part of the comic effect of this scene resides in Estefanía's hysterical accusations of the doctor. Her charges are partly pure comic (insofar as they spring from her passionate jealousy), but also partly serious, as they seem to have some validity outside the immediate context of the play. She attacks the unscrupulous behaviour of some doctors:

[ESTEFANÍA:]   Pues, dotor casamentero,
desde agora os notifico
que no entréis en esta casa,
ni aun a curar sus vecinos:
sabrá mi padre quién sois,
y os dirá si es permitido
que a mujeres de importancia
solicitéis con fingidos
y hipócritas pensamientos.
¡Bueno es, que habiendo salido
de vísperas catedrático,
que por mi prima perdido,
la de "prima" pretendáis!
(III.xviii. p. 1015b.)

More seriously, there is also a reference to the choice of a palace physician:

ESTEFANÍA: ¿Que no os vais? ¿He de dar gritos?
Desengañará mi padre
al Rey, porque esté advertido
de quién entra en su palacio,
y a quién su médico hizo,
el riesgo en que están sus damas,
la ciencia que en otros libros
estudiáis, no de Galeno,
sino de Marcial y Ovidio.
(III.xviii. pp. 1015b–1016a.)

This latter reference seems to be related to the contemporary concern over the appointment of palace doctors, a concern, which, as has been stated, produced echoes in other plays of Tirso's. Estefanía's anger, ironically, is appeased when, after a series of sex metamorphoses in which the doctor

moves from the male Barbosa to the female Marta disguised as her brother
and finally back to Barbosa, he confesses that he really loves Estefanía
and his disguise as a woman was motivated by love and jealousy, i.e., that
he is guilty of precisely the charges which Estefanía had only a moment
before levelled against him (III.xviii. p. 1018a–b.) The scene ends with
Estefanía accepting as her *esposo* the unscrupulous doctor of uncertain
sex, a factor which she, in her blind passion, curiously seems to have
overlooked completely.

Such unethical conduct on the part of the doctor finds not a little encour-
agement in the fact that Estefanía virtually throws herself at Dr. Barbosa.
This is especially evident in the medical examination scene (II.viii), which
is rich in comic meanings. The examination of the patient is itself a caricature of a medical examination; but this is on the level of farce. On a
much more subtle level is the delicate *quid pro quo* in the conversation
between doctor and patient. On the verbal level, Barbosa's comments and
questions, if isolated from their context, seem (if we make due allowance
for the exaggeration of caricature) normal and harmless enough. But Estefanía's interleaved asides leave us in no doubt that the examination is
for her an occasion for amorous communication:

ESTEFANÍA: (Aparte):
                            Amorosa
                sangre, decidle mi mal:
                sirva la arteria de boca,
                pues viene del corazón.
                                        (II.viii. p. 990b.)

She invites the doctor to examine her:

ESTEFANÍA: Abrásanseme las palmas
                de las manos: cuando tocan
                encienden; tentad, tentad.
                        (*Dale las dos manos*)
JERONINA: ¡Brava *intemperies*!
ESTEFANÍA: Soy Troya.
                                        (II.viii. p. 991a.)

There is, on the stylistic level, the ambivalent *double entendre*: the fire
is, in one sense, a fever; in another, it is her passion. On the level of
the medical satire, there is the obvious invitation to the doctor to hold
her hands and be inflamed: "cuanto tocan / encienden; tentad, tentad."
Barbosa's tacit connivance is loaded: his medical examination is, on the
moral level, unethical. But professionally he cannot but be unethical if he

would avoid the charge of being indifferent to the patient's welfare!

The situation is therefore a complex one (and would demand considerable skill and delicacy when acted on the stage). First, Jerónima's remarks must be neutral and professional enough to withstand the scrutiny of the bystanders (including the jealous, suspicious hawk-eyed Gaspar). At the same time, it is clear that the remarks, by virtue of their professional neutrality, must have the effect of parrying Estefanía's frantic advances. In other words, Dr. Barbosa knows that Estefanía loves "him," and sees the need for restraining her (for "he" is, after all, really a woman—a fact which, because of its undertones of sexual perversion, contributes not a little to the risqué comic suggestiveness of the scene). Thus Estefanía's declaration of her love is, in part, neutralised as the doctor takes up the image of burning but puts it into a medical context:

JERÓNIMA: Tenéis toda la región
              del hígado por la colera
              lesa, que la pituita
              quemándola se incorpora.
              Ahora bien, señora mía,
              vuesiría se disponga
              a preservar accidentes
              que la experiencia diagnóstica
              nos indica: lo primero,
              con dieta flemagoga
              y algo colagoga, enfrene
              cualidades licenciosas.
                          (II.viii. p. 991a.)

The last line, of course, is a discret hint to Estefanía that she should control herself. Again, when Estefanía aggressively and almost shamelessly offers herself to the doctor, the latter's professional solicitude helps to defuse the situation:

[JERÓNIMA:]   Espero en Dios de dejarla
              sana en distancia tan corta,
              que restituya alegrías
              y a sus mejillas sus rosas.
ESTEFANÍA: Haced vos eso, dotor,
              si mi salud os importa
              (que si gustáis, bien podéis),
              y de cuanto soy señora
              dispondréis a vuestro arbitrio.
                          (Aparte)

```
                    ¡Ay! ¡Si me entendiese!
JERÓNIMA:                                Sobran
                    voluntad y medicinas;
                    pero falta que se pongan
                    en ejercicio.
ESTEFANÍA:                      Por mí
                    recetad; que desde agora
                    estoy puesta en vuestras manos.
ÍÑIGO:              ¿Cómo te sientes?
```
(II.viii. pp. 991b–992a.)

Secondly, Jerónima realises that Estefanía's ambiguous speech cannot merely be countered on one of its levels of meaning, i.e., the doctor-patient one, which, in the context of the intrigue, is the less important. Thus the doctor's response, too, must be ambiguous. There is limited scope for further manoeuvre on the level of speech (which is rendered complex enough by Estefanía's ambiguities and the *quid pro quo* resulting from Barbosa's deliberate response on a professional level), but the doctor's *total* response can contain a reciprocal ambiguity, precisely because of the fact that "he" is a doctor. The second level of response is, of course, that of physical action: the examination of a patient can be less than an innocent process; and it is in the physical examination that the doctor responds to Estefanía's advances. He takes one pulse, then the other, and this does not pass unremarked by Gaspar:

```
GASPAR:             (Aparte):
                    ¿Que tenga un dotor licencia
                    tan amplia, que lo que goza
                    el tacto a mí se me niegue?
                    ¡Oh facultad venturosa!
```
(II.viii. p. 990b.)

Nor does the doctor hesitate to take the palms of the patient when the latter thrusts them forth, hot with love, for him to touch. This move is repeated a little later in the scene (after the passionate defence of youth and of personal cleanliness in doctors) when the doctor confirms Estefanía's almost miraculous improvement. But here, Barbosa's replies to Estefanía's questions themselves contain an element of ambiguity, for they can be interpreted as the flattery of a man addressed to a woman, and they are surely taken as such by Estefanía, since she rewards the doctor with two diamonds! Gaspar, of course, finds in this medical examination a confirmation of his worst fears:

GASPAR: (*Aparte*):
                     Por Dios, que soy si se nombra
                     medicina, y no amor, esto,
                     en uno y en otro idiota.
                                         (II.viii. p. 993b.)

The comedy of the scene is thus obvious, but its implications extend beyond the narrow boundaries of the plot itself. The insinuation here is that doctors are not all moral creatures, and will not hesitate to exploit any opportunity which presents itself. Gaspar has realised the truth of the situation and, in the ensuing scene (II.ix), his jealousy and anger are betrayed by his extreme irritability and his irrational calling into question of the doctor's competence. In a soliloquy in II.xi., his jealousy leads him into a wider criticism of doctors: first, he sees the dangers inherent in the doctor-patient relationship:

[GASPAR:]   Celos, ya empieza a temer
                     mi amor al dotor Barbosa.
                     Cuando no le ve, está triste,
                     él es despejado mozo;
                     cúrala, a su pulso asiste:
                     poco la sangre resiste,
                     si la ocasión la provoca:
                     si llega y arterias toca,
                     comunicaréle penas:
                     ¿quién vio que amor por las venas
                     hablase, y no por la boca?
                                         (II.xi. p. 996a.)

But almost immediately, the criticism is raised to the absolute level and virtually becomes a general charge directed at the medical profession at large:

[GASPAR:]   Médica jurisdición,
                     malicioso estoy: ¿qué quieres
                     de ocasiones y mujeres,
                     ella mujer, tú ocasión?
                     Oh médicos, qué inhumanos
                     con los cuerpos sois, dejad
                     las almas con libertad,
                     que ya perseguís tiranos!
                                         (II.xi. p. 996b.)

This line of thought is continued into Act III, when Gaspar directly accuses

Barbosa of unethical conduct:

[GASPAR:]
 que como consiste en tactos
 vuestra facultad, dotor,
 el médico y el amor
 todo es físicos contactos.

     (III.viii. p. 1007b.)

His charge stings the doctor into a passionate defence of the profession, a defence which, because of its heavy irony, can only succeed in eliciting a cynical guffaw fron the audience:

JERÓNIMA:
 Baste, señor don Gaspar,
 que no es noble el maliciar
 sino villano en su aldea.
 Yo soy hombre de opinión,
 y hasta ahora nadie ha habido
 que haya, cual vos, deslucido
 la médica profesión,
 ni la justa confianza
 que todo el mundo hace della.

     (III.viii. p. 1108a.)

But Tirso is not done with the profession yet. A further point taken up in the play is the social position of doctors. As has been pointed out already, Quiteria, in the opening scene of the play, remarks that in comparison with a doctor's profession, an executioner's is an "oficio de pobre honrado" (I.i. p. 972b). Doctors, in fact, are regarded as social outcasts, and Estefanía meditates on the ignominy of someone of her class loving a doctor: her haughtiness has made her fall into the depths of degradation:

[ESTEFANÍA:]
 ¿Por qué amáis desigualdades,
 ni posibles ni seguras?
 ¿Este fin será razón
 que tengan mis altiveces?
 Libertad, que tantas veces
 triunfó vuestra presunción
 ya que imitáis a Faetón
 cayendo, no os despeñéis
 sin que en todo le imitéis;
 pues aunque de seso falto,
 Faetón se perdió por alto,
 y vos por baja os perdéis.
 ¡A un médico amáis! Callad;

> que el publicarlo es locura.
>
> (II.v. p. 988a–b.)

The conflict between the desires of love and the demands of social conventions is also potentially present in Gaspar's love for Doña Marta. He,
in the blindness of his passion, is quite prepared to ignore her social status;
but the *gracioso* is by no means blind:

[TELLO:]	y advierta tu ciego amor
	que es hermana de un dotor.
GASPAR:	Mejor dirás ángel, Tello.

> (II.xiv. p. 1000b.)

His warning does not fall on deaf ears, for in III.viii, we see that Gaspar
is prepared to marry Doña Marta if he can find someone in the city "quien
vuestra limpieza apruebe" (III.viii. p. 1008b). The reference to *limpieza
de sangre* is significant, for doctors of Jewish origin were regarded with
suspicion at the time (as is made plain in *La prudencia en la mujer*). What
is more, *all* doctors were suspected of having Jewish blood in their veins,
and were thus socially undesirable characters.[19] Similar doubts persist in
Estefanía's mind, and, as late as III.xviii, she wants to be re-assured about
the doctor's suitability as a husband for her.

Now we can see why Jerónima, a member of the upper classes, acts
scandalously by becoming a doctor. She is not only undermining the
natural order, but also introducing chaos into the social. Such are the extremes of moral and social degradation to which the education of women
and feminist tendencies lead. This, of course, is only the negative and
comic side of the problem. But the play also contains a positive side.
Jerónima, by giving rein to her feminism, makes a plea, *ipso facto*, for
improving the status of doctors. It is implied that the medical profession
is used by some as a social ladder. Again, doctors not only rise in social
esteem in certain circumstances but also find medicine a lucrative profession. Dr. Barbosa, too, becomes royal physician (and implicity gains
some political power) and university professor, thus obtaining both status
and wealth. But he often affirms that his sense of vocation is genuine (as
it originally was, we know): he is neither a social climber nor a fortune-
hunter (III.viii. p. 1008b). His aim is to invest the medical profession
with a new dignity and importance. To achieve this, doctors must be well
trained and of unquestionable intellectual and moral calibre. Their new
position in society must be a reward for their merits, and that is why Dr.
Barbosa will not support his claim to a university chair with bribes (as is
the usual practice):

ÍÑIGO: Iré yo, mi casa toda
y cuantos títulos tiene
esta corte; y si os importa
hablar votos . . .

JERÓNIMA: Eso no;
mi justicia, señor, sola
es de quien he de valerme;
que los sabios no sobornan.[20]

(II.viii. p. 994b.)

Thus the play contains a constructive criticism of the medical profession in addition to being an overt condemnation of abuse and an exposure of ineptitude and ignorance by burlesque.

The satire of the medical profession is clearly not something extraneous. It contributes to the comic effect of the play through burlesque and the creation of ambiguous situations. More organically, Jerónima finds that being a doctor satisfies her feminist instinct, inasmuch as it constitutes an assault upon a traditionally masculine stronghold. Her success in storming it is of the highest importance in the fulfilment of her feminist aspirations. But, in addition to this, being a doctor (and therefore a man) is a perfect disguise for a love-stricken woman. Dr. Barbosa is none other than a new version of the old figure of the female page.

It is time to consider the feminine aspect of Jerónima's character, which is revealed in her relentless pursuit of the man she loves. Comic irony will have it that it is precisely her intellectual curiosity which leads to the emergence of her femininity: this is reflected, e.g., in the diction of the following extract:

[JERÓNIMA:]   Causó en mí este sentimiento
una curiosa impaciencia
y deseo de inquirir
si viven hombres de piedra;

(I.vii. p. 980a.)

But it is more than a mere intellectual curiosity. Gaspar's indifference towards her has offended her female vanity (I.i. p. 973b). Her reaction is in accordance with normal feminine psychology, as she herself points out:

[JERÓNIMA:]   En nosotras, ya tú sabes
que imperando la soberbia
se rinde por sus contrarios:
hombre que nos menosprecia,

> téngase por bien querido.
>
> (I.vii. p. 980a.)

Jerónima's pride has been reduced, and her surrender to love puts her on a level with all other "normal" women and in the same class as humbled man-haters. It is to be noted, however, that Jerónima's surrender is a *fait accompli* from the very beginning of the play. Tirso thus departs from the conventional treatment of a stock situation in comedy. We are not presented with a man-hater whose antipathy is gradually but inevitably overcome in the course of the play. Rather, from the outset, love and learning, nature and the intellect are housed in the same soul and, after an initial conflict, seem, surprisingly, to co-exist happily. This, of course, is in conformity with the binary pattern on which the play is built.

Jerónima, as we have seen from our examination of her feminist aspect, is strong-willed: "Yo sigo el norte / de mi inclinación" (I.i. p. 971b). And her *inclinación* is also towards the intriguing Gaspar (I.i. p. 973b). Just as her obsession with learning makes us consider her on one level as a humour, her new obsession with Gaspar threatens to make her a flat character, i.e., one given to violent obsessions. But her love, though violent, is always under control—if only just. She can devise a means of knowing whether Gaspar is ignorant of her presence in the house or not:

JERÓNIMA: Porque veas que te engañas,
                       anoche a la celosía
                       del patio le vi bajar;
                       y para que no tuviese
                       disculpas, porque se oyese,
                       dije en voz alta: "Aguilar,
                       ¿donde dejáis a mi hermano?"
                       Y respondióme: "Señora,
                       iba a la Alameda agora."
                       Entonces él, cortesano,
                       quitó a la reja el sombrero,
                       sin extrañar el oírme.
                       ¿Osarás ahora decirme
                       que no peca de grosero
                       quien sin hacer novedad
                       de escuchar que en casa había
                       hermana, la suponía?

> (I.i. p. 971a.)

She concludes from this that Gaspar must have another woman on his mind and spies on him:

JERÓNIMA: Vile anoche revolver
                papeles, sin advertencia
                de que acecharle podían.
QUITERIA: ¿Por dónde?
JERÓNIMA: Por el espacio
                de la llave.
QUITERIA: ¡Qué despacio
                tus desvelos te tenían!

                        (I.i. p. 973a.)

She is sure that his papers hold the clue to his distraction, and must see them: she is jealous (I.i. p. 974a). She decides to rifle his papers, and, significantly, Quiteria puts her two passions for love and letters on the same level:

JERÓNIMA: Las navetas los tendrán
                de aquel contador, que están
                sin llaves para guardarlos.
                Salgamos dese cuidado.
QUITERIA: Vamos, porque le asegures,
                y enferma, para que cures,
                la ciencia que has estudiado,
                que uno y otro es frenesí.

                        (I.i. p. 974a.)

This active scheming and planning on Jerónima's part make her not a humour but a wit. At times her passions threaten to overwhelm her:

[JERÓNIMA:]   En efeto, mis pasiones,
                sin saber dónde me llevan,
                me traen aquí, a ¿qué sé yo?
                ni ¿qué espero, aunque lo sepa?

                        (I.vii. p. 981a.)

But her intellect succeeds in containing and channelling them in a constructive and purposeful way.

    This is possible because Jerónima is a very self-conscious character, aware of her own nature and her own inconsistencies. This aspect is perhaps most effectively illustrated by the way in which she humorously accepts Quiteria's ironical remarks about her:

QUITERIA: ¡En verdad que en el estudio
                de la medicina medras
                lucidamente! Dotora
                que en vez de curar enferma,

	el diablo que le dé el pulso.
JERÓNIMA:	Decirme podrá el problema:
	"Dotor, cúrate a ti mismo."

(I.vii. p. 981a.)

She is not unaware that her books, which she originally thought of as her means of salvation, may be the cause of her perdition (I.ix. p. 984b). This belief coincides perfectly with the more pessimistic, comically sour attitude of Quiteria:

QUITERIA:	Yo no sé de qué blasona
	la ciencia en que te señalas,
	si a tal locura te obliga;
	pero diré que a la hormiga
	por su mal le nacen alas.

(II.xii. p. 997a.)

On the metaphysical level, Quiteria has a point, of course. Jerónima spreads her wings, but only to pursue Gaspar. It gradually becomes evident that all her energies are directed towards trapping the elusive male, and in this hunt, everything takes second place to the claims of love. Jerónima's machinations are evidence of her amazing ability to cope with almost any situation or development, expected or unexpected. The most obvious example of this trait is to be found in the scene in which she cleverly handles Estefanía, avoiding, by effecting a series of metamorphoses of sex, the scene which the latter threatens to create (III.xviii). These sex-changes are all part of the overall use of disguise by Jerónima throughout the play, and illustrate in the most extreme manner her chameleon-like ability to adapt herself to the situation with which she is confronted.

The conventional use of the device of the *mujer tapada* is one of the main features of *El amor médico*. Finding herself unexpectedly in love with an indifferent Gaspar, and piqued by his incivility, Jerónima finds the *manto* an effective weapon of offence as well as of defence. In the first act, her skilful manipulation of it allows her to conceal her own identity and at the same time to rouse Gaspar's curiosity so as to lure him into her net. His interest is initially awakened by a *tapada* who gives him news of Doña Micaela. Gaspar's enforced flight to Portugal, which threatens to frustrate this move of Jerónima's, does not, however, daunt our heroine, who follows him there. In Coimbra, Gaspar is the object of a three-pronged attack. He is shadowed by the Castilian *tapada* whom he had promised, as she claims to his mystification, to marry, while, at the same time, he is held prisoner by the beauty and promises of Doña Marta, who, by tantalisingly revealing to him a hand, an eye, and, finally, her entire face, makes him almost completely forget Doña Estefanía. In addition, the presence of Dr. Barbosa (the female-page version of Jerónima's disguise) also helps to keep Gaspar and Estefanía apart.

Jerónima's use of the *manto* also enables her to juggle with identities in such a way as to puzzle Gaspar. In fact, she has discovered a perfect way to keep Gaspar guessing. Tirso does not fail to exploit the comic potentialities of this. By being now Doña Marta and now, disconcertingly, the Sevillian *tapada*, Jerónima is able to "punish" Gaspar for his earlier indifference towards her (for the *tapada*, who now compels his attention, alternately fulfils and frustrates his expectations), while his slight, but obvious, basic emotional instability is exposed. Thus a large part of the comic effect of this play depends on the situations produced by the clash of the male and female temperaments, the process by which Gaspar is emotionally isolated, then confused, and finally captured. Jerónima has whole-heartedly devoted her talents and energies to capturing the man she loves. This signifies the triumph of her femininity.

But how can this femininity be reconciled with Jerónima's feminism? She herself had stated at the outset that the two things were incompatible. For Jerónima has not renounced her feminist aspirations. It is precisely in Act III that she appears to have won her greatest feminist triumphs. This development seems incongruous at this stage, when Jerónima's femininity seems to have gained the upper hand as her love has met more and more obstacles. However, a closer examination of the stages through which Jerónima's feminism passes reveals a curious situation.

Jerónima's feminism in its initial stages is at its most passionate: her opening speech reveals the warmth of her passion. Nevertheless, we note that, in the gardens of the *alcázar* in Seville, she uses the feminine *manto* as a means of disguise, i.e., she is a *mujer tapada*. When we meet her next, it is in Coimbra, where she seems to be pursuing her feminist aims with considerable success. Here, she is disguised as a man, and is practising her profession. The cures she effects earn her a considerable reputation which allows her to gain entry into Íñigo's house as physician to the Spanish ambassador. She immediately follows this up by becoming professor of medicine at the university of Coimbra and physician to the King, thus obtaining authority, social status, and the royal favour. But at this point, as we have seen, a tendency to caricature begins to creep into Tirso's portrayal of her: this is most marked in the farcical scenes with Tello. This is significant, although, at first glance, puzzling, as it signals the emergence of the latent plot.

For, of course, Jerónima has gone to Coimbra, not principally to practise medicine, but to pursue Gaspar: she enters Íñigo's house because
Gaspar lives there and is courting Estefanía, and Jerónima must prevent
their marriage; she wins authority and status so that Gaspar can have no
hesitation in marrying Doña Marta. In reality, therefore, she is pursuing
aims intended to give satisfaction, not to her feminist, but to her feminine
instincts. Her remarks at the end of the play make this quite plain. It was
her love for Gaspar which turned her into a doctor. And the aim of her
studies was to win him as her husband:

JERÓNIMA: Don Gaspar
                    es mi esposo, merecido
                    a precio de estudios tantos,
                    tanto disfraz y suspiro.
                                        (III.xx. p. 1020b)

But, paradoxically, she achieves all this while dressed as a man!

It is now clear that the various disguises are important in the revelation
of the heroine's character. One might almost say that with the assumption
of each new disguise a further layer of her soul in uncovered. The initial
disguise is that of the *mujer tapada*, and this corresponds to Jerónima's
most feminist stage. Male disguise is a part of Jerónima's scheme (here
the conventions of comedy are obviously at work, since Dr. Barbosa is a
"female-page" figure), and it is cleverly incorporated into the plot through
the theme of feminism. Male disguise is the ultimate and logical stage of
Jerónima's feminism. The assertion of equality between the sexes leads to
Jerónima's invasion of a masculine sphere of activity, which in turn leads
to a usurpation of the masculine personality. But by the time Jerónima
adopts male disguise, we realise that she is more intent upon trapping the
man she loves than upon asserting feminine equality, which she succeeds
in achieving in almost an incidental manner. Indeed, from the way Gaspar
is outwitted at every turn, one might be tempted to ask which of the
sexes is the unequal one! Thus, paradoxically, it is precisely when she
is a man that Jerónima is most a woman. Clearly, then, disguise has an
inversely symbolic role in this play. (The same is largely true of Rosalind's
disguise in *As You Like It*.) Now we can better understand why Jerónima's
initial disguise is the *manto* of the *tapada*, while, as her femininity gains
the upper hand, she switches to male disguise. Significantly, when the
tapada re-appears in Coimbra, she reveals herself in an oblique fashion
as Doña Marta, Dr. Barbosa's sister. But she is also accompanied by the
more mysterious Castilian *tapada*, whose identity is unknown, and whose

intervention threatens to frustrate any hope of marriage between Gaspar and Marta. The re-appearance of the *tapada* marks the beginning of the recapitulation: we have now come full circle.

But the inverse symbolism of dress, which has so far dominated the play, must somehow be re-inverted. This is achieved in III.xviii, whose organic function now becomes evident. Doña Marta has been introduced to Estefanía in scene xiii. In scene xviii, the doctor appears, claims to be Marta to pacify Estefanía, and then, to pacify her again, declares he is the doctor, who has visited her earlier (in scene xiii) disguised as his sister. It is as a man, therefore, that the doctor is accepted by Estefanía as her *esposo*. A woman's agreeing to marry another woman in male disguise is a stock comic situation of the time. But the real purpose of this apparently farcical mystification is to emphasise the fact that the doctor is "his" sister, i.e., that the man on stage is a woman:

ESTEFANÍA:	¿Luego no tenéis hermana?
JERÓNIMA:	El amor la ha convertido
	a ella y el dotor Barbosa
	en un cuerpo.

(III.xx. p. 1020b.)

And, the comic irony persisting to the last, it is in male dress (i.e., wholly a *woman*) that Jerónima is accepted by Gaspar as his wife:

JERÓNIMA:	Escuchad aparte.
	(Apártale)
	¿Queréis casaros conmigo?
GASPAR:	¡Jesús, dotor! ¿Estáis loco?
JERÓNIMA:	No juzguéis por los vestidos
	la persona. Doña Marta
	soy.

(III.xix. p. 1019a.)

It is in male dress, too, that Jerónima admits that she is a woman:

ÍÑIGO:	¿Luego sois mujer?
JERÓNIMA:	He sido
	quien a la Naturaleza
	con mi industria he contradicho.

(III.xx. p. 1020b.)

It is clear, then, that the use of disguise in this play allows a progressive revelation of the female mind, an exposure of Jerónima's character. By showing her to be really a woman underneath the surface trappings of a man, the play wittily equates feminism with femininity. The initial incongruity between the two has been overcome. We can proceed to consider some of the consequences of this.

Tirso is not an anti-feminist. He does not take the view that women are stupid creatures or that intelligent women are unattractive. Jerónima herself is an attractive woman, very clever, and, moreover, exceedingly intelligent. Nor, as is evident from this play, does Tirso believe that intelligence is incompatible with love.

B. Matulka, although (surprisingly) not referring to this play in her article on feminism in Golden Age drama, asserts that Tirso was a misogynist who, sceptical of the virtue of women, mocked them in his plays.[21] This play, however, can hardly be said to mock the amorousness of women. It is precisely Jerónima's love and her efforts to achieve its fulfilment which, as has been pointed out, save her from the deflation a humour must meet and convert her into a wit who controls the action of the play. *El amor médico*, like a number of other plays of Tirso's, celebrates the triumph of love and commonsense: in it, love and life win the day over medical learning and death.

This triumph, far from being a mockery of women, is an exaltation of Jerónima, of woman, and of femininity. If we laugh at Jerónima, it is not because we find her love ridiculous, but because she is made to realise that she cannot choose but love. She seems to have achieved a miraculous, harmonious reconciliation between learning and love—until we are made to realise that in reality the struggle between love and learning has ended in the triumph of the former, which cleverly converts the practice of medicine into yet another man-trap. Love threatens to destroy Jerónima's feminist aspirations, but, being the wit she is, she can quickly adjust to the changing situation. The intellect is used to achieve a natural end, while the professional garb and status are handy weapons in this battle of the sexes. Thus Jerónima, the wit, comes to the rescue of Jerónima, the humour, and saves her from absolute deflation. We have here a sly, gentle thrust at feminists, who are controlled willy-nilly by their own natures which they cannot deny. Their intellectual aspirations and desire for equality are but new manifestations of their age-old war against man: it is perhaps not so much a case of fatalism as of female wiles. Hartzenbusch saw the essential irony of Tirso's treatment of the theme, even though one would see less of philosophy and more of comic wit in it: ". . . es harto filosófico el pensamiento de pintar a una muger que pugna por salir de su esfera, que quiere competir con los hombres en sabiduría, y que sin embargo cede, como la menos avisada, a la propensión natural de su sexo, no sirviéndole

su ciencia sino para lo que le bastaba con su hermosura y despejo. . . ."
Thus it is that Tirso, with a light, gay touch, reveals to us the workings
of the feminine soul. We are meant to rejoice at the triumph of love and
life over death-dealing knowledge. The feminist theme is almost wholly
divested of all seriousness in order to afford a witty play on the concepts
of feminism and femininity. Out of a serious question Tirso has built a
comedy of wit.

So far, consideration has been given almost exclusively to the character
of Jerónima. This can be seen to have been justified, inasmuch as she is
the most important figure in the play: she controls the action (since she
controls the other characters); her portrayal is the one Tirso gives most
attention to, which is only natural, since the basic conflict of concepts
which constitutes the theme of the play is embodied in Jerónima herself,
and its resolution achieved in that of her psychological conflict. This
makes the study of this character crucial in any formal analysis of the
comedy. However, before we pass on to the consideration of other aspects
of the play's overall structure, it would be helpful to review rapidly the
more important secondary figures. These, as has been already stated, can
be regarded in large part as Jerónima's gulls. As such, they perform an
ancillary function, being auxiliaries in the dialectic of the play. They are
not drawn as fully as Jerónima. Yet this does not prevent them from being
reasonably interesting, while the continuance of the binary pattern in their
characterisations makes for certain ambiguities which help to create an
illusion (at least) of roundness.

Gaspar is Jerónima's antagonist. As such, he is a convenient mouth-
piece, as we have seen, for Tirso's criticism of the medical profession.
The jealousy he experiences as the result of Barbosa's interference in his
courtship of Estefanía makes the moral condemnation of the apparently
unscrupulous doctor natural and apposite on his lips. His indignation and
open attacks on the doctor are consonant with one aspect of his character,
which is a curiously ambiguous one.

As befits his secondary role in the play, he is introduced indirectly, in
the opening conversation between Jerónima and Quiteria. The two give
us conflicting opinions on him. Jerónima, as we know, considers him
uncivil and ungentlemanly because of his indifference towards her. She
has established that Gaspar is aware of her presence in the house: therefore
his failure to pay his respects to her must be set down to a lack of breeding.
On the other hand, Quiteria, who is not as emotionally involved, can find
nothing but praise for him, even considering him perfect:

QUITERIA: Yo en lo que he notado dél,
perfeto le considero:
la persona un pino de oro:
un alma en cualquiera acción;
de alegre conversación,
guardando en ella el decoro
que debe a su calidad;
en lo curioso, un armiño;
mas no afectando el aliño
que afemina nuestra edad;
mozo, lo que es suficiente
para prendar hermosuras;
mas no para travesuras
de edad, por poca, imprudente.
Júzgole yo de treinta años.

(I.i. p. 970a–b.)

She can explain away all apparent lapses into incivility. But not to Jerónima.

Gaspar's first appearance on stage follows in the next scene. Like Jerónima, he is provided with a confidant, Gonzalo, and his long speech provides factual background information about himself which supplements what we have learnt about him from Jerónima. The speech also tells us something about his character. He seems to be a man of principle—at least where his own honour is concerned. He does not hesitate to seek out and wound and even slay his slanderers. His attack on this breed of men is remarkable and betrays a considerable warmth of passion. However, it is clear that Gaspar's passionate impetuosity is as strong as his sense of honour.

Certain aspects of his behaviour during his courtship also help to confirm the view that he tends to be led by his emotions. His rash attack on the slanderers leads logically to consequences which Gaspar could not seriously have pondered: he has to flee from Toledo and then from Seville. Furthermore, it was his own indiscreet conduct of his courtship which gave the slanderers the opportunity to vilify both Doña Micaela and himself. The former, too, must have had ample knowledge of her fiancé's impetuosity to believe that it was Gaspar himself who penned the anonymous letter to D. Jaime. His rashness is a trait which persists through the play: we see it in his (almost slanderous!) attack on the doctor, his precipitate desire to marry Marta without properly knowing who she is, or, rather, in spite of his knowing that she is the sister of a doctor, and his swift, almost unreflecting acceptance of Barbosa-Marta as his wife at the end.

His attitude towards love is curious. His indiscreet parading of his affection for Micaela and of hers for him is only one aspect of this, and, as Jerónima informs us, Micaela has had to instruct him on how a discreet lover should behave (I.vii. p. 981a). For much of the play, however, Gaspar is anything but discreet. He tiresomely parades his love for Estefanía in Act II and in II.ii openly praises her to Rodrigo, which naturally arouses the latter's interest in her. It is not until he falls madly in love with Marta that Gaspar shows some discretion in his love-affair. In III.iii, for example, he is, for the first time, albeit perforce, secretive and indirect about his love.

Gaspar's boasting about his love-affairs may hint at some insecurity in his relations with women. But more significantly, it reveals the superficial, conventional nature of the attachments prior to his real passion for Jerónima. These superficial attachments can be attributed to two factors. The first is that, through a series of accidents, Gaspar is forced to lead a peripatetic existence. The second, and perhaps more important, is that social honour demands that a man should court a woman unless (and sometimes even if) he is married. This social convention encourages the so-called "double standard." That Gaspar should transfer his (admittedly conventional) affections from one woman to another is something he regards as quite natural. But he does not recognise a woman's freedom to do the same. (We find the same attitude in Don Lope of *Amar por arte mayor* and Don Álvaro of *Mari-Hernández la gallega* and there are interesting variations on the situations in *El Melancólico* and *Esto sí que es negociar*.) Thus, for much of the play, Gaspar is unable to maintain a valid and significant relationship with a woman. His affair with Micaela is a dismal failure, and all he gets out of it is a long opportunity for wallowing in self-indulgent pity and romantic fancies, as Jerónima's spying reveals to us. But this, too, is a conventional reaction, and Gaspar probably enjoys it. Then there is his curious attitude towards Gonzalo's sister, Jerónima. His courtship of Estefanía may have been motivated by either love or socio-economic considerations, or he may simply have been courting her on the rebound. Certainly his attitude in II.iv, as in I.viii, is too mannered, too polite, too correct, in short, too passive. This is not an ardent love. Even his jealousy appears too superficial: he does not challenge the doctor, but merely abuses him or, instead of trying to outrival the latter, complains about his fate in mannered, *culto* language:

GASPAR: (*Aparte*):
                   ¡Qué presto, recelo mío,
                   os muestra mi sol su noche!
                   ¡Apenas salió el aurora
                   del favor, cuando ya veo
                   nublados en mi deseo!

                                    (II.iv. p. 988a.)

His use of stylistic clichés would seem to indicate a personality whose re-
actions are likewise clichés: his concern for Estefanía's health is expressed
thus:

GASPAR: ¿A quién no dará cuidado
                   el ver el sol eclipsado,
                   señor, que entre nieve abrasa?

                                    (II.vi. p. 988b.)

That his love for Estefanía was at best a mere superficial attraction is
proved by his sudden and overwhelming passion for Marta which makes
him forget every other woman to whom he had been attracted: his initial
flirtation with the *tapada* in II.xiii is reflected in his mannered style; but
once he has seen Marta's hand, eyes and face, he loves her with all the
impetuosity of which he is capable, and, in the following scene (II.xiv),
his language is remarkably free of studied conceits: his emotions are too
powerful. Furthermore, in III.viii, Gaspar has so far forgotten his love for
Estefanía that he can offer the doctor a deal: he will surrender his rights
over Estefanía in return for Marta's hand. This bartering of womankind
strikes us as grotesque. But what is worse is the "disloyalty" this implies
towards his previous attachments. Therefore, the doctor chides him for his
"immoral" behaviour. In fact, the circumstantial evidence against Gaspar,
as arranged and presented by the doctor, is damning indeed:

[JERÓNIMA:]   ¡Muerto por vos en Toledo
                   un hombre, sin opinión
                   por vos doña Micaela,
                   con cartas que sin firmar
                   la intentaron desdorar!
                   ¡Civil y baja cautela!
                   ¡Una dama sevillana
                   que vuestros engaños llora,
                   y una embajatriz agora,
                   que despreciáis por mi hermana!

                                    (III.viii. p. 1009a–b.)

The doctor's warning underlines one of the most obvious weaknesses in Gaspar's character: his apparent emotional instability. As has been stated, he seems unable to establish a sound relationship with a woman. But can this be an indication of a superficial attitude to love, a confusion of love with idle flirtation? Several remarks in the play seem to confirm this. There is Tello's unvarnished aside at Gaspar's behaviour: "*(Aparte)*: ¡Miren allí qué meollo! / Tantas quiere cuantas ve" (II.xiii. p. 999b.). It is alleged, in the comic context of the intrigue, that Gaspar has already fallen for four different women, and Tello quite expects a further change in his affections at any moment (III.vii. p. 1007a). Tello's readiness to give credence to Barbosa's charge against Gaspar is not only comic, but helps to blacken the latter's character:

TELLO: Gallo en damas y después
                    gallo en el no te acordar.
                    No es mucho lo que te importo.
                    ¡Sin mí y en tal ocasión!
                    Cinco ya las damas son;
                    nos darás cinco de corto.[22]

                                (III.ix. p. 1009b.)

This systematic attack on Gaspar's morals is in part curious. Doña Blanca seeks to link it to circumstances outside the play, i.e., Lope's amorous exploits. There is even another passage which she might have quoted in support of her hypothesis, viz:

TELLO: Dotor para con chapines,
                    que con amarilla borla
                    puede llamarse Amarilis

                    . . . .

                                (III.iv. p. 1004a.)

The idea is an intriguing one, and would bear further investigation. The veiled hostility to Lope thus revealed would fit in well with R. L. Kennedy's account of the relations between Lope and Tirso at this period,[23] and also, perhaps, help to bring forward, if only by a year or so, the probable date of composition of the play.

Be that as it may, such a presentation of Gaspar is primarily comic. We know that Gaspar has in fact courted only three women—Micaela, Estefanía, and Marta—, but even these are too many for Tello, as we learn when he rebukes Gaspar for falling for Marta:

TELLO: Del [aire] de tus cascos me avisas,

                    según a todas acudes.
                    ¡Bueno es que en un año mudes
                    tres mujeres! ¿Son camisas?
GASPAR: Ellas ocasión me han dado.
                                        (II.xiv. p. 1000b.)

Gaspar's defence is to some extent valid, but we can hardly help thinking
that he is in part to blame for the failure of his affairs. But the other
two women whom Gaspar allegedly promised to marry are largely ghost
figures—the anonymous Toledan woman and his Sevillian hostess. Both
of these, we know, are in fact Jerónima, and are thus identical with Marta.
But their constant haunting of Gaspar produces a comic effect (just as the
green Don Gil haunts Martín), and also constitutes part of Jerónima's
scheme to trap Gaspar into marriage. On the whole, however, this aspect
of Gaspar's character marks him as a man basically hesitant in his relations
with women, perhaps an elegant flirt, who only learns what love is when
he meets Marta.

Gaspar, however, is not a simpleton, lacking in moral qualities. There
is a touch of nobility in his frank apology to Barbosa in III.iii, although
even here his apology is based on self-interest. In the same scene, he is
discreet about his love for Marta, but again his discretion is forced on
him and again motivated by self-interest. His preoccupation with Marta's
limpieza in III.viii, confirms that he can be concerned with the niceties
of social honour even where an overwhelming passion is concerned. In
III.xix, Gaspar is "hooked" in an almost casual manner: he enters and
agrees to marry Marta-Barbosa without much ado. To the last, he fulfils
his function as a foil—almost an instrumental foil—to Jerónima, who
throughout occupies the centre of the picture.

The minor characters, Estefanía, Rodrigo, Quiteria, are largely functional, but nonetheless interesting. I cannot consider them in detail here.
It will be obvious that they are used as vehicles for the satire in the play.
The way in which this satire is expressed through the clash between the
rivals, Jerónima and Estefanía, especially, is worthy of closer attention
than I can give to it here.

So far I have examined the witty implications of the theme and their
effect on the structure of concepts in the play as well as their embodiment
in the characters. It is necessary now to determine to what extent the play
possesses that overall structural unity which is indispensable in all good
works of art.

Notwithstanding the criticisms brought against the play and the faults
it undoubtedly contains, I have attempted to show that the real faults

are minor ones, whereas the apparently major ones can be regarded in a different light. The binary pattern noted in the thematic structure and the characters is also to be seen influencing the plot structure as well as the smaller sub-structures, thus ensuring a coherent unity within the comedy. In fact, a considerable amount of thought and care seems to have been devoted to the construction of the play.

The opening scene, for example, beautifully reflects Jerónima's inner conflict. It is a skilfully constructed scene which is ternary in structure and which grows out of the two thematic motifs of love and learning. We are presented, first, with Jerónima's exasperation at what she considers Gaspar's ill-breeding: her curiosity is aroused and her vanity offended. This is the love motif. The opening merges almost imperceptibly into the middle section, which introduces the learning motif. The final section constitutes a return to the love motif. From the outset, then, a basic pattern is established which both reveals the main theme and also, by its configuration—love-learning-love—, foreshadows the future thematic development. The structure also reflects the emotional and psychological state in which Jerónima finds herself. While learning and feminism seem to be at the core of her character, her present obsession is with love and jealousy. Furthermore, the learning motif, set as it is between the two appearances of the love motif and presented in the form of a flashback providing back-ground information, is already relegated to a secondary position and to the past. This is a good example of the skilful way in which structural configuration and the variation of tenses supplement and reinforce the sense of the actual words. It is interesting to note, too, that Jerónima's admission of jealousy comes after the motif of learning is introduced (with some warmth of feeling): this stresses the incongruity of her situation, and sounds a note of irony which is taken up in Quiteria's remarks. The transitions from motif to motif are effected smoothly and naturally enough, although this does not lessen the brusque effect deliberately created by the juxtaposition of opposing themes.

A similar ternary structure is also evident in the next scene where Gaspar's account of his tragic love-affair is enclosed between references to Castile and Portugal and their possessions in the East and West Indies. Again, there are two motifs, unrequited or frustrated love (and violent emotions) and travel, which are to be developed in the course of the play. Again, the transitions between them are smoothly effected.

The underlying binary pattern persists in the internal structure of a large number of scenes. A quick glance confirms that very many of them consist of a dialogue between two characters (often using the confidant technique—as for example, in I.i,ii) or a soliloquy in which an interior conflict is laid bare. The frequent use of such discussions and soliloquies harmonises with the basic dialectic which goes on in the play. This pattern also tells us something about the rhythmic structure of the comedy.

Nor is this careful patterning and symmetry restricted to individual scenes. The movement of the whole of Act I, for example, conforms to a beautifully symmetrical pattern. The act falls into two parts. The first opens with the conversation between Jerónima and Quiteria which introduces the basic motifs. The next scene brings in Gaspar with Gonzalo after the women have left the stage. There is a build-up of characters in this second *cuadro* to scene iv, and then a gradual reduction (in twos) in the number of characters—much like the reduction of stops on an organ—to the end of the *cuadro* (scene vi). The second half of the act follows a similiar pattern: a gradual build-up of characters, again in twos, introducing first Jerónima with Quiteria (scene vii) and then Gaspar with Tello (scene viii), comes to a climax in scene ix with the entry of Gonzalo who interrupts the *tête-à-tête* between Jerónima and Gaspar (just as in the first half Jerónima had interrupted the conversation between Gaspar and Gonzalo). This is followed by a withdrawal of characters: Gonzalo's exit is followed by that of Gaspar and Tello, which leaves the stage to Quiteria and Jerónima, who sees the plan she sketched out in the first scene apparently in ruins. The love-learning motifs, again in juxtaposed opposition, bring the act to a close. We have come full circle.

The inner conflicts in the main characters and their ambiguities can be seen as a continuation of the binary pattern. An instance of this ambiguity can be seen in the portrayal of Estefanía. Tello informs us that she loves to speak in Portuguese:

TELLO: La embajatriz mi señora,
                  que es digna de todo amor,
                  y me hace mucho favor,
                  por no decir me enamora,
                  da en hablar a lo seboso;
                  porque en nuestra tierra es fama
                  que en esta lengua una dama
                  tiene aire garabatoso;

                                      (II.iii. p. 986a.)

Furthermore, Estefanía is overcome by an inexplicable melancholy. This is characteristically Portuguese, but the real cause of her melancholy, which she admits only to herself, is her burning passion for her physician. This violent love, like the violent jealousy she experiences later, is also a Por-

tuguese characteristic. Portugal is traditionally, and always in Tirso, the
home of love: Rodrigo as well as Gaspar find love there, a love which, in
both cases, is sudden and violent, and, in the case of Gaspar, quite unlike
his earlier tepid affairs.

At the same time, ambiguous emotions, like Estefanía's, and obvious
internal conflicts, like Jerónima's, are salient features in the characterisation of the play, and are determined by the fact that the characters are,
to a large extent, to be seen as live dialectical elements engaged in an
intellectual play of wit rather than solely as living persons.

Since wit is a vital element in the dramatic structure, the play of ideas
naturally occupies a prominent position. This explains why, in spite of a
seemingly considerable amount of physical movement, there is in reality
comparatively little action in the play. The changes of scene and setting,
the quick changes in disguise, etc., are necessary to produce an illusion or,
at least, an impression of action. The dialectic in the play is indubitably its
most important feature, and the play of ideas can be illustrated in action
only to a limited extent. But more of this later. What we must note
at this point is the curious rhythm of the play: short bursts of physical
action alternate with relatively long periods of stagnation, during which
the dialectic is pursued. I.i,ii, for example, are, apart from the entrances
and exits, long narrations built on a number of motifs standing in mutual
opposition one to another. Scene iii to vi bring a perceptibly quicker pace
on the surface of the action. They also increase the psychological tension
by creating suspense in Gaspar's mind. The pace begins to slow down
in scene v, and there follows in scene vi a period of reflection, broken
only by the counterpoint of Tello's brilliant linguistic virtuosity. The next
scene (the "second exposition") continues this reflective mood. Though
tautological on the level of the action, it casts light on Jerónima's character,
stressing her obsession with her new experience of love to which Gaspar's
indifference and her own jealousy have given birth. This stagnation in the
action allows Jerónima to meditate on the nature of female psychology.
It is Quiteria here who ironically reminds her of her love of learning, a
trait which, as will be demonstrated later, finds only indirect reflection in
Jerónima's style. Jerónima's humorous reaction to Quiteria's irony reveals
an irony directed against herself. Scene viii brings no quickening of the
physical action apart form the entrance of Gaspar and Tello. But on the
stylistic level, the emotional tension increases as Jerónima's aggresive and
sarcastic remarks take a bewildered Gaspar quite by surprise. The tension
is maintained in the final scene with Gonzalo's sudden interruption and the
progressive dissolution of the cluster of figures on stage, leaving Jerónima

in despair and bewildered by the unexpected turn of events. This rhythmic pattern of a constant alternation between periods of surface action and episodes of stagnation with movement on the emotional and conceptual levels is maintained throughout the play, and is a direct consequence of the structure of wit employed by Tirso.

Wit also constitutes the unifying thread which draws together scenes and episodes which at first sight might appear unconnected. Three scenes in Act II provide us with as good an example as any: these are scenes iii, vii, and xiii. Scene iii is a humorous conversation between Tello and Delgado, the latter being essentially Tello's confidant. The shift of scene from Castile to Portugal has introduced complications, misunderstandings and ambiguities into the life of Tello, who explains to his friend the comic confusions which his partly deliberate misunderstanding of Portuguese produces. These confusions find a reflection in the *quid pro quo*'s of linguistic confusion. The comedy arises, of course, out of Tello's witty exploitations of homonyms: the same word (more or less) seems to mean one thing in Castilian, another in Portuguese. On the surface, this scene seems to have been inserted into the play for its comic effect. But the particular nature of the comedy, i.e., the confusions arising out of an ambiguous language, makes this scene a brilliant introduction to the ambivalent "medical examination scene" which follows in scene viii.[24]

This scene is doubly ambiguous. It is both a love-scene and a medical examination on the one hand, and, on the other, a courtship between a woman and a "man" who is in reality a woman: that is to say, the relationship itself is ambiguous on the sexual level. Scene viii presents to Gaspar only one meaning, however, for to him, as to Estefanía, Barbosa is a man. The other meaning emerges in scene xiii, which is complementary to scene viii. Here, Jerónima, as a woman, ensnares Gaspar by attracting him, just as in the earlier scene she had isolated him from Estefanía both by leading on the latter and also forbidding Gaspar to see her.

The use of wit to link scene to scene and to provide the conceptual opposition in the play with an ultimate synthesis does not, however, mean that the principle of causality is ignored. This principle operates to a surprising extent in the play: even the shift of scene form Seville to Coimbra is foreshadowed as early as I.ii, where Gaspar tells us of his intention to go to Portugal in order to embark for the East. Gonzalo's alternative suggestion is not allowed to materialise, and Gaspar is forced to flee to the Portuguese court in order to escape from the clutches of the Castillian law-officers. Thus the violation of the unity of place maintains the validity of the causal principle. The one real violation of causality is at the beginning of Act II, where there occurs the unexpected and unmotivated introduction of Estefanía and Rodrigo, who give rise to a new intrigue. At the same time, a change in scene would normally entail a change in circumstances: to maintain the old ones rigidly would constitute a flagrant violation of the probable. Also, as the main conflict is between Jerónima and Gaspar, Estefanía and Rodrigo (like Micaela) exist on the circumference of the main plot, and Estefanía can be seen as another obstacle in Jerónima's way, thus underlining Gaspar's emotional instability. But, as we have seen, Estefanía and Rodrigo are integrated into the plot in another way *via* the medical satire.

The binary pattern is manifested in other ways in the comedy, but I cannot go into that here. I should like only to note, briefly, some aspects of the Castile-Portugal opposition. On one level, the shifting of the setting after the first act to Portugal can be seen as a gratuitous violation of the unity of place. But this shift, if seen in symbolic terms, turns out to be intimately linked to the thematic development. Portugal and Coimbra especially, symbolise a purer, more innocent, less corrupt way of life than does Seville (cf. Gonzalo's speech in I.v. p. 979a). Thus it is in Coimbra that Gaspar finds true love.

So far, I have been dealing largely with the wit of situations and concepts in the play. Wit, of course, is a basic element in Tirso's style, and I shall now consider briefly some of the pertinent aspects of the play's style.

An obvious example of the persistence of the binary pattern on the stylistic level is the opposition of Spanish, the language used for most of the time in the play, to Portuguese, which is employed mainly by Marta/Barbosa as an element of disguise, and, for comic purposes, by Tello in a scene which has already been analysed.[25] The use of the two languages reinforces and enlarges upon the ambivalence which is at the root of the dialectic in the play.

But to pass on to wider considerations, we note that, as always in Tirso, the style employed in the play is brilliant. In the opening scene of the play, it is fluid and conversational. Jerónima's speeches betray the warmth of her passion for study as well as for Gaspar: they are long, well-argued and impassioned, indicating that she is carried away by the earnestness of her feelings, her exasperation at the incompetence of doctors, and Gaspar's indifference. The entire conversation in this scene is shot through with a liberal use of irony, initially unconscious on Jerónima's part and highly conscious on Quiteria's. The scenes in which Jerónima confronts Gaspar are particularly fine for their verbal fencing. In I.viii, Gaspar is no match

for Jerónima. Every remark he utters leaves his guard down, making
him vulnerable to Jerónima's penetrating thrusts. On the other hand, in
II.xiii, when Gaspar falls madly in love with Jerónima's hand, he finds
no difficulty in rising to Jerónima's level and maintaining a discreet and
witty dialogue in the flirtation.

One feature of Gaspar's speech is worth noting. This is his use of
Gongoristic language. As this Gongoristic style is employed almost exclusively by Gaspar, it is an aspect of his character and does not have a
structural function in this play. Gaspar tends to use this style in scenes of
heightened emotion. He expresses his gratitude to the mysterious *tapada*
in Seville thus:

> GASPAR: ¡Oh iris de mi ventura,
>   que disfrazada en tinieblas,
>   reflejos del sol retocas
>   colores con que me alegras!
>   Dame a besar esas manos.
>   (I.viii. p. 983a.)

He expresses his solicitude over Estefanía's poor state of health in the
following way:

> GASPAR: ¿A quién no dará cuidado
>   el ver el sol eclipsado,
>   señor, que entre nieve abrasa?
>   (II.vi. p. 988b.)

As has been suggested earlier, this use of a stylised language in moments of
presumed emotional tension indicates the conventional nature of Gaspar's
love. Also, one may go further and see in the limited use of this style a
foreshadowing of the elaborate and symbolic part it plays in the structure
of *La celosa de sí misma*. This is one point which would suggest that *El
amor médico* is earlier than *La celosa*.

Further support for this view would seem to be found in the limited use
of the religious word-play for comic effect in *El amor médico*. Again, this
stylistic aspect is associated with one person in the main, viz., Tello, and
is thus an aspect of his character. There are simple, obvious jokes such
as: "Y adiós, hasta la otra vida" (I.ix. p. 983b). Rather more elaborate is
the following:

> TELLO: (A QUITERIA)
>   Pueda
>   alcanzar yo algún favor

> dese retablo en cuaresma,
> ya que no corren cortinas
> aquí por pascuas, ni fiestas.
> ¿Eres dama motilona
> de la hermana compañera?
> ¿Fregatriz o de labor?
> No quiero decir doncella;
> que esa es moneda de plata,
> y como el vellón la premia,
> apenas sale del cuño,
> cuando afirman que se trueca.
> Dame un adarme no más
> de carantoña.
>   (*Va a destaparla, y pégale ella*)
> QUITERIA: Jo, bestia.
> TELLO: Bestia soy, pues que te sufro,
>   y Jo soy en la paciencia.
>   (I.viii. p. 982b.)

Perhaps the most developed example occurs when Tello condemns Gaspar for his fickleness:

> TELLO: que con ésta ya es la cuarta
>   que hemos mudado.
> GASPAR: ¿Qué quieres?
>   Entre todas las mujeres . . .
> TELLO: ¿Rezas?
> GASPAR: Sola es doña Marta
>   digna de ser adorada.
> TELLO: Yo que rezabas creía
>   por ella el Ave-María.
> GASPAR: Tello, ¿no es cosa cansada
>   verte siempre de un humor?
> TELLO: "Entre todas las mujeres,"
>   dicen, "bendita tú eres"
>   los que rezan. Si tu amor
>   da en hereje, ¿qué te espantas?
> GASPAR: No mezcle tu desatino
>   lo humano con lo divino.
> TELLO: Ni mudes tú damas tantas.
>   (III.vii. p. 1006b.)

But these examples, too, are isolated, and do not form a consistent pattern in the structure of this play.

However, there is, in *El amor médico*, a structure of images which is derived from the basic theme itself. Love is equated in the play with illness. This equation, as we have already seen, gives rise to a delicious *double-entendre* in some of the key scenes, based on the ambiguities of meaning which the equation allows. On the other hand, any illness calls for the services of a doctor, and the efficacy of his cure depends on his learning. Thus, the love-sickness, as the play implies, calls for the services of an *alcahuete* who is also a learned doctor. The ambivalent character of Dr. Barbosa is the source of much of the comedy in the play. His words and his actions are frequently double-edged. The ultimate irony in this play of wit is centred on the protagonist herself. Not only is she doctor and go-between: she is also a victim of the love-sickness. Thus she must be her own doctor and, therefore, *tercera de sí misma*. To this end she exploits her hard-earned knowledge and learning. In this way, the conceptual reconciliation of feminism and femininity is mirrored on the level of the action.

Seen in the light of these comments, the second exposition in I.vii takes on a new appearance. While, on the level of the action, it is tautological, on the level of character, and, more significantly here, on the stylistic level, it makes an initial step towards the reconciliation of the two opposing concepts first introduced in the opening scene. At first glance, Jerónima's speech is monothematic, in that it seems to repeat what we know about the birth and development of her love. This is an indication of the extent to which she has been carried away by her passion. But, significantly, her speech is shot through with terms and phrases drawn from educational jargon. Intellectual curiosity leads her to investigate Gaspar's character, as has been pointed out already. Her recognition of awakening jealousy is recalled thus:

[JERÓNIMA:]   Esto ya lo imaginaba
                 que A, B, C, de celos era,
                 que si a la postre presumen,
                 al principio deletrean.

                                        (I.vii. p. 980b.)

She reads and studies the accounts of Gaspar's love-affair:

[JERÓNIMA:]   Esto, Quiteria leí,
                 sospecho que en la postrera [carta]
                 de todas, con que animé
                 esperanzas y quimeras.
                 Estudié por las demás

todo el suceso y materia
destos trágicos amores:
¡fin más dichoso en mí tengan!
(III.xx. p. 1020b.)

The study motif has been assimilated into the love-motif on the stylistic
level, which indicates that Jerónima's learning is being turned towards
un-academic, if not unscholarly, ends. Thus, beneath its apparent repetitiousness, the scene indicates a modification in Jerónima's attitude as well
as a development in the dialectical process.

It is now quite clear that the comedy in this play exists both on the
stylistic level and also on the level of the stage action. Thus the implications of witty ideas which exist only in a germinal state on the stylistic
level—e.g., the love-illness equation, the doctor-*alcahuete* equation—are
fully developed only in the physical action on the stage, as in the medical
examination scene. Such a comic structure in which verbal wit is both developed and reinforced by physical situations makes for a comic language
of extraordinary compression, capable of being "read" at different levels
simultaneously. The resulting complex structure more than compensates
for the looseness and repetitions noted elsewhere in the play.

The binary pattern which pervades the whole play springs from the basic
thematic opposition between feminism and femininity, the reconciliation
of which is the aim of the play. So, too, in the violent structural and conceptual juxtapositions and oppositions which reflect the basic opposition,
there can be discerned a series of movements towards reconciliation. A
reconciliation between Castile and Portugal is hinted. The Barbosa-Marta
dualism finds a resolution in their being absorbed into Jerónima:

ESTEFANÍA: ¿Luego no tenéis hermana?
JERÓNIMA: El amor la ha convertido
               a ella y el dotor Barbosa
               en un cuerpo.
(III.xx. p. 1020b.)

Similarly, the male-female roles of Jerónima are resolved at the end by a
shedding of disguise:

ÍÑIGO: ¿Luego sóis mujer?
JERÓNIMA: He sido
               quien a la Naturaleza
               con mi industria he contradicho.
(III.xx. p. 1020b.)

The feminist doctor emerges as a feminine woman when feminism is shown to be another manifestation of femininity (or female wiles). With this, death-dealing, sterile learning is converted into a weapon which brings about the triumph of love. This event is simultaneous with Gonzalo's death, which ends the brother-sister conflict within the play on the personal as well as on the social level.

But this very event draws our attention to a final factor. While, in the majority of these cases, the oppositions established in the play dissolve with the final reconciliation of the main opposition, in a few significant cases, there is no real reconciliation, but rather a postponement of harmony which tempers the final gladness with a hint of an undecided struggle stretching into the future.

With Gonzalo's death, Jerónima, the second-born, inherits the *mayorazgo*. She is now head of the family and is required to return to Castile. This may be seen as no more than reasonable, but the situation is a bit more complex. Coimbra and Portugal have done their bit in achieving a certain harmony among the lovers, but realities require the main characters to leave their idyllic retreat in order to return to the corrupt, harsher Castile. Here, there is no real resolution to the Castilian-Portuguese opposition. It is put into cold storage. Perhaps this is a comment on the political situation of the early seventeenth century. Perhaps it is Tirso's way of saying that reality, however unpleasant, has to be faced, just as Shakespeare makes his characters, with the exception of the affected melancholy Jaques, return to the court at the end of *As You Like It*.[26] Coimbra, like the Forest of Arden, is no more than a temporary escape from reality.

Again, and here irony creeps in, Jerónima returns to Castile as the head of her family; but she returns as Gaspar's wife and is now subordinated to his authority. It is Gaspar, then, who in law takes over the *mayorazgo*. Jerónima has surrendered her desire for freedom in exchange for love, subordination and captivity. We have a comic situation in which the protagonist is forced to recognise the superior power of natural inherent limitations and to accept them freely. Such a freedom is, of course, little more than an illusion, although it may denote a certain wisdom. But the irony goes deeper. Our first movements of pity, or at least sympathy, for Jerónima are modified when we recall the sort of man Gaspar is and the ease with which Jerónima was able to outmanoeuvre him. Gaspar has been no match for Jerónima in the play, and is unlikely to be one in the future. Jerónima, at the end, it seems, has salvaged some little measure of freedom—if only freedom from the possible tyranny of a husband. Her voluntary submission, like Kate's at the end of *The Taming of the Shrew*, is only apparent.

These ambiguities and ambivalences in the ending ensure that echoes of the fundamental binary pattern persist to the end. The consistency of this pattern provides the play with a unity which, at first sight, seems all too absent. The oppositions in the play spring from the basic thematic opposition. That this is reconciled with the help of wit means that such a resolution is not absolutely valid: it is valid within the context of this comedy where the deeper metaphysical implications of the theme are avoided or only lightly and indirectly touched upon. The problem of whether the emotions can be reconciled with the intellect is one that brooks no thoroughly satisfactory answer.

How, then, does this play appear in the light of Kerr's ideas on comedy? In the play, love is presented as an obstacle to the intellectual aspirations of the heroine: being an emotion to which every person is subject, it constitutes a built-in physical limitation to any aspiration towards absolute human freedom. Jerónima realises this and willingly accepts the consequences. Is this voluntary abandonment of a desire for liberty to be seen in near-tragic terms?

Tirso, as has been said, avoids a deliberate exploration of the metaphysical aspect; all the same, there are certain implications in the ending. Freedom is willingly, and almost eagerly, surrendered for the captive state of marriage. This is reasonable within the play, for the pursuit of absolute freedom is absurd, inasmuch as it is a sterile, anti-vital, self-defeating activity. The linking of freedom through and in intellectual pursuits with the practice of medicine makes this point neatly in the context of seventeenth-century ideas and views. This voluntary choice of limitation in preference to freedom is an implicit attack on intellectual exclusiveness. Man is a limited being, and, by accepting the consequences of his limitations, may succed in partly transcending them. In this, the conventional view of the *comedia* which sets love above rigorous, inflexible ideologies, thought out *a priori*, prevails in this play, but it is presented in a new and more subtle way.

At the same time, a certain pessimism is attached to this necessary, albeit voluntary, renunciation of freedom. It is increased when we consider the nature of the life to which man must reconcile himself. *El amor médico* is, on the surface, a gay comedy of brilliant wit with only echoes of seriousness. Nevertheless, in it human beings are presented as almost helpless puppets of forces more powerful than themselves. The characters fall into the wits and gulls. The latter comprise all those who are deceived by Jerónima and her confidante. To achieve her end, Jerónima systematically deceives and tricks almost everyone else in the play. In this intrigue, good faith counts for naught and is mercilessly exploited by those who see how they can turn the naive credulity and frankness of others to their own profit. Even Rodrigo double-crosses his friend, Gaspar. But ironically, Rodrigo himself is a puppet controlled in part by love, in part by Jerónima-Barbosa. Rodrigo is more clever than Gaspar and thus naturally seeks to ally himself with Barbosa: he is open with the latter, but this frankness is not wholly reciprocated. Jerónima is the arch-deceiver who triumphs in the play: yet, powerful as she is, she, too, is helpless in the hands of nature: her only strength lies in her ability to recognise her situation and make the best of it. The whole intrigue is an elaborate pattern of deceit, schemes and counter-schemes typifying a way of life in which honesty and frankness are fatal flaws of character. Deceit and dishonesty (the ambiguous nature of which is reflected in the play's structure) are on the side of natural forces: the triumph of the latter in the comedy nullifies the negative moral effects of the former in practical terms. But do the means justify the ends? The overall view is a pessimistic one—as Kerr asserts the comic view to be—, and the implications no less than disturbing. It is this residue which makes the final, ambiguous tone of this comedy so apt. The whole play can be seen as a vast symphonic structure whose argument consists in a struggle between conflicting motifs which inter-act on one another as they recur periodically. The working-out leads to an uneasy reconciliation in the recapitulation: but we are meant to feel that the coda is not as merry as it seems to be: it only underlines the absurdity of life.

* * * * *

From the preceding analyses, it is now possible, by way of summing up, to draw some initial conclusions, which will serve as a guide to an exploration of the remaining plays to be examined.

First of all, there is the question of structure. In the three plays examined so far, I have shown that Tirso has used three different structures. This points not only to variety, but, more significantly, to experiments with the problem of dramatic structure. That we must hesitate before we accuse Tirso of being indifferent to dramatic technique, and, in particular, to structural soundness, is driven home by the perfect structure of *La celosa*: here not only is the notorious Tirsian *deus ex machina* missing— although the complication in the main action reaches an impasse—, but the *dénouement* is effected organically through the intersection or clash of the main and secondary actions: the two actions are thus linked not only thematically, as is normally the case in the *comedia*, but structurally, the development and unravelling of both being mutually interdependent. *Don Gil* and *El amor médico* exemplify two different approaches to dramatic construction: in their respective ways, both structures are novel. The Chinese-boxes structure recurs in a later play, *Amar por arte mayor*, while the use of wit as the structural basis of a play finds striking employment in *Por el sótano y el torno*. Those experiments in dramatic structure indicate that Tirso was working on the "frontiers of drama."[27] The dramatic structure of wit is perhaps his most interesting contribution here.

The way in which Tirso uses disguise is also noteworthy. Costume, in early plays, is symbolic of a character's social status: it is a form of short-hand by which the author helps us to "place" the character. Thus it is constant and fixed. In Tirso, the relationship between costume or dress and identity is explored more deeply, and the basic distinction between costume and disguise becomes more tenuous. Disguise ceases to be mere technical device to produce dramatic complication and acquires a more symbolic function, being more closely integrated into the theme and structure. This is clearly so in *Don Gil* and *La celosa*. The thematic importance is even more obvious in *El amor médico*, where the resolution of the thematic paradox is achieved symbolically by disguise.

That some of Tirso's best comedies are satirically conceived is made clear by the analyses of these three plays. In other words, certain social and literary conventions are satirised not merely in the words of these plays, but by the plays themselves, that is, by the way in which they are constructed. Satire, therefore, has an organic and not simply an incidental function in these comedies. Where Tirso goes beyond the conventional satire of social follies and moral failings found in so many other authors of the period is in his systematic exploitation of such satire for literary ends.

Closely associated with Tirso's satirical attitude is his love of absurd situations. This is exemplified in all three of the comedies examined. While it must be recognised that the term "comedy of the absurd" has existentialist overtones to the contemporary reader, it is at the same time a description which, if we are willing to forgo the existentialist nuance, suits Tirso's plays perfectly.

The three plays also illustrate Tirso's development technique. *Don Gil* carries to its extreme limit the conventional dramatic figure of the female page. In *El amor médico*, the use of two forms of disguise increases the complication. Some of the motifs in this play are developed in *La celosa*. A similar process can be discerned on the stylistic level: the structural use of imagery, although not absent in *Don Gil* and *El amor médico*, is much more marked in *La celosa*.

Finally, these three plays throw some light on two of the theories of comedy examined in the introduction to this book. It is evident that the attempt to apply the cathartic theory of comedy to *Don Gil* and *El amor médico* does not provide us with an entirely satisfactory explanation of these plays: woman emerges as a force for order, stability, sanity and morality in a world where male domination tends to produce selfish self-centredness, chaos, immorality and confusion of values.[28] While *La celosa* would seem to provide us with an instance of a woman producing chaos, the situation is really absurd, and the frustration of Magdalena within the play obviates the need for the cathartic theory to make us see in the play a restoration of harmony in the world. The charge, too, that Tirso's comedies are immoral is seen to be without foundation and clearly based on a misinterpretation of his plays.

At the same time, *El amor médico* provides obvious support for Kerr's view of comedy as the dramatic form which pessimistically draws attention to man's limitations. The freedom-limitation opposition is no less evident in the other two plays. In *Don Gil*, however, the freedom Martín seeks is escape from responsibility. This is denied him in the interests of moral (and, therefore, social) stability and order. Martín's individual identity is also one of his limitations—but fortunately so, we feel in this case. The escape from self is presented in its absurdity in *La celosa*. But the metaphysical implications are not explored.

These three plays thus illustrates what can be termed the "ambiguous tonality" of the *comedia*. The most striking example is, perhaps, *Don Gil*, a sparkling comedy which sounds deep and serious issues, and in which, as I have pointed out, the "diffused responsibility" which Parker has shown to be a central feature of Calderón's tragedy can also be discerned. It seems to have been one of the fundamental assumptions of the age that life is both comic and tragic. In the one is the other, necessarily and inevitably. That, at least, if the *comedia* is a faithful mirror of life.

NOTES

1 In her introduction to this play in *Tirso de Molina. Obras dramáticas completas*, II (Madrid, 1962), pp. 961–69.

2 In his review of *Por el sótano y el torno*, ed. A. Zamora Vicente (Buenos Aires, 1949), in *Symposium*, IV (1950), 187–90.

3 Cf. R. L. Kennedy: "*La prudencia en la mujer* and the Ambient that Brought it Forth," *PMLA*, LXIII (1948), 1131–90.

4 This date is suggested by R. L. Kennedy in her article "On the Date of Five Plays by Tirso de Molina," *HR*, X (1942), 183–214.

5 R. Sancho de San Román: *La medicina y los médicos en la obra de Tirso de Molina* (Salamanca, 1960), p. 65.

6 This feature is similar to Tirso's so-called "Self-plagiarism," already noted by critics. See, e.g., G. E. Wade, "Tirso's Self-Plagiarism in Plot," *HR*, IV (1936), 55–65. One aspect of this developing technique is also discussed by E. Calderà in "Un motivo delle commedie 'de enredo': l'elaborazione de 'El melancólico' " in *Studi tirsiani* (Milan, 1958), 95–110.

7 This date is suggested by Ruth L. Kennedy in her article "On the Date of Five Plays by Tirso de Molina," *HR*, X (1942), 183–214.

8 This is noted by A. Zamora Vicente and M. Josefa Canellada de Zamora on p. 88 of their ed. of this play (Madrid, 1956).

9 In his review of *Tirso de Molina: Comedias* II (Clás. Castellanos, Madrid, 1947), eds. V. Zamora Vicente and M. J. Canellada de Zamora, in *NRFH*, IV (1950), pp. 68–71.

10 In his *examen* of the play in *Teatro escogido de Fray Gabriel Téllez* vol. VIII (Madrid, 1840).

11 J. M. Viqueira, on p. 229 of his interesting monograph, "La lusofilia de 'Tirso de Molina,' " *Biblos*, XXXVI (1960), 265–489, sees the play as exemplifying two types of freedom: the freedom to love and the freedom to act. This, in a sense, is true enough. Yet, there is an assumed incompatibility between these two types of freedom in the play—until a way of reconciling them is found. One type of freedom, in other words, limits the other type. This is what helps to maintain the dramatic tension in the play.

12 Cf. the following passage from *Marta la piadosa*:

> JUAN: Don Diego, hele de matar.
> DIEGO: ¿Sois vos médico?
>   (III.xviii.)

13 José M. Viqueira, in his study, *Coimbra en las letras españolas* (Coimbra, 1964), refers briefly to the play's dualism which, as he points out, suits the character of the city.

14 Quotations are taken from Doña Blanca de los Ríos's ed. already mentioned. References are to Act, scene, and page. In a few cases, Zamora Vicente's ed. in Clás. Castellanos, mentioned above, provides a more satisfactory reading.

Where there is a significant difference between the two texts, this is noted. Obvious misprints have been corrected.

15 In *The Structure of Literature* (Univ. of Chicago Press, 1962, c 1954), Chap. III, "Comic Plots," pp. 82ff.

16 In his *examen* of the play, mentioned in note 10.

17 "The Optics of Love: Notes on a Concept of Atomistic Philosophy in the Theatre of Tirso de Molina," *PMLA*, LVIII (1943), 108–21.

18 I.xiii, p. 561b in vol. III of B. de los Ríos's ed., (Madrid, 1958).

19 The large number of Jewish doctors in Spain and the essentially social reasons for this have been noted by E. Glaser in "Referencias antisemitas en la literatura peninsular de la edad de oro," *NRFH*, VIII (1954), 39–62.

20 The emphasis on personal merit as the basic criterion in determining the individual's position in the social hierarchy is a constantly recurring theme in Tirso. Doña Blanca de los Ríos has sought to connect this with her hypothesis of Tirso's illegitimacy and his consequent attitude towards bastards and *segundones*. G. Mancini has pointed out, however, that the *segundón* is a common enough character in the drama of the period in his article "Caratteri e problemi del teatro di Tirso" in *Studi tirsiani* (Milan, 1958), p. 12. The self-made man who stakes all on merit and personal achievement is, of course, a typical figure of the Renaissance.

21 "The Feminist Theme in the Drama of the Siglo de Oro," *RR*, XXVI (1935), 191–231. Feminism is, of course, also a real-life social phenomenon of the period. Both Doña Blanca and Zamora Vicente discuss some feminists of the day in their introductions to the play. Bomli, in chap. IV of the first part of his *La Femme dans l'Espagne du siecle d'or* (La Haye, 1950) examines the phenomenon, making passing reference to this play of Tirso's.

22 "Importo/corto:" this is Zamora Vicente's reading.

23 "A Reappraisal of Tirso's Relations to Lope and his Theatre," *BC*, XVII (1965), 23–34 and XVIII (1966), 1–13.

24 Cf. R. Cantel's article "Le Portugal dans l'oeuvre de Tirso de Molina," in *Mélanges d'études portugaises offerts a M. Georges le Gentil* (Chartres, 1949), pp. 131–53.

25 Zamora Vicente makes a brief reference to the relationship between language and personality in *El amor médico* in "Portugal en el teatro de Tirso de Molina" in *De Garcilaso a Valle-Inclán* (Buenos Aires, 1950).

26 For a discussion of this point, see Jan Kott's "Shakespeare's Bitter Arcadia" in *Shakespeare our Contemporary* (2nd ed., London, 1967).

27 The phrase is, of course, taken from U. Ellis-Fermor's book *The Frontiers of Drama* (2nd ed., London, 1964).

28 A similar point has also been made with respect to Calderón by A. A. Parker in his article "History and Poetry: the Coriolanus theme in Calderón." In *Hispanic Studies in Honour of I. González Llubera* (Oxford, 1959), pp. 211–224. Cf. also K. Muir's statement on Shakespeare's heroines in his introduction

to *Shakespeare. The Comedies*, ed. K. Muir (Prentice-Hall, Inc., Englewood Cliffs, N.J., *c* 1965), p. 7. This view of woman in drama may perhaps be linked to the feminist question and this, in turn, to the general ferment in the intellectual and social climate of the seventeenth century. See, e.g., P. W. Bomli, *La Femme dans l'Espagne du siècle d'or* (La Haye, 1950) and María del Pilar Oñate, *El feminismo en la literatura española* (Madrid, 1938).

Marta la piadosa.
The "Religion of Love"

Marta la piadosa, which was probably written in 1615,[1] was first published in the *Quinta parte* of Tirso's plays. This collection bears an *aprobación* by Calderón, which contains the following words:

antes hay en ellas [i.e., las comedias] mucha erudición y exemplar doctrina por la moralidad que tienen encerrada en su honesto y apacible entretenimiento, efetos todos del ingenio de su autor. . .[2]

As E. M. Wilson has pointed out, there is little doubt that Calderón's words are meant sincerely.[3]

Later critics, however, seem to react rather differently to the play. Perhaps owing to a conscious or unconscious association with Molière's *Le Tartuffe*, many have considered *Marta la piadosa* a study in hypocrisy. As a result, there is a conflict of opinion over the precise meaning of the play. A. Lista has some penetrating comments to make.[4] He stresses that Marta's hypocrisy is feigned and not real. It is an attempt to cope with a situation:

Así su gazmoñería es producida por las circunstancias, pero no está en su corazón. Esta combinación produce un buen efecto dramático, y es de ridiculizar la conducta y el lenguage de los hipócritas, sin hacer odiosa a la que se valió de la gazmoñería para librarse de una violencia injusta, porque de tiempo inmemorial están convenidos el auditorio y los actores, en que todos los ardides útiles al amor son disculpables. La ridiculez cae toda entera sobre un viejo tan crédulo como avariento. . . (pp. 449–500)

But Lista is not quite happy with the play. Not only does he disapprove of the supposed "indecencies" in it, but he also finds the moral condemnation of hypocrisy not strong enough: "Para la hipocresía no basta el ridículo: es necesario la odiosidad" (p. 453). Tirso's play is, for him, a mere trifle. But we know that Tirso's criticism is never as crude and as heavily moralising as Lista would have it be. Furthermore, Lista puts in the centre of the picture the ridicule of religious hypocrisy, which is really a secondary aspect.

Hartzenbusch sees a clear moral purpose in the play: "Téllez, que se propuso escarnecer la hipocresía en la persona de doña Marta, se adelantó a Molière y a Moratín en este pensamiento moral."[5] But he also realised that, even though Tirso's purpose may have been to ridicule hypocrisy, Marta was not condemned: "Supone después que ha hecho voto de castidad; pero es cuando se ve colocada entre un joven a quien ella quiere, y un viejo que la destinan para marido; de modo que su ficción es harto disculpable" (p. 241). All her naughty pranks are amusing, "porque se ve que nacen de la astucia y del amor, y no del vicio" (p. 241). What Hartzenbusch says is apt; but here again a slight shift in focus would enable us to see the play more clearly.

P. Chasles states what must be regarded as an extreme and untenable view: "Une fois seulement Téllez s'est avisé de médire des femmes, et c'est aux dévotes, à ses propres ouailles, qu'il s'est attaqué. *Martha la Piadoza* est le portrait comique d'une Tartuffe femelle, peinte des couleurs les plus vives et les moins indulgentes."[6] This judgment is clearly based on a mis-reading of the play. Marta is by no means painted in an unfavourable light, nor is it accurate to say that she is criticised.

More modern critics have, like Lista, stressed the essential difference between Marta and Tartuffe. While M. Romera-Navarro's judgment is still equivocal,[7] A. F. G. Bell rightly points out that Marta ". . . is not a hypocrite. . . . She simply adopts hypocrisy to attain her purpose."[8] In this, he follows Hartzenbusch, but perhaps ignores some of the more serious implications of the play. These are not sidestepped by A. Valbuena Prat, for whom the play represents "el triunfo del amor sobre los convencionalismos sociales, la risa de la vida. . . ."[9]

Not all critics share Valbuena's point of view, however, and some of the most serious criticisms of the play have been made by M. Penna, whose views are almost diametrically opposed to Calderón's.[10] He considers that Tirso's plays are hardly the sort of thing one would expect from a friar. As for *Marta la piadosa*, the subject itself is offensive and borders on the sacrilegious: "Tutto codesto—non dimentichiano, nello sfondo, l'ombra del fratello ucciso—a noi oggi fa l'impressione di qualche cosa poco meno che sacrilego, e costa fatica pensare che sia stato scritto da un frate" (p. 131).

The outcome of the play is also morally objectionable in Penna's eyes. He is disturbed by the fact that Marta and her associates triumph in the

CHAPTER IV

end. Marta organises an outing at which she is surprised by her father. A complete change of feeling is undergone by many, which leaves all happy and satisfied: Lucía, for no good reason, renounces Felipe and marries the Alférez; Urbina gives up Marta; Gómez "dimentica francescanamente il figlio ucciso per accettare in santa pace l'uccisore come genero" (p. 132). There remains, contends Penna, ". . . insoluto il problema della carenza morale che in taluni momenti sembra sfiorare la profanazione." What is worse, Marta escapes scotfree, having made fun of all, and, not only is she made the central figure of the play, but she is never condemned.

Penna also finds the ending unsatisfactory on the structural level: the *desenlace* is absurd. The solution is improbable; nothing leads up to it, and the attitudes of Lucía, Urbina, and Gómez in the final scene are inexplicable and inconsistent with their earlier behaviour. In other words, the construction of the play is weak, or, as Penna contends, Tirso's plays are not constructed: an improbable ending puts an end to a fantastic game. As will be evident, the structural problem (as Penna sees it) is directly connected with the moral problem posed by the play.

If, in fact, Marta has been merely playing a gratuitously heartless and immoral trick on others, one might agree with Penna's views. The latter's own explanation is that Tirso, probably a bastard son of Osuna, was really an unwilling friar, who had to make the best of his life in a monastery. Art provided an escape for the basically worldly-minded Tirso, who, by writing profane and risqué plays, managed to maintain his mental equilibrium. Tirso's was a case of "due vite parallele ma diverse riunite nella stessa persona," and the situations he created in his plays were essentially examples of wish-fulfilment.

This explanation is very ingenious, but is perhaps over-subtle, and is demanded by a rather naive view of the play. Moreover, to grant the validity of the argument is to say that Calderón was a hypocrite, a charge Penna is ready to make. Yet, there is a possibility that Calderón may have seen something in the play which Penna overlooked. In fact, there is no doubt that Tirso is on Marta's side (and so are most of us), but *Marta la piadosa* is no more sacrilegious than is *Le Tartuffe*, nor does the play shock our moral sensibilities if we take the trouble to examine it carefully.

E. Juliá Martínez, in the introduction to his edition of the play,[11] approaches it from a slightly different angle, which complements Valbuena's view. Juliá states that "El problema que plantea Marta no es de hipocresía, sino de explotación de la falsa religiosidad de cuantos le rodean" (p. 15). Social satire, which consists of the ridicule of the credulous, is, for Juliá, central to the play and its main distinctive feature: "la sátira social la eleva de categoría estética, singularizándola entre la copiosa y selecta producción del dramaturgo mercedario" (p. 16). The centre of gravity in the play is thus shifted:

en Marta no hay hipocresía, antes bien, un juego para explotar en provecho propio la credulidad y candidez de quienes admitan la verdad de los hipócritas: este juego está presentado con toda gracia, y para mostrar que, en la gradación del obsesionante problema de la salvación, a más de la predestinación y el olvido de la justica divina, había el descuido temporal que, no teniendo raíz en la propia alma, puede ser extirpado fácilmente, constituyendo un accidente en el vivir, más atacable a la artificiosa sociedad que al propio individuo. (pp. 17–18).

This seems to me to be an apt comment on the theme of the play. Our attention is to be forced not on the criticism or condonation of religious hypocrisy but on the satire of the overcredulous. At the same time, this view can be widened in scope to include not only those who are deceived by apparent religiosity, but also those who are too ready to conform to social conventions and be over-awed by the trappings of authority. In this analysis, therefore, I propose to develop further the statements of Juliá Martínez and Valbuena Prat.

One indication of the rather wider scope of the play's satire—and simultaneously a confirmation of the validity of Valbuena's and Juliá's views—is the function of Juan and Diego in this play. In as enigmatic a play as this (if the puzzled and conflicting opinions of the critics mentioned above are anything to go by), the roles of these two characters appear even more enigmatic. Hartzenbusch's view is that the two characters are superfluous and constitute a minor blemish in one of Tirso's best plays: "Tampoco hacían falta los personages de don Juan y don Diego, que casi siempre hablan al paño" (p. 242). Doña Blanca de los Ríos, following Hartzenbusch, implies the same.[12]

It is true that Juan and Diego are minor, secondary characters. We see so little of them that it is difficult not only to decide whether they undergo any development, but also to form a very clear picture of them. They are tenuously connected to the story by being made suitors of Marta and Lucía, but it is clear from the beginning that they are doomed to failure. They play no part in the plot of the *comedia*, nor do they influence the action. They appear on stage only three times—once in each act. Quick reflection will show that they can easily be removed from the play, and that, had Tirso wished to do so, he would only have needed to suppress a few scenes and make minor alterations here and there to a few others. Nevertheless, it appears that Tirso insisted on dragging them into the play, and the fact that, for the most part, they appear in virtually self-contained scenes suggests that they might have been added as an afterthought. Their presence, therefore, becomes even more intriguing, and an examination of the scenes in which they appear may help us to find a justification for their inclusion in the play.

The first appearance on stage of Juan and Diego (they always appear together, and their observations are generally complementary) is at the end of the first act (I.xiv–xv). They have entered secretly to witness the betrothal of Marta to Urbina, but they do nothing, whereas Felipe, who, like them, has also secretly entered the house, contrives to draw Marta's attention to himself, thus strengthening her in her resolve not to marry Urbina. The function of the two friends is therefore reduced to that of spectators and commentators, and what they have to say is obviously important. In I.xiv, they condemn the practice of forced marriages:

DIEGO: Casallas quiere el padre con violencia.
JUAN: No es en eso prudente, aunque atrevido,
                que en este tiempo no parece justo
                casar las hijas contra el propio gusto.[13]
                                    (I.xiv. p. 368a.)

In the following scene, Diego further disapproves of Marta's marriage to an old man: "No ha seguido su padre buen consejo." (I.xv. p. 369a.) Diego and Juan, then, seem to belong to what we may call the enlightened section of the public. They move with the times and do not seem to follow traditional ways blindly.

This impression we have of their good sense is confirmed in II.v, when they frankly ask Gómez for permission to marry his daughters. Their behaviour is commended by the father, who, however, is unable to grant their request. Neither action nor plot has been advanced by this scene, which is, consequently, useless from a technical point of view. But it has served to bring the two characters on stage, and their role as commentators continues in II.vi. We realise that, not only are they sensible and intelligent, but that Juan is not lacking perspicacity when he recognizes the falsity of Marta's saintliness: "esa buena persona / es mona de hipocresías." (II.vi. p. 380b.) Her religiosity is only on the surface:

                Es Marta disimulada
                zorra, que no vale nada
                la carne, sino el pellejo.
                                    (II.vi. p. 380b.)

Diego, who loves Marta, is not wholly convinced, but we see that at least one section of the public is not deceived by Marta's feigned religiosity.

The third and final appearance of the two friends towards the end of the play (III.xvii to end) comes almost as a surprise to us. We have almost forgotten them. What is even more surprising, however, is that Juan's attitude is far from being sensible. His abortive attempt to kill the Alférez turns out to be an unnecessary piece of melodrama. This time it is Diego who leads the way with a display of good sense. He restrains the insanely jealous Juan, pointing out to him how irrationally absurd and unfounded his hostility towards the Alférez is. The point is that an emotional reaction to a situation blunts the keen sense of perception of both Juan and Diego. Just as Diego is unwilling to believe that Marta's saintliness is assumed, Juan cannot understand that his hostility towards the Alférez is misdirected. However, it is not only love which is capable of preventing the two, on the whole, intelligent characters from making a just assessment of certain situations.

Scenes xix and xx are interesting: now that Tirso has put Juan and Diego on the stage, we should normally expect further comments on the situation from them. Instead, the two friends, for all their good sense and perspicacity, are made the victims of a *burla*. Both Juan and Diego are persuaded (the latter, it is true, only against his will) that Marta is a Portuguese Duchess, in spite of the fact that Juan recognizes Lucía and speaks to her, and that Diego's heart and eyes tell him that the "Duchess" is Marta. The fact that Marta is disguised as a Duchess—"su traje la asegura," affirms Juan (III.xx. p. 401b.)—, that Pastrana speaks in Portuguese, and that the outward comportments of Felipe and Marta are consistent with that of high nobility all combine to deceive, surprisingly, even the shrewd Juan and Diego.

Juan and Diego are here deceived by appearances: dress and language combine to make them deny their own feelings. It has been pointed out that their critical apparatus tends to be blunted by emotion. It is because Diego loves Marta and Juan loves Lucía that their judgment vacillates. In the final scene, they are again blinded, but this time by the trappings of false nobility. It is significant that the false nobles have only lately been false saints who have contrived to deceive others.

To sum up, the analyses of the three appearances of Juan and Diego confirm that they play no indispensable part in plot or action. They are, however, important, as commentators, and even more important as the representatives of an enlightened attitude towards life. But while, on the whole, they are not deceived by religious appearances and refuse to accept traditional attitudes blindly, the fact that they are taken in at the end of the play is significant, for they are thus assimilated into that body of characters who are deceived and ridiculed—Gómez, Urbina, Lucía, and the public in general. The deception of Juan and Diego, then, is the culminating point of a series of deceptions. Thus these two characters are related thematically to the main plot.

The central problem in the play arises out of a stock situation in Golden Age literature. Gómez wishes to marry his daughter to a rich, old man. Such a marriage, although unnatural, is not only attractive to the greedy Gómez, but is sanctioned by social custom. Social custom, too, endows Gómez with that paternal authority over the life and happiness of his daughter, which he would wield tyrannically. These conventions are criticised in the play. Juan, as we have seen, declares that forced marriages are unjust (I.xiv), while Pastrana and Marta, in I.xv, stress the incongruity of a marriage between an old man and a young girl (p. 369a).

There are two other obstacles in the way of Marta's happiness. One is Lucía's rivalry. The way in which this obstacle is overcome has comic rather than social or moral implications. Lucía is outwitted in the game of love. The final obstacles are provided by social conventions. One has already been referred to above. Another is that Marta loves a man whom society expects her to hate—or, at least, persecute—for having killed her brother. But revenge is not man's highest moral duty, nor is it reconcilable with love, Christian or otherwise.

At first sight, the cards are all stacked against Marta. In order to marry the man she loves, she has to defeat her father, her sister, and and a powerful body of social conventions. There are two alternatives open to her. The first is rebellion in order to assert her freedom. But open rebellion against paternal and social authority is, by convention, in the tragic mode. This is so in, for example, Calderón's *La devoción de la cruz*. The other alternative, which is adopted by Marta, is to resort to a trick by which the obstacles can be circumvented; the situation can then be treated as a battle of wits. This is, of course, in the tradition of comedy: emphasis is shifted from the tragic assertion for individual freedom to the comic exploitation of the limitations of others. The particular form which this trick takes is that of an appeal to authority—the highest authority, namely, religion.

The appeal to religion has the advantage of allowing Marta to cope with the demands of her father, the rivalry of her sister, and the pressure of social convention. The success of her trick depends upon the weight which authority in its diverse forms carries with the vast majority of people, who constitute the gulls of the play. They are the social conformists who follow convention blindly, who respect authority because that authority claims a respect which they are too ready to grant, and who, consequently, are dazzled by the trappings of authority—of nobility, of religion—, equating, to use Juan's words, the *pellejo* with the *carne*. It is the familiar mistaking of appearance for reality, a favourite theme in Golden Age literature.

The gulls in the play suffer from the defect of being deficient in intelligence to a greater or lesser degree. They are not wholly fools, however. But their rational faculties are blunted by their emotional, instinctive impulses, which are strengthened by social conventions. They then lapse into a sort of mental automatism. This is a clear instance of the automatism to which Bergson referred, and which is one of the human limitations which Kerr sees as the basis of comedy.

The wits in the play exploit this general human limitation in order to have their own way. The division in the comedy between the wits and the gulls is a clear-cut one: even Juan and Diego, who seem to be ambiguous characters, in the first two acts, are seen at the end to belong, for all their intelligence, to the gulls. In this relatively early play of Tirso's, there is as yet no sign of that complex irony, which he will exhibit in later plays. Tirso's art is comparatively simple here. Marta is conscious of her superiority and of her more flexible approach to life, and delights in the ease with which she can manipulate the human robots who are her opponents. According to Romera-Navarro, "Uno de los principios de la fórmula dramática de Tirso es el contraste entre la iniquidad y la justicia, entre la agudeza y la necedad, entre la audacia y la timidez, etc., de cuyo contraste sacó gran partido sistemáticamente" (p. 344). *Marta la piadosa* is an excellent example of a play built upon this system of contrasts. Let us examine more closely the ways by which Marta's opponents are defeated.

Lucía, Urbina, and Gómez are systematically deceived throughout the comedia. The opening scene gives a sample of what is to follow. Here, Marta traps Lucía, although the latter is on her guard, into admitting her love for Felipe. The immense superiority of Marta over Lucía is made clear from the very start. The two opening sonnets illustrate superbly the differences in mentality between the two sisters. The theme of both sonnets is the same; but whereas we know immediately the cause of Lucía's despair, Marta's sonnet gives nothing away. We know only that she despairs—"no puedo esperar ni aun esperanza." Marta's thought is expressed in poetic images; Lucía's words are more concrete. Marta is more circumspect, Lucía more simple. This contrast is emphasised throughout the scene, which ends with Marta's reflection: "¡Qué fácil es de engañar / cuando es boba una mujer!" (I.i. p. 357b.)

But not only is Lucía, as a person, less cunning than her sister. She is also slow-witted and naive. In I.iii, she fails to realise that Gómez's perplexity at being told that Felipe has been arrested is proof that Marta had lied to her. Instead, she is puzzled, which allows Marta, with a show of infinite sisterly kindness, to calm her suspicions and lull her back into a sleep of complacency. Similarly, when Lucía's suspicions that Berrío is Felipe are confirmed, Marta finds it easy to persuade her sister that she plans to marry her to Felipe, while in fact manoeuvering her into marrying the Alférez. Lucía, then, is a gullible and relatively passive creature, easily convinced by protestations of kindness and friendship.

Her naiveté is again exploited in III.vi–vii, this time by Felipe, who finds it easy enough to appease her by promising to be her husband when she threatens to disclose his identity to her father. He bases his technique upon a dual appeal to her love for him and her jealousy of Marta. It is amusing to note, however, that his persuasion is so effective that he has some difficulty later in convincing Marta that it was all a pretence. Significantly, the arch-wit, Marta, is deceived, albeit momentarily, only by another wit, her accomplice in deception, Felipe. The momentary misunderstanding between these equals threatens to produce tragic results, but this threat dissolves into a delightfully comic scene (III.ix) in which the lovers' tiff and kiss of reconciliation only serve to convince Gómez and Urbina of Marta's saintliness (III.ix p. 392a). Where the intellectual discrepancy between protagonist and antagonist is so great, tragedy is impossible.

But to return to Lucía, it would be inaccurate to say that she is completely stupid. She is not a hopelessly unequal rival to Marta, and, in the opening scene of the play, holds her own until Marta informs her of the arrest of Felipe and his imminent execution. Until then, she is at least the equal of Marta in her use of biting irony and sarcasm.

Nor is Lucía taken in by Marta's show of saintliness:

LUCÍA: Es muy grande socarrona
                mi hermana, o muy recogida.
                No me pago de su vida,
                por más virtud que pregona;
                que aunque no tan adornada
                como yo, en fin se deleita,
                y algunas veces se afeita,
                y así es virtud afeitada.
                            (II.viii. p. 381b.)

In fact, Marta does not depend on it in order to deceive her sister. Her deception of Lucía starts before her own "conversion": Lucía can be handled in a different way.

There is the occasional flash of fire and show of initiative to be seen in Lucía. She instantly recognizes Berrío as Felipe, and decides to help Marta in persuading their father to allow Berrío to remain in their house. But she then loses the initiative to Marta when she allows Inés to lead her away (II.ix). In III.vi, she gives vent to jealous rage and threatens to reveal Berrío's real identity to her father, but is easily deceived by Felipe. In III.xii, she ventures to use ambivalent language, pretending to address words of love to the Alférez, when they are, in fact meant for Felipe. The fact that she is unaware of being deceived by Felipe makes her even a slightly pathetic figure here.

However, despite her intelligence, Lucía is too naive, too credulous, too passive, and too timid. He who hesitates in love, as in other things, is lost, and Lucía has to be content with the Alférez. But more important is the fact that it is her emotions which blind her to the reality of things. Her love for Felipe is something which both Felipe and Marta can exploit: the promise of marriage to Felipe is the illusory carrot held out to her. Also, she too easily believes that Marta's attitude towards her is sincere and free from duplicity, for her knowledge that Marta was deceiving others, including their father, should have been a warning to her. But by then, perhaps, Lucía is already convinced of her sister's sincerity:

LUCÍA: Callar quiero, que ya advierte
                 mi sospecha, hermana mía,
                 que los celos que tenía
                 de ti eran sin razón,
                 pues que con tanta afición
                 me favoreces.
MARTA: Lucía,
                 los celos son el tributo
                 que dan intenciones malas,
                 ruin el árbol como el fruto.
                              (I.iv. p. 359b.)

The readiness to believe that a sister is unlikely to deceive one, i.e., trust in the solidarity of the family, is another of Lucía's weaknesses. She is thus "punished" by being made to marry the Alférez, but not too severely, for the latter's love for her is genuine.

The *indiano*, Urbina, is a variation on a familiar type in Golden Age drama. His life has been dedicated to making money, which he confidently expects will compensate for other failings he may have. In this, he reflects the values of the society in which he lives. With his money he hopes to buy a wife; like the present-day successful businessman, he expects money to be an adequate substitute for the love and affection he cannot offer. His attitude is unnatural and anti-vital and that is why his ambitions are frustrated.

As A. Urtiaga has pointed out, Urbina is not an unpleasant person.[14] He seems to take the shock of discovering that Marta is vowed to chastity quite well, and is ultimately philosophical about it—as well as about the final discovery that he had been deceived all along. In III.i, he promises his nephew eight thousands ducats as a wedding present. And, to show his love for Marta, a love which is "ya no humano, mas divino," he contributes an equal sum towards the asylum which she is establishing (III.i. p. 385a). Later on, he even remembers Marta's "hospital" (perhaps that is where his heart is):

URBINA: La obra que tenéis tan bien trazada
                 del hospital, señora, se comience,
                 porque cuando yo vuelva esté empezada.
                          (III.xiv. p. 397b.)

He is utterly convinced of Marta's saintliness: "Es una santa," he declares (III.iii. p. 388a).

In all this, Urbina is not ridiculous. Where he is ridiculous is in wanting to marry a young girl who does not love him. That is why he is ridiculed. We may think at first that the loss of his money is a bit hard on him—that his "punishment" is excessive; but, on reflection, we can see that he is really learning to get his values straight—albeit the hard way. An old, rich man, Tirso seems to be saying, would use his wealth more properly in works of charity and in helping his younger relatives than in grotesquely trying to secure personal, physical pleasure, which he cannot enjoy; he ought to be looking to his soul. Perhaps Urbina's declaration that his love is "divino" and his noble gesture at the end indicate that he has learnt his lesson. Marta's appeal to religion (her excuse of being bound to a vow of chastity has grotesquely comic undertones, since her marriage to Urbina would have been a "chaste" one in any case) seems to have been not without some positive influence on the old man's character.

Gómez is the most extreme example in the play of a person who completely and unquestioningly accepts the prevailing values of his society. This acceptance is perhaps not reluctantly given, for his innate greed for money, which is his most deplorable trait, is at once satisfied and aggravated by the social conventions to which he subscribes. Thus he seeks to marry his daughter to a man who is as old as himself. He is not unaware of the unsuitability of this marriage, but he rationalises the problem:

> La misma edad que yo tiene
> el capitán; mas pues viene
> con más de cien mil ducados,
> años que están tan dorados
> reverenciarlos conviene.
> Darále Marta la mano,
> que no es viejo el interés,
> aunque el capitán es cano;
> y menos enfermo es
> el invierno que el verano.
> Invierno viejo es mi yerno;
> verano suele llamar
> la juventud a amor tierno;
> pero bien podrá pasar
> con tanta ropa este invierno
> mi hija; que della fío
> que ha de hacer el gusto mío
> y del que escribe esta carta;
> que es viejo, y compra esta marta
> para remediar su frío.
>
> (I.ii. pp. 357b–358a.)

This speech would well repay a closer attention than can be given to it here. Not only does it anticipate the religious developments in the play ("reverenciarlos conviene"), but it also betrays a tension which springs from the incongruity between the apparently closely reasoned argument and the latter's failure to conform to fact. Gómez must admit that Urbina is old, although his money is not. But since the two are inseparable, Gómez must justify his choice of husband on the grounds that winter is more salubrious than summer: "y menos enfermo es / el invierno que el verano." That this is so in reality is by no means established. But there is even another objection: the analogy is clearly false in the light of human experience: if winter is a healthy season, old age is not characterised by good health. Gómez finally concedes that the marriage must be a loveless one, but there are, to his mind, adequate material compensations: "bien podrá pasar / con tanta ropa este invierno / mi hija." Here we see not a father's solicitude for his daughter's welfare, but a rationalisation of a sordid business transaction. His daughter is not a woman to be married, but a piece of fur to be bought by an old man "para remediar su frío." Marta's life and happiness are to be sacrificed on the altar of the selfishness of two old men. This instrumental relationship of father to daughter is extended to include Lucía. Gómez takes both his daughters to Illescas and, with all the pride of a merchant displaying his wares, says to Urbina: "Celebraréis vuestras bodas / con la que más deseáis." (I.viii. p. 362b).

We must also conclude that Don Gómez feels—or felt—no great love for his dead son; we never see him grieving over his son's death, and, in fact, he never seems to think of it unless the subject is mentioned by others—his daughters or Pastrana. In spite of Marta's protests in I.ii, all respect for her brother's death goes overboard. Gómez's glee at the prospect of renewing his friendship with Urbina can hardly be concealed. Friendship (or should we say the possibility of selling a daughter?) excuses all (I.ii p. 358a).

When Gómez is told by Lucía (who has herself been deceived by Marta) that Felipe has been arrested, he does no more than pay lip service to a desire to see the offender punished. But even this is subordinated to his eagerness to visit Illescas: (note the significant use of enjambement in the last sentence, and the socially obligatory stress on "justa"):

> dará el homicida
> justa venganza a mi pecho.
> De todo a informarme voy,
> y porque partamos hoy
> a Illescas, voy a aprestar
> un coche en que caminar.

(I.ii. p. 358b.)

However, we notice that in I.viii, although Gómez has arrived in Illescas, no mention is made of his having found out whether Felipe has been arrested. This comparative indifference of Gómez's to whether his son's murder is avenged continues throughout the play, and is only substituted by a real interest when Pastrana suggests in III.xiv that Gómez should go to Seville in order to witness Felipe's execution and claim his wealth. (Thus we see, incidentally, that there is no real contradiction in Gómez's character in the final scene when he accepts "in santa pace l'uccisore come genero"—to use Penna's words.)

We see, then, that Gómez's lust for money, his greed, constitutes his driving force. To this all else is subordinated; his daughters are articles he hopes to sell, his relationship towards them is instrumental, and he obviously treats his son's death as a little bit of spilt milk. He adopts a tyrannical attitude towards his children, seeks to violate their individual liberty (an action always fraught with dangerous consequences in Golden

Age drama) and is thus unjust towards them. He deliberately deceives Marta in I.ii ("Encubrille el casamiento quiero"), does not consult her wishes, and flies into a rage when she refuses to do his bidding (I.xv. p. 369b). Thus both in his arranging a "suitable" marriage for Marta and in his attempting to compel her to agree to it, Gómez is abusing social conventions for selfish, unnatural and immoral ends. He is morally culpable.

It is not surprising that Marta should rebel (I.xv. p. 369b). Her inspired plan, conceived on the spur of the moment (for the marriage proposal takes her by surprise), seems to owe not a little of its ingenuity to Pastrana's cynicism as expressed in I.ix: the fact that men are men, and therefore, vain, gullible, and venal makes them more manageable than bulls. (The witty connexion between this speech and the theme of the play is obvious.)

While Marta's deception of Lucía starts from the very beginning of the play, she does not start to deceive her father until the end of Act I, when she is forced to invent a "lie" in order to avoid marrying Urbina. From here onward, the deception of Gómez is systematic. He is convinced that Marta has renounced the worldly life (although he hopes that it is but a passing phase); he is persuaded to give shelter to his son's killer. He helps to put Berrío to bed in II.xi and, ironically for once, feels an affection for Marta which he had never shown before: "¡Hay tal virtud! ¿Quién no ama / tal hija?" The superb Latin lesson scene (III.ii), which Valbuena has described as "un logro único del fraile malicioso," serves to underline Gómez's stupidity.

Gómez, however, is not only the dupe of Marta. He is also deceived by Felipe, who plays the part of a palsy-stricken theological student perfectly. Even more important is the fact that Gómez is taken in by Pastrana. By his diligent efforts, "Don Juan Hurtado con pestañas de Mendoza" effectively prevents Gómez from suspecting that Felipe is much nearer to Madrid than he thinks. Gómez is here dazzled by Don Juan's illustrious lineage—"¡Honrados títulos goza!", he exclaims in II.viii—without realising that Don Juan's surname would be more appropriately written with a small "h." Here Gómez is deceived by name and position. It is Pastrana, too, who, by exploiting Gómez's lust for money, persuades him to leave for Seville (III.xiv. p. 397a). Gómez agrees: "Todos me aconsejáis; de todos sigo / el gusto y parecer." This does not mean that Gómez is as weak-willed as his words seem to imply, although they do indicate his readiness to be influenced by others. The prospect of getting his hands on Felipe's wealth is highly agreeable to him, and we must think that he undertakes his journey to Seville joyfully—especially as he has hopes of getting this extra wealth cheaply (III.xiv. p. 397a).

Let us now consider the question of revenge. As I have suggested, Gómez does not appear to be excessively concerned with his son's death or with a desire for revenge. At the very most, justice and vengeance interest him only in so far as they are financially profitable. And as far as Marta and Lucía's case, it is a simple matter of love being stronger than the social demands of vengeance or justice. This is also true in the case of Marta, but, in addition, the moral implications of such a choice, to which little or no consideration is given in Lucía's emotional attitude, are deliberately brought to the fore. There is a real problem here, but from the beginning, Marta leaves the matter in God's hands (thus anticipating, dramatically, her subsequent "conversion") (I.i. p. 357a). Later on, of course, Marta is freer to preach that vengeance is incompatible with the Christian way of life:

[GÓMEZ:]	Mi venganza cumpla Dios.
LUCÍA:	Señor, sí, en Sevilla queda
	preso el que mató a mi hermano.
GÓMEZ:	Castigue Dios al tirano.
MARTA:	No le castigue aunque pueda.
GÓMEZ:	¡Qué decís vos!
MARTA:	Yo, señor,
	que en conciencia, y para abono
	de mi alma, le perdono,
	y que el matalle es rigor.
GÓMEZ:	No es contra la justa ley
	dar la muerte a un enemigo;
	Dios es quien hizo el castigo,
	y después de Dios el Rey.

(II.vii. p. 380b.)

On one level, this can be seen as a comic example of the Devil's citing of Scripture; but on another, Marta's attitude is Christian, and it is the only attitude which can provide a suitable justification for her continuing to love Felipe—or, rather, she pardons him out of love for him. We may also remember that we are never told why Felipe was led to kill Antonio. Tirso himself leaves the matter vague, and this perhaps implies that the reasons are not important, the conventional implication (in comedy) being that the victor had acted in self-defence. The fact that Felipe is the man who killed Antonio is what is really pertinent in the play.

The ambivalence inherent in this attitude is characteristic of the handling of the religious question in the play as a whole. The overall comic effect derives mainly from two basic stylistic features. The first is Marta's use of religiosity as a cover for love, the second, Felipe's feigned "illness." The disguise of amorous meanings in medical and religious terms is a stylistic reflection of the situation in the play.

The fact that Felipe pretends to be a palsy-stricken student sets up the equation: love-illness. Just as love is traditionally seen as an illness, the traditional cure for such an illness is, of course, love (although religion, too will do). Whereas in the later play, a doctor is at hand to administer the cure, in *Marta la piadosa* we have the equivalent of a religious nursing sister. Marta's sense of vocation is so strong that she intends to found a hospital (II.iii. p. 377a). We are told, in the same scene, that Marta has been visiting the sick, to which Gómez objects: she, however, insists on performing such works of charity (II.iii. p. 376b). So worthy is she, in fact, that in II.ix the mountain comes, in the shape of the disguised Felipe, to Mohammed. We are to get an illustration on stage of Marta's charity. She sees this as an excellent opportunity to practise her skills (II.ix. p. 382b), and the cure starts immediately. In return, Felipe offers to teach Marta Latin, and the nature of the skills to be imparted is quite clear:

MARTA:	Deseo yo leer latín.
	Decid: ¿no me enseñaréis?
FELIPE:	Y aun gramática, hasta tanto
	que empecéis a conjugar.

(II.ix. p. 384a.)

The second equation of basic importance of the play is love = religion. The fact that love ("charity") is a central feature of the Christian way of life introduces into the play an ambiguity whose potentialities are fully exploited. The implications of this equation are perhaps more complex than those of the first, i.e., the love = illness equation. For whereas, in the main, illness is merely a disguise for love, and we simply read "love" wherever "illness" occurs, the ambivalence in the love = religion equation is maintained intact; that is, love can mean both Christian charity and passion. Much of the comic effect arises out of the fact that Marta's religiosity is taken at face value by Gómez and Urbina, while Lucía sees it wholly as a pretence. In reality, it is both. Thus Marta is not really lying about having made a vow of chastity, as the following lines show:

| GÓMEZ: | ¿Que castidad prometiste? |
| MARTA: | Sí, señor.   (*Aparte*) |

> Yo sé con quien.
>
> (I.xv. p. 370b.)

Similarly, Marta's appeal to religion in order to circumvent her father's plans and also to justify her forgiveness of Felipe is more than deception: it is a genuine and serious appeal to the highest authority. This is an important factor in the question of Marta's "hypocrisy."

But, as is to be expected, the comic effect is greatest, if not quite as subtle, where the element of deception is most apparent to the audience. II.ix is a superb instance of a practical demonstration of Christian love and charity: in the name of religion, Marta can admit her lover into her house and embrace him in front of her father. The comedy arises out of the audience's awareness of the discrepancy between appearance and reality. The fact that Gómez is taken in by appearances introduces the satirical note into the comedy.

This presentation of human love in religious terms derives obviously from the so-called "religion of love." But whereas in the latter phenomenon, religious terms are only a sort of disguise for amorous-sexual ones, with the religious terms virtually emptied of all really religious significance, in Tirso's play, the religious terms are not solely a disguise, but retain (or, rather, are re-invented with) their literal meanings. This allows for both the seriousness of Marta's religious utterances and also the ironical statements such as Lucía's:

LUCÍA:	(*Aparte*):
	¡Oh qué devotos que están!
	¡Bien rezan, por vida mía!
MARTA:	¡Ay dulce dómine mío!
FELIPE:	¡Ay mi hipócrita amorosa!
LUCÍA:	(*Aparte*):
	¿Esta es Marta la Piadosa,
	y éste el dómine Berrío?
	Con tales dominaciones
	también me seré yo buena;
	(III.v. p. 388b.)

In other words, the religion of love is to be taken in a much more literal sense than it generally is.

The fact that illness and religiosity are both used in the play as substitutes for love links the first two phenomena in passages such as this:

| MARTA: | ¡Mi infierno! |
| FELIPE: | Vanos recelos |

asaltan mi corazón,
y como en el alma son
los celos pesados hielos,
siempre que el temor los cría,
sin poderme defender,
por tu ocasión vengo a ser
enfermo de perlesía.
MARTA: Pues si le sana el calor,
y amor mis deseos abrasa,
perlático de mi casa,
llega al fuego de mi amor.
                              (II.x. p. 384b.)

Here love produces illness in Felipe: he is to be nursed back to health by
Marta, which is made possible by love. This, in scene x, is, of course,
passion. In scene xi, which takes up the motif introduced in scene ix, it
shows itself as charity.

The link between illness and religiosity is fairly clear in terms of the
ideology of love prevalent at the time, which springs from the ideas of
courtly love. However, it is not clear why Tirso should have chosen
precisely palsy, a sort of falling-sickness, as it turns out to be, with which
to afflict the amorous Felipe. It is just possible that this falling-sickness
is balanced by Pastrana's malicious reference to Marta's levitation in the
third act (III.xiii. p. 395a). If we were to transfer the "palsy" to Marta
and the "levitation" to Felipe, it will be seen that these manifestations
of "illness" and "religion" are linked directly, and not only indirectly,
through their metaphorical connexions with love. On the stylistic level,
Tirso's ironical use in this play of literacy and ideological conventions
associated with love is evident. By explicitly maintaining the ambivalence
of the language of the religion of love in our consciousness, he satirises
the tradition.

The comedy, of course, is not mere farce. The comic scenes are part
of the deception of Gómez and Urbina and thus an integral part of the
social satire of the play. The basis of their deception is their inability to
distinguish true religion from false religiosity, like the public at large:

GÓMEZ: Tu virtud es de manera
que eres Marta la piadosa.
Toda la corte te da
este nombre que has ganado.
MARÍA: (Aparte):
¡Ay Dios! ¡Qué engañada está!

(III.i. p. 386a.)

It is this willingness to take appearance for reality which Marta exploits in order to attain her end. There are some who are not taken in by her saintliness, but she has other means of dealing with them: almost all persons are capable of being deceived by appearances.

The religious satire is effected in various ways. The most obvious is Marta's awareness of the effectiveness of her assumed religiosity in deceiving the public. But there are also direct comments on certain aspects of religious practices. A good example is Marta's expressed desire to learn Latin—so that she can understand her prayers:

MARTA: Siempre que llego a rezar
en las horas a algún santo,
me pesa de no entender
lo que allí se significa.

(II.ix. p. 384a.)

Even more explicit are her words in the preceding scene:

PASTRANA: ¡Rosario de cocos!

MARTA: Pues.
así se llaman. ¿Qué quieres,
si hacen cocos las mujeres,
porque anda el mundo al revés?
A lo bueno en estos días
la devoción va expirando,
pues si rezan ya, es cocando
hasta las avemarías.

PASTRANA: En algunas no son vanos
los cocos, pues si reparas,
muchas, cocos en las caras,
llevan cocos en las manos.

MARTA: Profánanse ya las suertes:
ya la devoción es gala.
Traigan todas, noramala,
unos rosarios de muertes,
que sirvan de centinelas;
que yo desde hoy pienso hacello.

PASTRANA: ¿Muertes en rosario al cuello?
Parecerán sacamuelas.

(II.viii. p. 382a–b.)

Then there is Marta's own comment on the freedom which the dress of a *beata* confers on one:

MARTA:	Linda sangre y humor cría,
	Pastrana, la hipocresía.
	Nunca tuve libertad,
	mientras que viví a lo damo,
	como agora; si intentaba
	salir fuera, me costaba
	una riña: ya no llamo
	a la dueña, al escudero,
	ni aguardo la silla y coche,
	ni me riñen si a a la noche
	vuelvo: voy a donde quiero.

(II.iv. p. 378a.)

This is not merely a humorous comment on her own situation, but surely also a reference to real hypocrites is society.

It would be convenient to review here the moral values contained in the play as they have emerged from the preceding analysis. Our assessment of them must depend on our view of the deception practised by Marta and her accomplices.

On the plot level, the deception of Gómez, Urbina and Lucía brings about a successful end to the problem. This, we recall, was produced by Gómez's cupidity and his slavish obedience to social conventions. By exploiting these factors, Marta can hold Gómez and Urbina at bay until she can present them with the *fait accompli* of her marriage to Felipe. Ironically, her opportunity for doing this is brought about by precisely those factors which initially produced the problem. Thus the ending of the play is not forced. Gómez, Urbina and, to a lesser extent, Lucía, have been checkmated because they are victims of their own follies. At the end of the play, they can only passively accept the situation. The only alternative is, of course, a violent ending, which would solve nothing. (This is something to which comedy often points; a violent ending in tragedy generally does lead to a solution).

The gullibility and follies of these characters are ridiculed through their frustration. This is what gives the comedy its satirical tone. As I have tried to point out, the play satirises all those who are too easily taken in by the trappings of authority, by appearances, perhaps because they themselves obey the letter (often distorted) rather than the spirit of laws and conventions, since it suits them to do so for personal and selfish reasons. While the main weight of the satire falls on the gullible, there is also an ironical amount of religious satire in the comedy.

This brings us to the portrayal of Marta herself. While Tirso shows us the workings of the ways of the religious hypocrite, it is clear that he does not do so by presenting us with a hypocrite. In Marta's case we seem to be on equivocal terrain. In the play, those who are taken in by her consider her a saint; those who see through her pretence regard her as a hypocrite. Juliá Martínez points out that the play does indeed contain a potential portrait of a real hypocrite, drawing attention to Marta's words:

[MARTA:]   Diréis, hermana Lucía,
que no entendéis ni alcanzáis
qué es esto, y que hablar yo así
parece gran novedad:
pensaréis que fue fingida
mi mesura artificial,
y engañosa en la apariencia,
como en rosa el alacrán.
No, hermana; pero el que es bueno,
con su virtud natural
licencia tiene unos días
para poderse alegrar.

(III.xv. p. 398a.)

And Hartzenbusch is at pains to contrast this play with Moratín's in order to stress that Marta is not a hypocrite. These critics are, of course, right. The last four lines of the above passage stress that virtue does not imply asceticism or puritanism. For Tirso, the pursuit of cheerfulness does not mean the abandonment of virtue. Thus one of the more interesting effects of the play is to lead the spectator or reader into a consideration of the nature of hypocrisy. More than ever we are aware of the change which intention or motive can produce in an action. What is only a trick on Marta's part can, with a different aim and a different intention, and in different circumstances, unhesitatingly be recognized as hypocrisy. It is Penna's failure to see the morally subtle ground on which the play moves which, quite understandably, makes him uncomfortable about its implications. Few, indeed, can read Tirso without experiencing unease.

Admittedly, it is difficult for us to reconcile ourselves to what Tirso seems to be saying in this play, especially if we are accustomed to think, in the abstract, of moral actions as absolute. I do not mean that Tirso is proposing at a deep level the thesis of the relativity of morality, although it may appear so on the surface. The question (only one of the many raised in the play) is how are we to evaluate the morality of our actions. It is a question of the relativity of judgment. We may think that we know what hypocrisy is once we are alerted to it. But Tirso here presents an extreme case where few, if any, of our criteria of judgment are valid. The mere fact of deception is not sufficient, although deception is an integral part of hypocrisy. Religiosity is used as a mask, but this is not condemned. We must penetrate beyond actions, appearances and means in order to arrive at a ground firm enough for judgment. For, ironically, if it is the appearance of religiosity which enables us to define hypocrisy, Marta's hypocrisy is, in its turn, only mere appearance.

Marta's ultimate aim is a justifiable one: marriage to the man she loves is moral and natural. There is a possible conflict between this aim and her father's wishes, between love and duty, personal desire and obedience to authority. But Tirso is careful to point out that for Marta to place duty above love, that is, to do the apparently moral thing and obey Gómez, would be immoral. Thus we arrive at the paradox that, if morality is to prevail, there must be a violation of morality: Marta must break one of the Commandments. This can only be done, within the comic context of the play, by invoking a higher authority, religion, in which morality is vested. This appeal also allows her to overcome the obstacle of marrying the man who killed her brother. Not only are the circumstances attending the killing deliberately vague, but, for Marta, as for Lucía, love forgives all. By refusing to apply the old law of an eye for an eye, she upholds the new law of love, leaving God to judge. Therefore she refuses to kill. And that, too, is Christian.

In other words, we see how Marta manages to do what is, at first sight, immoral and socially outrageous and yet escape condemnation; for what she does is, by absolute moral standards, perfectly moral. The demonstration of how what is immoral is really moral contributes not a little to the overall comic effect. Thus Tirso cleverly links a conventional comic plot to a truly Christian attitude. The situation is an extreme one; but this is toned down both by the use of a conventional situation and also by the ambivalence of language and situation so frequent in comedy. The point is nonetheless serious enough.

Marta la piadosa, therefore, can hardly be regarded as an immoral or sacrilegious play. What Penna sees as a condonation of immorality is, in reality, its frustration. The means by which this frustration is achieved are indirect, roundabout ones because this is comedy. Rebellion would produce tragedy. Where suffering and death would serve no purpose and are avoidable, there is no need to insist on them. Suffering is necessary in tragedy to achieve some measure of freedom only when there are no other means of achieving it. But in this play, we do not have a contest between nearly equal forces. Freedom is achieved by the discomfiture of those who have deprived themselves of freedom by becoming the prisoners of their own passions and society's conventions. Nor should we be scandalised by the discomfiture of elders and their ridicule. Nowhere in Tirso's plays is there any support to be found for a parent who abuses his authority or who attempts to compel his children to perform immoral or unnatural actions. This is not to say that Tirso is suggesting that one should not honour one's parents. He is merely stating that parents should not forfeit their right to honour, obedience and respect. In this, he is scrutinising social customs and conventions, the relationship between different members and classes of society, and, ultimately, the structure of that society itself and the moral values on which it is based. These problems, as we know, are to be explored, often in the tragic mode, by Calderón.

NOTES

1 See G. E. Wade, "Notes on Tirso de Molina," *HR*, VII (1939), 69–72.
2 Reprinted in E. Cotarelo's introduction to his edition of *Comedias de Tirso de Molina*, I (Madrid, 1906), p. xvii.
3 "Seven *Aprobaciones* by Don Pedro Calderón de la Barca," in *Homenaje a Dámaso Alonso*, III (Madrid, 1963), pp. 605–18.
4 *"La beata enamorada o Marta la piadosa*. Comedia de Tirso de Molina, refundida en cinco actos," *El Censor*, X (1821), 449–53.
5 In his *examen* of the play in *Teatro escogido de Fray Gabriel Téllez*, I, ed. J. E. Hartzenbusch (Madrid, 1839).
6 *Italie et Espagne. Voyages d'un critique à travers la vie et les livres*, II (Paris, 1869), pp. 337–50.
7 Cf. "El arte de Tirso ha logrado . . . hacernos tolerable y a ratos simpática a la protagonista: es hipócrita sencillamente porque ama con pasión a un hombre y no quiere entregar su cuerpo a otro." In his *Historia de la literatura española* (Boston, *c* 1928), p. 337.
8 "Some Notes on Tirso de Molina," *BSS*, XVII (1940), 172–203.
9 *Historia de la literatura española*, II (4th ed., Barcelona, 1953), p. 409.
10 *Don Giovanni e il mistero di Tirso* (Turin, 1958).
11 Clásicos Ebro (4th ed., Zaragoza, 1958; 1st ed., 1943).
12 "De Tirso de Molina al refundidor de *Marta la piadosa*. Carta," in *Del Siglo de oro* (Madrid, 1910), pp. 81–97.
13 All quotations are by act, scene and page and refer to vol. II of *Tirso de Molina. Obras dramáticas completas*, ed. B. de los Ríos (Madrid, 1962).
14 *El indiano en la dramática de Tirso de Molina* (Madrid, 1965), pp. 116–124, 174–175.

PART II

SOCIAL RELATIONSHIPS AND
THE SOCIAL STRUCTURE

CHAPTER V

El melancólico and Esto sí que es negociar. Love and Class Barriers

(a) El melancólico

El melancólico, published in Tirso's *Primera parte*, had for long been considered one of his early plays. Doña Blanca, following Cotarelo, assigned it to the year 1611, on the assumption that it contained a reference to the *premática* against coaches issued in that year.[1] Ruth L. Kennedy, however, put forward a strong argument for considering *El melancólico* a late play, dating it c. 1622–23.[2] The cumulative evidence she puts forward is compelling, even though one must bear in mind the reservation that *El melancólico* may have been an early play which underwent considerable textual revision to give us the play as we have it. Perhaps the only point (and one which carries very little weight) which would make one hesitate over the dates suggested by R. L. Kennedy for the play is the absence of any satire of the *culto* poets. There is a fairly long passage written in *culto* style, viz., Rogerio's description of Leonisa when he fell in love with her (I.x), but the tone does not seem to me to be that of satire or parody. However, in the absence of any stronger evidence for an earlier date, I shall accept R. L. Kennedy's dating as valid. The fact that the play was put on by the Valencianos also suggests that it is a late one, and, as I shall indicate in my analysis of *Amar por arte mayor* in Chapter VI, Tirso's late style is characterised by its serious use of the *culto* style.

The aspect of *El melancólico* with which I am principally concerned is the satire contained therein of social conventions regarding class. This is effected by stressing the absurd and ridiculous nature of the situation in which the protagonist, Rogerio, finds himself. The clash between the demands of love and those of social convention, which is one of the central aspects of the play, has been indicated by Varela Jácome and A. K. G. Paterson.[3] This social satire is also linked to the satire of a literary convention. These are the points which I propose to develop here.

The opening scene of the play introduces the vestigial sub-plot, viz., the love-intrigue between Firela and Carlín. It fades out after the end of Act II, when Firela, her mechanical function fulfilled, seems to be cast out of the play because of her moral flaws—her betrayal of her friendship for Leonisa, her willingness to be suborned by Filipo (which is linked to a sort of misguided friendship for Leonisa), her blackmailing of Carlín. The latter soldiers on to the end of the play, but, for the last act, he is without a mate (or even a thought of one, for that matter). But while the sub-plot fizzles out, it does, while it lasts, cast light on the implications and problems of the main plot.

Carlín's humorous courting of Firela sounds the principal motif of the play: love and social precedence. In the burlesque pastoral tone with which the play opens—half realistically rustic, half artificially pastoral—, his anecdote about the donkeys presents us with an embryonic version of the story to come and its central problem: love at first sight, the perfect "courtesy" of the *burro*, the honesty of the *burra*—and the resulting impasse. The suffering that results at once foreshadows, on the farcical level, the physical beating Carlín is to receive before the act is out, and, on a more serious level, the emotional and spiritual suffering which Rogerio and Leonisa have to undergo. The absurdity of the impasse created in the main action is brought about, ironically, by the fact that Rogerio and Leonisa hold to a view of "perfect" love. In order to examine the implications of this for the plot, it will be necessary to look briefly at these characters.

El melancólico has long been singled out for special commendation on the grounds that it is a play with a "character." Hartzenbusch states this quite firmly.[4] Doña Blanca agrees with him, although she would stress Tirso's powers of characterisation somewhat more strongly. Ruth L. Kennedy, too, concurs. On the other hand, E. Calderà senses something mechanical, artificial in the portrayal of Rogerio: the latter is drawn, so to speak, too much according to textbook rules.[5] The truth, as is generally the case in such situations, is probably somewhere between these two views.

There is little doubt that Tirso has laid much stress on Rogerio's character. But the obvious consequence of this shoud be noted: there is very little purposeful surface action in the play; most of it is desultory. That is because the action is, to a large extent, internalised: the real action is psychological, not physical, and the purposeless acts reflect an internal state of mind. The explanation for that is the fact that Rogerio's will is paralysed, the sources of action have dried up. Hence his melancholy.

Late Romantic criticism, which lasted well into this century, sought character above all in drama. The warm praise given to *El melancólico*, which not only has a "character," but also a melancholy one, is easily understood.[6] But if the commonsense view that drama is action is adopted (a view at least as old as Aristotle and more recently defended by E. Bentley),[7] the plot of *El melancólico* seems to be particularly sketchy. This is a point to which I shall return later.

The dominant feature of Rogerio's character is his melancholy, which gives the play its title. Almost invariably in Tirso, the standard cause of melancholy is unrequited or frustrated love, and this play is no exception. Curiously enough, there is little or no sign of Rogerio's melancholy in Act I, the exposition. It is in the second act that the melancholy Rogerio appears. To the puzzled Duke, his father, he gives two main reasons for his melancholy: his unexpected luck has put him in the same catergory as opulent fools, and at the same time has frustrated his personal ambition to make himself, that is, to owe what he is to his own merit and efforts (II.i).

But these, as Rogerio immediately afterwards confesses, are sophistical rationalisations: he does not resent his good luck. He is melancholy because he is in love and his newly acquired social status makes its fulfilment impossible:

[ROGERIO:]   Perdíte; ya no es posible,
        en desiguales estados,
        dar alivio a mis cuidados,
        ni ver tu rostro apacible;
        pues amar un imposible
        será eterno padecer;
        no amarte, no puede ser;
        pues, amarte, y no esperar
        padecer, y no olvidar,
        es morir y no poder.

                         (II.iii. p. 235b.)

(Here we see the beginnings of Tirso's new, "Calderonian" manner, which I shall consider at greater length in my chapter on *Amar por arte mayor*.) The son of a Duke, he can no longer marry the peasant-girl, Leonisa. It is thus the frustration of his love which brings out his melancholy.

Rogerio is, of course, susceptible to melancholy precisely because he is intelligent and learned. This is important, because it throws some light on the nature of his predicament. There is a constant stress on Rogerio's great learning from the beginning. He is introduced indirectly at first, the audience being prepared for his entry by Leonisa's and Firela's discussion of him in I.ii. The quality they emphasise most is his great learning. The fantastic, Gargantuan scope of his education is made clear when he at last enters with his supposed father and teacher, Pinardo (I.iii). As the latter here points out, there is nothing which Rogerio does not know.

But, Pinardo insists, he is not yet a perfect, i.e., a complete, man. While the rational side of Rogerio has been developed fully, his emotional side has remained dormant, if not stunted. This latter should also be developed, and Pinardo quotes Plato in support of his argument:

[PINARDO:] Si el filósofo admirable
       llamó animal racional
       al hombre, Platón, su igual,
       le llama animal sociable.
       El que no es comunicable
       no es hombre, según Platón,
       y siguiendo su opinión,
       te hará tanta sequedad
       bruto por la voluntad,
       aunque hombre por la razón.
            (I.iii. p. 224b.)

The crucial role of love in the development and perfection of man is thus stressed. At this point, Pinardo urges Rogerio to practise on the village girls:

[PINARDO:] y un discreto, si lo ignoras
       llamaba a las labradoras
       espadas negras de amor.
            (I.iii. p. 224b.)

This attitude has ugly undertones, the least offensive of which is the social arrogance of class. Rogerio, too, is not innocent of such arrogance, but his contempt for the village girls is a question not so much of social pride as of intellectual conceit:

ROGERIO: Aquí, señor, no hay sujeto
       en que lograr esperanzas,
       ni entre groseras labranzas
       mi amor halla igual objeto.
       Si me tienes por discreto,
       y amor es similitud,
       ¿por qué culpas la quietud
       que en mi libertad desprecias?

¿Es bien que serranas necias
malogren mi juventud?
Viva el alma libre y franca,
pues en su estudio me alegra.

(I.iii. p. 224b.)

Rogerio's attitude soon undergoes a drastic change when he falls madly in love with the *villana*, Leonisa:

ROGERIO: Es precipitado
amor. Vine, vi y perdí
la libertad, no el cuidado.
Ya juzgaré por mejor
potencia la voluntad
que el entendimiento: Amor
de su noble facultad
hoy me ha hecho profesor:
desde hoy cursaré su escuela.

(I.x. p. 227b.)

So drastic, indeed, that the violence of his passion amazes and even frightens Pinardo, who argues that Rogerio is not to go from one extreme to another, but to love in moderation. He should no take his love too seriously—it is, for Pinardo, only a technical emotional exercise (I.x). But Rogerio is too far gone: he cannot love by halves. Ironically, at the precise moment at which he gives his heart to Leonisa and promises to be hers, the Duke, his real father (as it turns out) has other plans for him.

These, principally, are his transfer to the court, his legitimisation, and his marriage to Clemencia. The first means only a separation from Leonisa, and is but the first test to which his love will be put. The second two are much more severe ones. With Rogerio's new life, there begins a conflict which, as Paterson has stated, by putting his love to the test, teaches him about the true nature of love—love as Christian charity.

Here, I am more interested in the nature of this inner conflict, the particular form which it takes in the context of the play. It is, at bottom, a conflict between those two fundamental aspects of man, the rational and the emotional. While learning characterises the "animal racional" that is man, it is love which perfects him as an "animal sociable" by awakening his soul. If the fundamental *necessity* of love is postulated, there arises a genuine conflict in the wise man, which can be formulated thus: how can the wise man bring himself to subordinate reason to passion? It turns out, at the end of the play, that there was no real conflict between these two.

This may seem to suggest that the conflict was artificially set up so that Rogerio's love could be tested. I shall return to this presently, but first I should like to examine the causes of the inner conflict.

Rogerio, to perfect himself, falls in love. But when he reveals to Pinardo that the woman he loves is their vassal, Leonisa, Pinardo is disturbed. He warns Rogerio not to take his love too seriously, especially since Leonisa is his social inferior (I.x. p. 228b). However, Rogerio tosses this warning aside: for him, the distance between a *caballero* and a *villana* is not too great for his love to bridge.

Yet, when he becomes a Duke, Rogerio, in spite of precedents, cannot allow himself to marry Leonisa. In this decision, his intellect plays the crucial part. Yet there is more that a hint of intellectual arrogance in his self-esteem:

> [ROGERIO:]   Si yo de Pinardo fuera
> hijo, cual pensé, y te amara,
> cuando a mi ser te igualara,
> poco tu suerte subiera.
> Soy Duque: ¡ay, fortuna fiera!
> tormentos con honras das:
> ya yo sé que igualado has,
> midiendo amorosas leyes,
> los pastores a los reyes;
> mas yo soy sabio, que es más.
> En cuanto rey, no era mucho
> llevarse de mi pasión;
> en cuanto sabio, es acción
> en que mi deshonra escucho.
>   (II.iii. pp. 235b–236a.)

At the same time, while refusing to marry Leonisa, because of her social inferiority (or, rather, his newly acquired superiority), he is also unwilling to marry his social equal, Clemencia, because he still loves Leonisa and means to be faithful to her.

This highly intellectual approach to what is a vital problem lands Rogerio in an insoluble dilemma. For most of the time he refuses to question the pre-eminence of reason. This is why his "wisdom" is continually stressed in the play. He firmly persists in using his intellect as his guiding force. In II.iv, his refusal to be annoyed by Enrique's insults and his dignified response to them is a clear example of that. Another, perhaps even more interesting, example is found in the episode of the "homework" on the court suitors he has to deal with in III.ii–iv. He gets his secretary,

Filipo, to obtain information about the suitors so that he can deal justly with them. This allows him to impress the audience enormously, and one suspects that this episode may have been intended as an object lesson in kingship for Philip IV. Compare the following lines:

ROGERIO: Pretendo saber las faltas
que tienen los pretendientes
de mi corte y de mi casa;
que aunque es bien premiar servicios,
no será razón que se haga
menos que con suficiencia
de las partes.
FILIPO: La ignorancia,
señor, y poca noticia
de algunos príncipes causa
que sin méritos se den
injustamente las plazas.

                         (III.ii. p. 249a.)

Yet, in spite of his enormous intellectual control of himself, Rogerio's passions at times threaten to get the better of him. The enigmatic words he addresses to Filipo in I.vi, soon after the scene with the suitors, provide one instance when his strong passions (in this case jealousy) seem to break through his iron control. The speech, though enigmatic, contains a sinister threat:

ROGERIO: Filipo, la juventud
también es enfermedad:
disposiciones curad,
sangraréisos en salud.
Corales que adornan cuellos,
no generosos, villanos,
afrentan los cortesanos:
sangre muestran, sangraos dellos.
FILIPO: Señor, la que los perdió
gusta.
ROGERIO: Yo soy vuestro amigo:
que os sangréis dellos os digo;
no aguardéis a que os sangre yo.

                         (III.vi. p. 252a.)

Rogerio recognises immediately afterwards that his passions are hard to control:

ROGERIO: Por más que callar procuro,

> habla mi desasosiego;
> que en fin, donde amor es fuego,
> brotan celos, que son humo.
>
> (III.vi. p. 252b.)

Therefore, when Filipo spills ink instead of sand on the letter he has written to Clemencia, it is further proof of his enormous self-control that he does not use that as an excuse for inflicting a severe punishment on Filipo in order to give vent to his feelings of jealousy.

But there are obvious limitations to an intellectual approach to life. In contrast to an early play like *La elección por la virtud*, where there is an exaltation of learning, in a number of later plays Tirso seems to express a certain disillusionment with learning: *El amor médico* and *Ventura te dé Dios, hijo* are obvious examples. This disillusionment seems to be present in *El melancólico* as well.

There is, without doubt, a positive side to Rogerio's intellectual approach to life. The conflict which it provokes allows him to learn something about love: the social obstacle to his marrying Leonisa means that this love must be a Platonic one, spiritual and unselfish, i.e., nonpossessive. For love of Leonisa, he must be prepared to make what is for him the ultimate sacrifice and marry Clemencia. When he shows he is ready to do so, Leonisa's supposed father conveniently dies so that she can discover that she, too, is of noble birth. The obstacle has been an artificial one, imposed arbitrarily by the dramatist, and, consequently, the final solution is not an organic one.

But the obstacle can be seen as less artificial and more organic if we consider the negative side of Rogerio's intellectual approach to life. It is this which leads him into one absurd situation after another and which, simultaneously, prevents him from realising the absurdity of these situations. Take, for instance, the "ultimate" sacrifice he is willing to make because of his love for Leonisa. This is noble, but, at the same time, it is, paradoxically, absurd: it entails marrying a woman he does not love and, more important, being untrue to Leonisa to whom, all through the play, he has considered himself engaged.

Once this ultimate absurdity is perceived, Rogerio's earlier actions also appear equally absurd. It is absurd for him to argue that his change in status makes it impossible for him to marry Leonisa, whom he was prepared to marry while he was only a *caballero*. His argument is based on the assumption that social position or status (the "dream" of Calderón's famous play) is an integral part of the individual, and that personal relationships are controlled by social factors. This argument is based on a misapprehension of values and of the nature of reality. For Rogerio, appearances are more important than reality, status and social honour more important than love and honesty in personal relationships. Ironically, it is precisely because of the importance which Rogerio gives to the intellect that he thus misconstrues reality and thinks he has incontrovertible proof of Leonisa's love for Filipo. So the wise Rogerio will not marry Leonisa, nor will he marry Clemencia. But he will not allow Filipo to court Leonisa either. He is content to settle for a perpetually hopeless love and melancholy. Such a pure, non-sexual, Platonic love may be all very well in theory, but in practice and in reality it is little more than an absurdity. Love between a man and a woman (and this is love as passion, not friendship: Rogerio's description of Leonisa in I.x proves that) is not intended to be an unnatural, disembodied, ethereal phenomenon.

That it is not, in any case, is proved by the fact that Rogerio is capable of experiencing intense jealousy. His love is, therefore, possessive—aggressively, but also absurdly so, since we realise that it is of the dog-in-the-manger variety. To prevent a marriage between Leonisa and Filipo (and anticipate the possibility of her falling in love with Filipo), Rogerio takes his rival with him to court, ostensibly to honour him, in reality to separate him from Leonisa. This we may agree is cunning, born of jealousy, but hardly the action of a "sabio."

An apparently, disinterested, noble act of generosity is promised when Rogerio, convinced that Leonisa returns Filipo's affections, decides to marry her to Filipo. But is this anything more than self-pity, we wonder. He dramatises the nobility of his gesture. But, as he says the words, he knows that he cannot consent to it:

[ROGERIO:]   Casarlos mañana intento,
                    y mostrar cuán sabio soy,
                    pues venciéndome a mí, doy
                    corona a mi sufrimiento.
                    Esto dice el pensamiento,
                    mas no el amor en que excedo
                    a la ley que admito y vedo.
                                  (III.viii. p. 254a.)

His jealousy, too, is without foundation. Seeing Leonisa and Filipo struggling over her necklace, he jumps to conclusions. He deduces from the evidence that they are in love. But he, the wise Rogerio, is deceived. It is Leonisa who points out how fallible his reasoning is:

ROGERIO:	Diréis que le aborrecéis:
	corales vi yo por trueco
	de eslabones, que, dorados,
	yugo son de vuestro cuello.
LEONISA:	También yo vi que os llamaba
	Bretaña sabio y discreto,
	sin merecer este nombre,
	quien preciándose de serlo,
	es tan fácil en creer.
ROGERIO:	¿Los ojos cuando mintieron?
LEONISA:	Cuando no los rige el alma,
	ni alumbra el entendimiento.

(III.xvii. p. 257a.)

And surely this is the point of the play. Rogerio the wise is far from being wise, because he depends too much on his intellect. His blind confidence in its infallibility makes him ignore the desirability of subjecting its workings to dispassionate, intellectual scrutiny. And yet he seems unaware of the extent to which his intellect is influenced by his emotions. In this problem of love, the limitations of the intellect are clearly revealed. In Rogerio's misinterpretation of the struggle between Leonisa and Filipo in III.xviii, as in his refusal to marry Leonisa because of his change in status, he is committing the error of paying too much attention to external appearances, and not enough to inner reality.

Thus it is that Rogerio's ultimate professed self-sacrifice is his greatest absurdity, compounded in that it comes after he has been disabused of his jealousy and has again promised to marry Leonisa. He should have realised earlier that the real mark of a disinterested love would have been to sacrifice his own false sense of social decorum by marrying Leonisa. That would have been true humility and true love. But Rogerio loves himself too much. This is not to say that his final act is without nobility. But the trick he devises fools no one, and hardly does credit to his intelligence. The emphasis is on the ridiculing of Rogerio.

Perhaps it is convenient to point out here that Rogerio, unlike Mireno in *El vergonzoso* and Rodrigo in *El castigo del penséque* and its sequel, is not *shy* in love. His hesitations spring not from a sense of his own inferiority, as is the case with the other two, but from a sense of his own superiority, or, rather, the inferiority of others. In this play, it is Filipo, rather, who is the hesitant one. Rogerio, for all his learning and wisdom, accepts society's conventions unquestioningly. Thus his dilemma arises from what he sees as a choice between two goods. The dilemma would be tragic if Rogerio were less blind. Consequently, I should hesitate to group Rogerio along with Mireno and Rodrigo, as Calderà does.

If Rogerio's ignorance in the midst of so much learning surprises us, so does Leonisa's passivity. In one crucial respect, namely, her lack of initiative and determination, she is unlike the heroine one normally associates with Tirso. If we would look for an exemplary, pure love in the play, we should look to Leonisa's love for Rogerio.

The opening scene of the play, set in the country, is, as I have said, ambiguous in tone. This means that Leonisa can be seen both as a rustic peasant-girl and as a pastoral shepherdess. It is in her role as a Neo-Platonic pastoral shepherdess that Leonisa gives us a striking description of love which helps to bring into focus the central problem of the play. Her companion, Firela, is arguing that Rogerio is wise, proud, and noble: therefore Leonisa would do well to forget him and love someone who is her social equal. Leonisa replies magnificently:

LEONISA: ¿Pues qué importa que esté el fuego
        cebado en la tosca leña
        o en la despreciada paja?
        ¿Por eso es razón que pierda
        su inclinación generosa
        y que el subir no apetezca?
        Pues ¿qué importa que mi amor,
        cebado en alma grosera,
        humilde sujeto abrace
        si experimento en mí mesma
        que, a pesar de mi ser tosco,
        subir al valor intenta
        de Rogerio, noble y rico,
        que es el centro donde sosiega?
        Todas las almas, amiga,
        son iguales: la materia
        de los cuerpos solamente
        hacen esa diferencia.
        Alma noble me dio el Cielo.
        No te espantes si con ella
        el amor, fuego con alas,
        intenta subir y vuela.
        A Rogerio he de adorar.

           (I.ii. p. 223a–b.)

To her, what really matter are love and the soul, which is love's province. Love is one of those human experiences, like birth and death, which cut

across all social classes and prove the common humanity of all men. In
a sense, it even transcends birth and death, since it is a quality of the
immortal soul: it is one of the ultimate realities which man has to face.
Love, then, is what encourages Leonisa to aspire to Rogerio's affections,
for she, too, has a noble soul.

The events of the play do indeed prove the nobility of the soul. Leonisa,
for all her theoretical boldness, seems prepared to accept the dictates of
social convention, but that is so only because she is led to believe that
Rogerio means to marry Clemencia. Yet she will be constant and love
on. Leonisa, much more that Rogerio, is interested in perfect love in all
its manifestations. In II.xiii, she upbraids Firela for debasing the love of
friendship—"friend," on Leonisa's lips, is a word full of meaning:

LEONISA: ¿Qué desvarios,
                     Firela, te descomponen,
                     o la lealtad, o el juicio?
                     ¿Tú eres mi amiga?
FIRELA: Por serlo
                     esposo te solicito
                     igual, ya que no a tu estado,
                     a tu pensamiento altivo.
                                   (II.xiii. p. 243b.)

She then proceeds to describe her own love, pure and perfect, seeking not
its own:

[LEONISA:]   Mi amor es sólo potencia
                     del alma, que no apetito;
                     y el amar por sólo amar
                     es perfección, si es martirio.
                     Que se case o no Rogerio,
                     ni con Clemencia compito
                     ni se amortiguan las llamas
                     de mi amor perfecto y limpio.
                                   (II.xiii. p. 243b.)

Ironically, it is because she tries to recover her necklace from Filipo in
II.xviii, convinced that to allow him to retain it would constitute a blot
on her love for Rogerio, that she gives rise to Rogerio's suspicions and
jealousy.

The fact that Leonisa's love for Rogerio is "perfect," leads to a situation
similar to the one familiar in the pastoral novel. An impasse is reached.
The crucial difference in the play is, of course, that this impasse is not

brought about by unreciprocated love, but by Rogerio's unwillingness to compromise (as he sees it) his social honour: "Mi amor no quiere a Clemencia, / ni mi nobleza a Leonisa" (III.xvi. p. 256b.). This is not to say that Leonisa is wholly passive. At the end of Act III (xvii to end), she does make an attempt to reassure and disabuse Rogerio. The latter creates a scene of jealousy, thus himself going against the sound advice he had given out in III.iv, and at the same time, contributing to endangering the life of Leonisa. The latter does finally succeed in calming his jealousy— ironically by taking her necklace from Filipo and putting it around his neck. Rogerio might now well regret his earlier condemnation of Filipo's effeminacy (which we, of course, know was primarily a manifestation of jealousy). Leonisa's initiative is not wholly successful, however, for she is imprisoned. It is now Rogerio's turn to demonstrate his perfect love: but his trick for securing Leonisa's release deceives no one, and it is only the revelation of Leonisa's real identity which prevents an unhappy ending.

The love of the main characters is thus a "perfect," pure, spiritual love. It is, perhaps, purest, most unselfish in Leonisa. Rogerio, too, affirms the perfection of his love:

ROGERIO: Yo te he querido, Leonisa,
       con el amor más perfecto
       de cuantos su deidad honran;
       vi tu mudable sujeto;
       déjame, y ama a Filipo.
            (III.xviii. p. 259a.)

But, as I have suggested, it is inferior to Leonisa's, principally in that it is too selfish. Rogerio, for most of the play, thinks too much of himself: there is too much of self-love in his love. Another mode of self-denying love is presented in Clemencia: she loves Rogerio passively, silently, knowing that he loves another.

The effect of portraying this type of suffering, "perfect" love is curious in dramatic terms. The passivity of the characters is evident: they all suffer from a virtual paralysis of the will. While the real obstacle in the play springs from Rogerio's character, from his inner conflict which derives from a misapprehension of values and a misconstruction of the evidence of the senses (both ironical in a wise, learned man), no other character has the determination and initiative required to break the stalemate of wills and actions. All suffer in silence, waiting for a sort of miracle, one might almost say, which does occur to bring the play to an end.

The point the play is making seems to be that such perfect, Platonic, spiritual love has severe limitations and is productive of more unhappiness than happiness. Rogerio's final solution is quite absurd, for, reduced to its simplest terms, it means that he is prepared to marry Clemencia because of his love for Leonisa. This may be Neo-Platonism or Christian charity (though, ironically, it has been brought about by Rogerio's initial failure to understand truly the nature of Christian charity). But it is not life or love as ordinary humans understand them. Hence the need for an artifical solution, almost in the pastoral tradition. The discovery that Leonisa is Clemencia's sister allows the old Duke to arrange a marriage between Leonisa and Rogerio, and at the same time removes the sole objection Rogerio had to a marriage with Leonisa. But the ending is all the same ironical: Rogerio, even from the socially conventional point of view, would have lost nothing and done no wrong had he exercised true Christian charity and married Leonisa thinking that she was a peasant girl, but one whom he loved.

These, then, are the dramatic problems posed by *El melancólico*. On the surface the play might appear to be unsatisfactory, not because it is carelessly constructed (one might say quite the opposite), but because the ideological premises of the play do not and cannot permit an organic solution, unless Rogerio undergoes a conversion. Rogerio's character, too, no matter how interesting it may be as a case-history, is also a stumbling block. This is not to say that the play is a failure: its lack of dramatic viability is precisely the point it is supposed to make: the apparent failure of the play is really the practical failure of a conventionally "perfect" love in a human situation. That this failure is deliberately created by Tirso is indicated by the consistent burlesque of dramatic conventions in the play (which I shall touch on when I discuss *Esto sí que es negociar*). The play satirises both a literary and a social convention by demonstrating their absurdity. But the majority of Tirsian heroines are real women of flesh and blood who will not wait for time and fortune to favour them.

* * * * *

(b) Esto sí que es negociar

In my analysis of *El melancólico*, I suggested that in that play Tirso was drawing attention to the limitations of a so-called "perfect" love between a man and a woman by illustrating the absurdity to which it can lead. It is this literary idealisation of human love (which can ultimately be traced back to Platonic and Neo-Platonic philosophy) which Tirso takes delight in deflating. I suggested, too, that this "perfect," spiritual love was really the frustrated love of a man and woman for each other, and that the frustration could be attributed to Rogerio's subscription to false values. Because of the philosophical premises concerning the nature of perfect love, the conflict born of Rogerio's love for Leonisa and his unwillingness to marry her, a conflict essentially social in nature, could have no organic solution.

In *Esto sí que es negociar*, the *refundición* of *El melancólico*, an attempt has been made to re-cast the play so that an organic solution to the conflict is possible. The main problems remain the same, but the emphasis is shifted slightly in order to underline the fundamental absurdity of Rogerio's dilemma. The philosophical premises, too, are altered, which allows Leonisa, like the majority of Tirso's heroines, to resolve the problem by the exercise of her initiative and will.

In assuming that *Esto sí que es negociar* is Tirso's, I have followed all Tirsian critics. While this play is published in the *Segunda parte* and does not carry Tirso's "signature," so to speak (as does *Por el sótano y el torno*, for example), the fact that it so closely resembles *El melancólico* makes it unlikely that Tirso would have included among the plays by other authors one which would be such a flagrant plagiarism of his own *El melancólico*. There is the possibility, if we admit that *El melancólico* is the later play, that the plagiarist was Tirso, but that would make us question his veracity when he asserts that he is not a plagiarist. At the same time, Ruth L. Kennedy has commented on the obvious bad humour revealed in the last lines of *El melancólico*:

CARLÍN: ¡Alto! Vayan
                    por otra para Carlín,
                    que esta comedia se acaba
                    sin bodas. Tirso la ha escrito:
                    a quien la juzgase mala,
                    malos años le dé Dios,
                    y a quien buena, buenas Pascuas.
                                  (III.xxvii. p. 265b.)

Could Tirso be referring here to an author who was so dissatisfied with *El melancólico* that he re-wrote it as *Esto sí que es negociar*? The closing lines of the former could have been written in the course of a revision, which would have been effected after the composition and staging of *Esto sí que es negociar*. This can only remain a speculative question at the moment. In the absence, therefore, of any positive evidence to the contrary, I shall take it that *Esto sí que es negociar* is Tirso's.

I have also assumed that *Esto sí que es negociar* is the *refundición* of *El melancólico*. While the majority of critics have though so, Ruth L. Kennedy suggests that *El melancólico* may be the later play. This is just possible, but, because of the technical superiority of *Esto sí que es negociar* and the bringing into clearer focus of the central issues of the play, it seems to me unlikely. The main point of a *refundición* is, after all, the re-casting of an earlier play in order to produce a technically superior one. But it must be borne in mind that this may not always be the dramatist's aim.

I shall now examine some of the differences between *El melancólico* and *Esto sí que es negociar* in order, first, to stress that the latter play is technically superior to the former; to identify, secondly, the shift in emphasis from *El melancólico* to *Esto sí que es negociar*, and, thirdly, to suggest that this shift, depending as it does on the creation of an absurd situation through the use of disguise, has something in common with Tirso's later comedies such as *La celosa de sí misma*.

Hartzenbusch, while recognising the importance of the characterisation of Rogerio in *El melancólico*, regards *Esto sí que es negociar* as the superior play on technical and stylistic grounds.[8] Doña Blanca de los Ríos, following Hartzenbusch, affirms that *Esto sí que es negociar* is the *refundición* of *El melancólico*, which, though less finished, is superior to the former in its characterisation of the protagonist; she also values it highly as an autobiographical document by virtue of its audacious satire of the rich and the foolish and of the unjust law of the *mayorazgo*.[9]

First, I should like to indicate several small, but significant features which, by showing *Esto sí que es negociar* to be the more unified and tauter dramatic structure, would indicate that it is the later play.

The most obvious difference is that Leonisa, and not Rogerio, is the protagonist in *Esto sí que es negociar*. In *El melancólico*, as has been stated, the idealised love between Leonisa and Rogerio leads to an impossible situation. Leonisa is a very passive creature, prepared to love even if her love is unrequited. Apart from pointing out to Rogerio his error, she never makes fun of him. Even her disguise in the final comic scene is a poor trick engineered by Rogerio to secure her liberty. But the satiric potentialities of this episode are realised in *Esto sí que es negociar*.

This accounts for the enormous development of the Margarita episode in *Esto sí que es negociar*, where it is initiated in the middle of Act II and used to create the crisis as well as to effect the *dénouement*. This is fully consonant with the orthodox technical use of disguise in drama, but its implications go further, as I shall argue later.

Closely connected with the Margarita episode is the fact that, in *Esto sí que es negociar*, the revelation of Leonisa's true identity comes only after Rogerio's personal decision to marry her, come what may. In *El melancólico*, this revelation leads to the Duke's decision to marry Rogerio to Leonisa (III.xxii), though Rogerio himself is prepared to marry Clemencia to secure Leonisa's release from prison. In this play, too, Clemencia's reconciliation with Leonisa is too forced and abrupt, and the whole episode of the discovery is artificial, although, as I have argued, necessarily so.

A further consequence of making Leonisa a aggressive female protagonist is the subordination of Rogerio to Leonisa in *Esto sí que es negociar*, whereas in most respects he towers over the other characters in *El melancólico*. In fact, Rogerio, the grave, wise, almost omniscient man of *El melancólico* is deflated and ridiculed in *Esto sí que es negociar*. This ridiculous aspect of Rogerio is already present in *El melancólico*, although it is not systematically exploited.

Enrique, on the other hand, plays a more important part in *Esto sí que es negociar* by virtue of the fact that he joins forces with the scheming Leonisa in order to solve the problem of who is to marry whom.

Similarly, the sub-plot dealing with the love-affair between Filipo and Leonisa is more closely woven into the fabric of *Esto sí que es negociar*. Leonisa's feigned marriage-preparations force Rogerio into a ridiculous situation and also set the scene for the solution. This incident helps to underline the social satire of the play.

Thus there is no doubt that the changes help to produce a more tightly-knit structure. This would seem to indicate that *Esto sí que es negociar* is the later play. But, at the same time, there is also a shift of emphasis in the theme of this play.

Perhaps that is why some critics are not entirely happy with *Esto sí que es negociar* in spite of its technical superiority. Doña Blanca says that *El melancólico*, a psychological play, is converted in *Esto sí que es negociar* into a "linda novela escenificada," a "vulgar comedia novelesca." And she seeks some additional reason for this not entirely happy change. Rightly, I think, she rejects the hypothesis put forward by Hartzenbusch.[10] But her reasons, while perhaps more interesting, constitute an over-statement of her case. She regards *El melancólico* as too obviously autobiographical. Its attacks on the concept of hereditary nobility, the law of the *mayorazgo* which led to "la servidumbre y despojo de bastardos y segundones" were unacceptable to the public and were therefore toned down in *Esto sí que es negociar*. But this seems to contradict Doña Blanca's own statement that "No era Tirso hombre que se dejase imponer por nadie" (Vol. II. p. 701b). Nor are the changes satisfactorily explained by Doña Blanca's hypothesis of a reconciliation between Tirso and the Girones.

Ruth L. Kennedy's suggestion, based on the view that the satire of opulent fools is central to *El melancólico*, is suggestive, but does not seem to be entirely convincing. This satire is clearly an important aspect of the play, but Tirso did not need to re-write it, merely in order to include a passage of topical satire. The satire of opulent fools does not seem to me to be thematically central: its organic function lies in the fact that it heightens the irony of the situation in which the limitations of Rogerio's wisdom are exposed. He, who makes such scathing remarks about opulent fools and the social conventions which favour them, turns out to have limited reasoning powers, because his intellect is handicapped by the conventions he previously despised but now passively accepts. Such an ironical treatment of a protagonist is, of course, a recurrent feature of Tirso's plays.

The problem which confronts Rogerio is adumbrated in *El melancólico* and developed in *Esto sí que es negociar*. A consideration of the way in which it is developed indicates that there is a case for arguing that in the latter social satire is a central feature and that this satire has wider implications than it does in the earlier play. We can perceive a shift from the exposure of the absurdity of an idealised form of love (in which a social convention is only a convenient obstacle) to a ridicule of this convention through the ridicule of Rogerio's actions. The social obstacle, which is almost an excuse for the exploration of one form of love in *El melancólico*, comes to the fore in *Esto sí que es negociar*.

In this play, Tirso sets out to ridicule Rogerio, who, suddenly transferred to a higher social class, is led by his learning to adopt blindly a conventional set of values which require him to give up the woman he loves (II.iii. p. 716a–b). These values are false since they are contrary to nature: Rogerio claims that: "Hijo de un Duque, trocó / la suerte mi amor" (I.ix. p. 713b). But he is unable to love Clemencia. How absurd these conventions are is shown by the fact that he is prepared to love Leonisa-Margarita and marry her because she reminds him of his Leonisa. Such a marriage would, of course, be technical adultery. Rogerio objects to Enrique's marriage to Leonisa for just such a reason:

[ROGERIO:]   pues si ha de ser Margarita

> mi esposa, y a esotra imita,
> quien della está enamorado,
> de mi esposa lo estará,
> porque es semejanza amor,
> y ofenderéis vos mi honor
> si esa permisión se os da.
>
> (III.ix. p. 738a.)

Here, the disguise of Leonisa has become symbolic, and Rogerio is prepared to take the shadow for the substance:

> dividido mi amor crece
> adorando mi interés
> en mi serrana lo que es
> y en la otra lo que parece.
>
> (II.xx. p. 729a.)

Rogerio is brought to his senses and taught true wisdom by Filipo. The latter, an *hidalgo* himself, is eager to marry Leonisa, for he recognises her true worth. Marriage to Leonisa cannot be a stain on his nobility: "no mancha al mar una gota / de tinta" (III.i. p. 730a). Furthermore, as Pinardo points out:

> Pobre y serrana es Leonisa;
> mas en tal desigualdad
> la virtud es calidad.
>
> (III.i. p. 730a.)

Leonisa has compensatory virtues that are more lasting than skin-deep beauty. This is why Filipo realises that Leonisa will make him a worthy wife. And love is what can create an "imagen soberana" (III.i. p. 730b). Rogerio's eyes are opened: he agrees with Filipo that: "el alma es quien da nobleza; / la virtud es calidad" (III.i. p. 731a).

In his soliloquy in III.ii, Rogerio realises how stupid he has been. He would have seen what Filipo saw "si mi amor no fuera necio." He now realises her full worth:

> el cielo ha encerrado en ella
> discreción de más valor
> que la calidad mayor;
> y es ignorante bajeza
> despreciar por la corteza
> lo que es noble en lo interior.
>
> (III.ii. p. 731b.)

Rogerio now sees a justification, based on nature, for his marriage to
Leonisa:

> O soy bárbaro, o ignoro
> que amor, hortelano astuto,
> en sazonado tributo,
> si la voluntad es huerto,
> estima en más el enjerto
> de dos almas, que otro fruto.
>
> (III.ii. p. 731b.)

(This horticultural image, it may be noted in passing, is a favourite one
of Tirso's.)

In *El melancólico*, as I suggested, the social problem is not resolved
organically. A happy discovery enables the Duke to marry Rogerio to
Leonisa, whereas this discovery in *Esto sí que es negociar* comes only
after Rogerio, held to his promise, finally determines to marry Leonisa at
all costs. The social aspect is stressed when Rogerio, finding he has to
choose between obeying the dictates of love and obeying those of society,
chooses love:

> Su esposo tengo de ser,
> aunque el patrimonio rico
> pierdo que en Bretaña adquiero,
> y otra vez viva estos riscos.
> Sé que he de perder la vida
> luego que pierdo el arrimo
> que hasta agora la sustenta;
> y ansí el menor daño elijo.
>
> (III.xv. p. 742a.)

It is, in fact, a choice between life and death. Although not as senti-
mentally heroic or pseudo-heroic as the melancholy Rogerio's would-be
self-sacrifice on the altar of a marriage with Clemencia (one differentiat-
ing feature of the Rogerio of *Esto sí que es negociar* from the Rogerio
of *El melancólico* is the former's reluctance to dramatise his situation),
this choice is, perhaps, even more of a sacrifice, since it is formulated in
extreme terms. Thus the revelation of Leonisa's real identity in *Esto sí
que es negociar* can be seen as a symbolic reward for Rogerio. But the
latter's conversion is not wholly the result of intellectual persuasion. He
must be made to realise how absurd his attitude is. Leonisa plays a vital
part here.

The love of Rogerio and Leonisa in *El melancólico* is so passive that no real conflict is produced. If their love cannot be fulfilled, they resign themselves to unhappiness and self-sacrifice. Such an impossible love is all well and good as the subject for pastoral novels and for sonnets where the Petrarchan woman is set on a pedestal and worshipped from afar. But it is of no use for a flesh-and-blood woman like the Leonisa of *Esto sí que es negociar*. The aggressive Leonisa, then, can be seen as a burlesque of the passive Petrarchan woman, and, in particular, the passive Leonisa of *El melancólico*.

But if the latter is burlesqued, what is the underlying reason? This is to be sought in social conditions. A woman may be content to be set on a pedestal and idolised because of her femininity, her beauty, her virtue, etc. But in real life such idolising is rare, and often has nothing to do with choosing a wife. Men base their love on *interés*; they want a wife who is rich, or noble, or both, and they are ready to abandon one woman when a better one turns up. Social conventions as they exist are detrimental to sound human relationships and hostile to emotions. Rogerio, by bowing to the demands of his social class, has rejected and thus offended Leonisa. This is unjust.

Therefore, Leonisa, wounded in her self-esteem and affronted, will challenge society. She explains the problem: "¿Cómo, siendo labradora, / seré de un Duque mujer?" (II.v. p. 717a). She exalts her Titanic efforts to scale the heavens:

> Yo, que de mi esfera salgo
> con mejores pensamientos,
> animando atrevimientos,
> merezco más, pues más valgo.
>
> (II.iv. p. 716b.)

But, unlike the Titans' efforts, hers is not one of brute force, an achievement requiring the piling of mountain on mountain in order to scale the heavens. On the contrary, her art is very deft and subtle, and of the essence of femininity. She determines to show the absurdity of Rogerio's stand, and of the social conventions which hinder their marriage by ridiculing Rogerio's proud wisdom.

Leonisa has recourse to disguise, which creates an absurd complication —Rogerio is engaged to two women simultaneously—in order to show how the existing clash between nature and society is absurd and also immoral. Rogerio's marriage to "Margarita" would lead to spiritual adultery. The situation itself leads to moral and social confusion: is Rogerio to marry two women? Or is he, like the dog in the manger, to prevent Leon-

isa from marrying Filipo, and "Margarita" from marrying Enrique, and yet
marry neither? He is being unjust not only to Leonisa by rejecting her for
an aristocratic Leonisa, i.e., "Margarita," but is also unjust to "Margarita"
by loving her not for herself but for being a Leonisa-substitute.

The use of disguise is also symbolic of social attributes; it is equivalent
to *corteza*. It can be put on and taken off, and has nothing to do with the
intrinsic worth of the real person. Not only can it hide one's real, inner
nature (Leonisa, although apparently a *serrana*, is of noble birth and also
noble in character), but is also hostile to love. That is why Firela and
Carlín comment cynically on the ornate dress of "la hermana Duca":

FIRELA: Trabajo tendrá quien la ama,
               con tanta ropa y botín.
                                        (I.v. p. 707a.)

And Carlín adds:

               El que la llegue a abrazar,
               por fuerza se ha de picar,
               según la guarnecen puntas.
                                        (I.v. p. 707b.)

Furthermore, a person is not to be judged by what he or she wears:

CARLÍN: Dad al diablo la mujer,
               que gasta galas sin suma;
               porque ave de mucha pluma
               tiene poco que comer.
                                        (I.v. p. 707a.)

Rogerio, for all his learning, finds himself in a thoroughly ludicrous situation. He loves Leonisa, and also loves "Margarita," not for herself, but
because she wears a different dress, i.e., her *corteza* is different. Yet she
is really Leonisa.

As has been already pointed out, real wisdon is imparted to Rogerio
by Filipo and Enrique. Rogerio, now brought to his senses, will marry
Leonisa. But he has more than once been brought near to tragedy. Because
of a false generosity and unquestioning obedience to convention, he is
prepared to sacrifice his own happiness and that of Leonisa by allowing
her to marry Filipo. But then, to avoid losing Leonisa, he gets himself
engaged to her after having promised to marry her "shadow," Leonisa-
Margarita, in a weaker moment. It is only our knowledge that Leonisa
and Margarita are one and the same person which allows the situation to
remain on a purely comic level: but it is potentially tragic. Fortunately,

the real Margarita appears. This solves Rogerio's problem: he has been taught his lesson.

To sum up, one may say that if a *refundición* almost invariably is better constructed than its source-play, the fact that *Esto sí que es negociar* is technically superior to *El melancólico* and also seems to echo situations found in the latter would indicate that it is the *refundición* of *El melancólico*. Secondly, the technical changes seem to be due not only to a wish on Tirso's part to write a better constructed play but also to a desire to bring into clearer focus a critical view of a social convention. In thematic terms, this means that there is a shift of emphasis from the satire of a literary convention to the satire of a social convention. And, finally, the way in which this satire is effected, namely the manoeuvring of the learned Rogerio into a frankly absurd situation through the use of disguise (the absurdity of Rogerio's situation being adumbrated in *El melancólico*, but the satirical use of disguise to underline the theme being a new addition in *Esto sí que es negociar*), seems to place this comedy during the period of composition of some of Tirso's late plays, which are characterised by their subtle irony and strong sense of the absurd.

The element of social satire coming to the fore in *Esto sí que es negociar* raises a number of interesting points. First, we can discern a straight line of development leading from the early *El vergonzoso* to the later plays analysed in this chapter. Ruth L. Kennedy's dating of *El melancólico* and *Esto sí que es negociar* is, of course, crucial here; but if it is accepted, Calderà's attempt to establish the chronological order of Tirso's plays on the basis of a development of a character seems to call for modification. A crucial factor in his argument is his view that Rogerio's character (in *El melancólico*) is lacking in subtlety and too schematic in outline. This, by any view, is a questionable interpretation. Another of Calderà's points is that Tirso moves away from the court-country opposition to a more courtly type of play. This may well be possible, if the date I assign to *Amar por arte mayor* is correct. But it seems to me that such a change, if it does take place, is later than Calderà implies, and cannot validly be used as a criterion for dating the plays he discusses. The view I suggest avoids such difficulties by seeing a thematic development as the basic explanation for these various treatments of the shy lover. The basis of this thematic development can be seen as an increasing preoccupation with social problems. In the later plays, these are presented in sharper focus, with a greater degree of social realism, which contrasts with the strong romantic element in *El vergonzoso*.

NOTES

1 In her introduction to the play in *Tirso de Molina. Obras dramáticas completas*, I (Madrid, 1946), pp. 207–219. All quotations refer to this edition.

2 "Studies for the Chronology of Tirso's Theatre," *HR*, XI (1943), 17–46.

3 Valera Jácome in the introduction to his ed. of the play (Madrid, Aguilar, 1967) refers to it in the section entitled: "Conflicto social," pp. 22–24. Paterson also touches on this aspect in his discussion of the play in the introduction to his ed. of *La venganza de Tamar* (Cambridge University Press, 1969).

4 "*Observaciones*" on *Esto sí que es negociar* and *El melancólico* in *Teatro escogido de Fray Gabriel Téllez*, IX (Madrid, 1841), p. 333.

5 "Un motivo delle commedie 'de enredo': l'elaborazione de *El melancólico*," in *Studi tirsiani* (Milan, 1958), pp. 95–110.

6 Valera Jácome, in fact, refers in his introduction to the play to this so-called "melancolía prerromántica." But the melancholy individual was well-known in the 17th century. See, e.g., L. C. Knights' discussion of this figure in 17th-century England in Appendix B: "Seventeenth-Century Melancholy" to his book: *Drama and Society in the Age of Jonson* (Peregrine Books, 1962; 1st ed., 1937).

7 *The Life of Drama* (London, 1965).

8 In his "*Observaciones*" to the two plays, referred to in note 4 above.

9 In her introduction to the two plays in *Tirso de Molina. Obras dramáticas completas*. Vol. I (Madrid, 1946), pp. 207–219, and Vol. II (Madrid, 1962), pp. 697–702. *Esto sí que es negociar* is in Vol. II, from which quotations are taken.

10 Hartzenbusch suggested that the reason for the writing was Rogerio's close resemblance to Philip II: "*Observaciones*," p. 331.

CHAPTER VI

Amar por arte mayor.
Its Formal Structure and Satirical Content

Amar por arte mayor is, it seems, a late play, and a remarkable one at that.[1]
In a number of ways it harks back to some of Tirso's earlier works. In
structure, it resembles *Don Gil*. The background to the action resembles
that of *El amor médico*. Lope, like Gaspar, is forced to flee, leaving
behind the woman he loves, who marries another man. Both men, in love
with other women, allow themselves the right to criticise the "fickleness"
of their former loves—Lope in II.viii p. 1186, Gaspar in II.i p. 984.[2]
Doña Blanca's machinations bear some resemblance to Jerónima's: both
pretend to be the *tercera* of a former love; both make similar accusations
of infidelity and fickleness to the man they love. Doña Blanca, too, is a
typical man-hater, like so many other women in Golden Age drama; and,
like Tisbea of *El burlador*, Serafina of *El vergonzoso* and Jerónima of *El
amor médico*, she is reduced to love. The fundamental absurdity of the
situation, too, in which Elvira and Lope love each other and express their
mutual affection by pretending to hate each other and love Ordoño and
Blanca is typically Tirsian. The abuse of power and situation, which we
detect in the earlier *La elección por la virtud*, recurs in this play. The scene
in which Elvira and Ordoño wrangle over a partridge (I.vi–vii), which
gives rise to Lope's jealousy, recalls a similar scene in *El melancolico*
where Rogerio's jealousy is aroused when he sees Leonisa and Filipo
struggling to obtain possession of the former's *corales* (II.xviii–xx).

   Yet, for all these echoes of earlier plays, *Amar por arte mayor* is dis-
tinctively different. The tone and style are quite different from the ones
we normally associate with Tirso. This play seems to be essentially a court
play. The Tirso of *Amar por arte mayor* is, in fact, more Calderonian than
Lopean. If Calderón is influenced by Tirso, which seems probable, this
surely is the Tirso who influences him. At the same time, we cannot dis-
count the possibility that the younger playwright may also have influenced

the older.

The new manner of Tirso can be noted in the studied artificiality of the structure. The parallelism and symmetry noted in earlier plays appear here perfected and employed with fine delicacy. Consider, for example, the situations in III.xii, xiv, where it is precisely the artificially contrived symmetry and parallelism of the plot-structure which allow Elvira and Lope to employ ambivalent language. The number of characters, too, is small by Tirsian standards, and almost all of them have organic roles in the play, the only real exception being García, who in fact is merely one of the King's attendants (I.vii. p. 1175). We have a further move towards dramatic economy.

But, above all, the new manner is most apparent in the style. What we recognise as a Calderonian note is struck in the long, opening speech by Tello. The long, intricate periods and the profusion of "learned" metaphor and simile, used seriously, are far removed from Tirso's earlier style. The exposition in the opening scene (which requires a silent, attentive audience from the start—there is no question here of imposing silence on a noisy audience, which suggests that this play was not conceived primarily for the public theatre) is narrated, not presented in action as it often is in earlier Tirso (*El vergonzoso, El amor médico*). There is, of course, less "typically" Tirsian stage-action in this play. The conflicts are essentially internal ones, and this is reflected in the language of the play. The Calderón-like formulation of an internal dilemma is easily recognised in this play: note, e.g., Lope's soliloquy in II.xi:

> Remató
> la fortuna con mi seso;
> echó el resto a sus rigores:
> ¿No fuera mejor, temores,
> acabar conmigo preso?
> Si doña Elvira me trata
> con desprecio, he de perder
> la vida; si llego a ver
> amor en mi hermosa ingrata,
> el rey ha de aborrecerme,
> la infanta ha de perseguirme:
> mudable, en efeto, o firme,
> voy, desdichas, a perderme.
>
> (II.xi. p. 1189a–b.)

Phrases which we consider typically Calderonian abound: Lope mentions a "confusa ilusión" in III.ii. p. 1196a, and says a bit later: "¿Queréis

sacarme, desdichas, / del golfo en que desespero?" (III.iii. p. 1198b).
Such expressions are not, of course, confined to Lope. Elvira's soliloquy
expressing her dilemma, in II.xiii. p. 1190, is equally "Calderonian." It
may be noted here that there are considerably more soliloquies in this play
than is normal in Tirso—another so-called Calderonian feature: two occur
in Act I (iii, v); six in Act II—or, perhaps, five, since II.vi is not really a
soliloquy (iv, vi, ix, xi, xiii, xviii); and four in Act III (i, iii, viii, x).

The artificial, courtly style is standard. Note, e.g., I.i, and Blanca's
remarkable lyrical soliloquy in I.iii. This does not mean that Tirso no
longer satirises the excesses of the Gongoristic style. Bermudo lets himself
go in a splendid piece of burlesque in II.v:

> mas usiría, muchacha
> brillante, esplendora, armiña,
> candor, crepúsculo, amago,
> aroma, coturno, pira;
> usiría que enjaulando
> el copete que entroniza
> solapa una ratonera,
> de tanto moño tarima,
> ¿ya en esa edad gruñizón?
>
> (II.v. p. 1183a.)

But, by this play, Tirso is clearly attracted by the dramatic possibilities of
the *culto* style, stripped of its excesses. (The mannered style in this play
is, of course, also to be noticed in Tirso's prose.) I cannot here do more
than call attention to this new, Calderonian manner in the late Tirso, which
clearly requires a separate study. I shall now pass on to the examination
of some other aspects of the play.

I have suggested that the formal structure of *Don Gil de las calzas
verdes* can be best likened to a set of Chinese boxes or to a series of
concentric circles of diminishing radii. A moment's reflection makes it
clear that symmetry and parallelism are the inevitable concomitants of such
a structure. We are, of course, familiar with the secondary intrigue in the
comedia which centres around the *gracioso* and parodies the main action:
the one in Tirso's *Mari-Hernández la gallega* is a striking example, in that
the sub-plot is a close and systematic parody of the main plot. Tirso is
also given to using symmetry and parallelism in plays of more orthodox
construction, as, for example, in *Marta la piadosa*. Such features are
indicative of a certain care in construction and would seem to go against
the traditional view that Tirso was indifferent to the niceties and even
basic requirements of plot-construction. However, the "telescopic" form

referred to above is a distinctive one in Tirso's theatre and reappears in *Amar por arte mayor*.

The outer frame or circle of the plot is provided by Lope's coming into conflict with King Sancho over Isabela. Lope is obliged to flee to Asturias where he falls in love with Elvira, and this begins the action proper of the play. At the end of the comedy, the reconciliation between Lope and Sancho brings the action round full circle, thus ensuring an overall formal unity.

The struggle between two persons for the possession of a third object or person is the basic motif on which the plot is constructed. The main action of the play, which deals with the clash betwen Lope and King Ordoño over Elvira, is a reflection of the situation which constitutes the outer frame of the story. The secondary action is a further reflection of the initial situation, in that it presents the struggle between the Infanta Blanca and Elvira for Lope's affections. Obliquely, Ordoño's attempt to marry his sister to the Duque de Vizcaya against her will makes the Duke an indirect rival of Lope's for the Infanta, a situation which is paralleled by the fact that the Infanta of Navarre is an indirect rival of Elvira's for Ordoño. Finally, on the symbolic level, the scene in I.vi–vii, where Ordoño and Elvira wrangle over a partridge is once more a repetition of the main motif. The central couple, Lope and Elvira, through being the common factor in all of these incidents, form, so to speak, the centre common to all the circles. Formal structural unity is thus secured by a central group on whom all the situations are hinged, and a common motif on which a number of variations are played. The opposition of morality to power ensures dramatic tension.

The central problem of the play is the presence of obstacles, in the forms of King Ordoño and his sister, to the love of Elvira and Lope. As we have seen, this love is the direct result of Lope's clash with Sancho. The structural reasons for the introduction of the earlier love and conflict will be discussed later. But the new love-affair leads to another and similar conflict between King and vassal, with the added complication that Doña Blanca has designs on Lope.

In their attempt to indulge their passions, Ordoño and Blanca abuse their power and authority. Ordoño, falling in love with Elvira, orders her to forget the man she loves (I.vii. p. 1176b). Later on, when he suspects that Lope loves Elvira, he practises what virtually amounts to emotional blackmail on Lope:

[ORDOÑO:]   A ponderaros

> vine lo que me debéis,
> porque cuando libre estéis,
> deudo, vasallo y amigo,
> de la suerte que os obligo,
> mercedes desempeñéis;
> por mayordomo mayor,
> mi casa, Lope, os recibe.
>
> (II.iii. p. 1182a.)

Then he explains to Lope how he can repay this debt:

[ORDOÑO:] Prenda en mi corte tenéis
que os sacará de deudor.
Baste esto, si pretendéis
cumplir con vuestro acreedor.

(II.iii. p. 1182b.)

Ordoño's generosity has been, in fact, an attempt to bribe Lope.

We also note that Lope and Elvira are virtual prisoners in the palace. Act II opens with Lope in prison; he is set free physically by Ordoño, but is made a moral debtor, and cannot be really free until he has paid off his debt—with Elvira. By being made "mayordomo mayor" he is also confined to the palace, where Elvira is being held. The latter, by being appointed lady-in-waiting to Blanca, is brought to the palace so that Blanca's blandishments and Ordoño's wooing may persuade her to love the King (II.i. p. 1181a). Blanca, however, is not only an advocate of her brother's cause, but has her own axe to grind. It is to her advantage that Elvira should marry Ordoño, since she herself is in love with Lope. Tirso's treatment of Blanca is, as is to be expected, interesting. When we first meet her, she protests against the violence done to her liberty:

[BLANCA:] Bien pudo
un consentimiento mudo
quejaros en mí de la ley
que introdujo la costumbre
en las de mi calidad,
pues contra la libertad
dan al alma pesadumbre.

. . . .

¡Triste cosa que hayan dado
las coronas inhumanas
en desterrar sus hermanas
por sola razón de estado!

(I.ii. pp. 1169b–1170a.)

Regretting that the individual freedom of a ruler is severely curtailed by
political obligations, which may at times go against personal inclinations
and desires, Blanca envies the absolute freedom of the wilds, the complete
self-sufficiency of the phoenix:

[BLANCA:]   ¿Quién imitaros pudiera
                   gozando entera exención
                   de ajena jurisdicción,
                   por más grave, más severa?
                        . . . .
                   ¡Feliz Narciso en amores
                   que no admitió compañía!
                   ¡Feliz el Fénix también
                   que privilegia desvelos
                   y jubilado de celos,
                   sólo a sí se quiere bien!
                                    (I.iii. p. 1170a–b.)

She contrasts the liberty of the pheonix with the servitude of the princess:

[BLANCA:]   ¿Qué mucho que en dicha tanta
                   envidie a una ave una infanta,
                   esta esclava, aquella reina?
                                    (I.iii. p. 1170b.)

Her confessed envy of Narcissus is revealing: Blanca is self-centred. She
can think only of herself. But she is soon to discover that true love is
directed towards others, in other words, that man must live in society;
and Blanca must then learn that gregarious living demands a measure of
self-sacrifice, which increases with one's social responsibilities, which, in
turn, depend on one's position in society. But, at first, Blanca moves
only from her desire for absolute freedom to her love for Lope. Her
egocentric attitude leads her to exploit her position and power in order
to gain her own ends. She pretends to Lope that she is acting on behalf
of the abandoned Isabela. But she gradually reveals her true intention.
Lope is to love Isabela, but to reserve a place in his heart for another
woman, i.e., herself (III.ii. p. 1198a). Veiled threats are not absent either.
After Lope, to satisfy the King, has "pretended" to woo an angry Elvira,
Blanca's parting speech makes her intentions clear:

BLANCA: Mucho, Lope, os debe el rey
                  si son fingidas las muestras
                  de amor que Elvira no admite.
                  Mucho también Isabela,

> y yo mucho más que todos;
> pero si son verdaderas
> (que para fingidas, Lope,
> vi mucho espíritu en ellas),
> que os guardéis de mí os aviso,
> porque al paso que agradezca
> puntualidad en servirme,
> castigaré inobediencias.
>
> (II.xvii. p. 1194b.)

Few authors indeed have managed to reproduce so well those perversely ambiguous speeches (the despair of lovers) in which women manage to say yea and nay simultaneously.

A direct, open conflict between rulers and vassals is avoided because an ambiguous situation is maintained throughout. To avoid coming to grief, Lope and Elvira must circumvent the obstacles to their love with the utmost care and discretion. They hit upon an ingenious trick which allows them to express their love for each other while ostensibly expressing their affection for the King and Princess. At this point, one reason for making Lope come into conflict with Sancho over an earlier love-affair becomes apparent. Blanca has exploited this for her own purpose, although Lope is only momentarily puzzled by Blanca's news of Isabela's "arrival" in León. But he goes along with Blanca's game, for this allows him to lull the King's suspicions, and also to deceive Blanca into believing that he loves her. On the other hand, the fact that Ordoño and Blanca have promised to marry the Infanta of Navarre and her brother respectively in order to end the war between Navarre and León is a conveniently ambiguous factor which Lope and Elvira can exploit. The ambiguous speeches prepare the way for the climax which comes with the exchange of written messages: Elvira's letter to Ordoño contains within it a message for Lope, while Lope's letter actually has three different messages for three persons! (III.vii–xi).

The climax of the play is thus produced by a brilliant display of ingenuity and technical virtuosity. It will be clear that such a climax is best suited to the telescopic structure of the play, providing, so to speak, the apex of the cone. The parallel with the "Gil cluster-point" in *Don Gil* is obvious.

Ordoño and Blanca are clearly the victims of an outrageous *burla*. King and Princess are not only frustrated in their pretensions, but ridiculed. The fact that they are deliberately deceived by Elvira and Lope also means that they have been affronted by their vassals. But ultimately, it must be admitted, they are not so much the victims of the deception practised upon them by the two lovers as they are victims of self-deception. They deceive themselves into believing that the power and authority vested in them by reason of their position in society, (and, consequently, the obedience to them required of their vassals) can be exploited for the satisfaction of their own selfish desires and passions, even at the cost of violating the rights of their subjects and negating the responsibilities of King to subject. It is only because they are blinded in this way that they can be deceived, to their ultimate discomfiture and shame, by an outward show of submission, acquiescence and obedience. The old Spanish formula of "obedezco pero no cumplo" is excellently illustrated here.

The trick played by Lope and Elvira is, of course, a potentially dangerous one. This is consonant with the ambiguous tonality of the play. There is a perceptible change in tone during the course of the play. In the first two acts, especially, there are dark and troubled undertones. As I shall suggest, this is probably due to the nature and implications of the theme. That may help to explain why the third act is emotionally low-keyed. Even so, tragedy is never far away. Towards the end, Ordoño discovers that Isabela is married in France. His previous defiance of Sancho (due not so much to his refusal to surrender Lope as to the selfish reasons underlying this refusal) brings the two nations perilously close to war, but tragedy is avoided, thanks to the good sense of the reformed Sancho, who reveals the true state of affairs to the King and thus brings about the "reformation" of Ordoño and Blanca.

The entrance of Sancho seems, from one point of view, arbitrary. We are not prepared for the fact that Elvira has written to him, asking for his help. But, in terms of the structure of the play, Sancho's intervention here balances his intervention in the earlier affair. It was he who disrupted the social harmony at the start, and it is he, now a reformed man, who comes to restore it at the end. With his arrival on the scene, the various circles which form the plot are completed. This is the second main reason for the existence of the Sancho-Lope-Isabela intrigue. Both Kings have to learn self-control through the frustration of their selfish desires. Sancho's self-mastery makes it easier for Ordoño and Blanca to dominate themselves. The marriages between the Kings and the Infantas, which ensure international peace, reveal that they have grown aware of their duties and obligations. Blanca herself, who had erstwhile rebelled against a marriage "por razón de estado" on the ground that it violated her liberty, and who was yet prepared to ride roughshod over the liberties of her vassals, is made aware of her duties to her subjects and to the state. Her conversion, effected in two stages, is complete: she is no longer a man-hater, nor is she a wilful, irresponsible Princess.

On the other hand, there is also a point to the arbitrary ending of the play. W. Kerr, in his book, *Tragedy and Comedy*, discusses the arbitrary nature of the happy ending in comedy. It is deliberately arbitrary to call our attention to the pessimism inherent in the comic view of life. "Substitution, compromise, resignation—of such stuff is our merriment made" (p. 61). Compromise and resignation are necessary, because in comedy (as often in real life) they are the alternatives to despair. "Within comedy," says Kerr, "there is always despair, a despair of ever finding a right ending except by artifice and magic. . . . There is something about comedy that has no future" (p. 79). Thus "To be comic, the ending must forcefully call into question the issues of 'happiness' and 'forever after.' Comedy is not lyric, not rhapsodic, not reassuring; putting its last and best foot forward, it puts it squarely down in dung" (p. 79). This view of the arbitrary comic ending seems to me to be very pertinent to the ending of *Amar por arte mayor*. There is compromise and resignation, because they are the only alternatives to violence. Tirso, in this comedy, has brought us to the edge of the tragic pit, and our final merriment is tinged with hysteria. The hint is subtle but not for that any less meaningful. The full implications of this, especially for Tirso's audience, will, I hope, be brought out by the points I now propose to make.

The abuse of regal power and authority is, of course, the theme of *Amar por arte mayor*. This theme is treated in a number of Golden Age plays, of which the most famous is the tragedy, *La Estrella de Sevilla*. In Tirso's play, a tragic ending is avoided by a delicate managing of passions which, throughout the play, constantly threaten to get out of hand: Elvira, offended by the accusations of the jealous Lope in I.viii, has him arrested and imprisoned. Later, in II.xiv, Elvira's jealousy again breaks out in dangerous fashion (and the unflattering reflection on the King who is in a woman's power is not to be missed):

[ELVIRA:]   Tengo a Ordoño en mi poder,
                 y como le hice prender,
                 le haré cortar la cabeza,

                          (II.xiv. p. 1191a.)

Now, just as the structure of the play is reflected in the climactic device of the use of letters which contain several messages, it seems that the theme of the play can likewise be interpreted in different ways, the first interpretation being in terms of the story itself, i.e., at a purely artistic level, and the second, in terms of the historical implications, literary as well as social, of the story.

We note, first of all, that some incidents in *Amar por arte mayor* seem to recall similar incidents in the anonymous *La Estrella de Sevilla*. The main situation is similar in both: a King loves one of his subjects, who, because she loves another man, refuses to accept the King's love. In both plays, the King attempts to abuse his power: while this is largely limited to threats in Tirso's play, it leads to Busto's murder in *La Estrella*. In the latter, the King attempts to bribe Busto by conferring favours on him; in *Amar por arte mayor*, Ordoño frees Lope from prison and makes him "mayordomo mayor." In both plays the King's designs are frustrated, although the endings differ. Finally, there seem to be other echoes of *La Estrella* in Tirso's comedy: Tello tells of Lope's refusal to draw his sword in the King's presence:

[TELLO:]   Bien pudiera retirarse,
                  o a no estar su rey presente
                  vestir de nuevos esmaltes
                  el siempre temido acero,
                           . . . .
                  No lo hizo por leal,
                  ni lo otro por turbarse.
                                        (I.i. p. 1168a–b.)

Busto, of course, attacks the King, pretending not to believe he is the King. The confrontation in the tragedy comes when Busto prevents the King from gaining access to Estrella's room, while in the comedy, it is the King who surprises Lope in Isabela's room. Whereas Busto is murdered, we learn that Sancho's resolve to kill Lope was frustrated in the nick of time (I.i. p. 1168b). Lope, in I.viii, refers to the suborning of judges by the King (I.viii. p. 1179b). At the end of the third act of *La Estrella* we recall that the King tried to persuade the judges to let Sancho off with only a token punishment. These similarities are pointed out, not in order to prove any deliberate borrowing by Tirso from *La Estrella* (although, as I shall later point out, there seems to be some connexion between the two plays), but to suggest, first, that they are recurrent situations in a certain type of play, and, secondly (and more important), that they may be references to events and situations which actually took place. In any case, it seems reasonable to assume that there are echoes of *La Estrella* in Tirso's comedy. (We may bear in mind that a King Sancho appears in both plays, and also that a Don Gonzalo de Ulloa appears in *La Estrella de*

Sevilla. We meet him again, of course, in Tirso's *El burlador de Sevilla*.)

It has often been suggested that some of the incidents in the plot of the anonymous *La Estrella* seem to be references to actual historical events.[3] In fact, the close resemblance between the murder of Busto at the King's orders and the murder of Juan Escobedo in 1578 and, more pertinently, that of the Conde de Villamediana in 1622, supposedly at the instigation of an outraged and jealous King; the resemblance, also, between Busto's attack on the King while feigning ignorance of his identity, and the drubbing supposedly administrered by the Duke of Albuquerque to Philip IV and Olivares when the former attempted to seduce the Duchess, seem to indicate that the play was intended as an attack on Philip IV's irresponsible philandering and his abuse of power.[4] In view of this, it is no surprise that the play is anonymous, and that even such stylistic analysis as has been attempted has been of no help in establishing its authorship.

Furthermore, a curious feature is that a number of Golden Age plays with similar or related themes seem to have been composed during the period 1623 to 1631. C. E. Aníbal points out that *La Estrella* may have imitated Lope's *Servir con mala estrella* (published 1615).[5] This is, admittedly, an early date, but the theme of abuse of regal power seems to have become especially popular with Golden Age dramatists in the early years of Philip IV's reign. S. E. Leavitt, following Cotarelo, argues that *La Estrella* seems to have been composed in 1623.[6] Aníbal, in his article mentioned above, also argues that the *fiestas* referred to in the play were most probably those held in honour of the visit of the Prince of Wales (7th March to 9th September, 1623). This argument is convincing, although a further detail may be pointed out. The play opens with Sancho's entrance into Seville, and much is made of the setting of the play in that city. In view of the generous praise accorded Seville and the detailed references to it, it seems highly probable that the play was written to be performed initially in Seville. (In passing, we may bear in mind two points here: first, Tirso, in various plays mentions and praises Seville; secondly, setting is often very important in Tirso: compare *La celosa*, *Por el sótano* and *El amor médico*, to name three obvious ones. The exploitation of setting is a feature of Tirso's dramatic art.) Now, early in 1624, Philip IV made his first visit to Andalucía, and the highlight of this trip was his visit to Seville. He arrived in that city on Thursday, 28th February, 1624, and his official entrance was on the first of March. His arrival caused a great stir in Seville, the inhabitants of which were favourably impressed by the King. Philip left Seville on March 13th.[7] *La Estrella de Sevilla*, then may have been composed in 1624, perhaps just after Philip's departure from the Andalusian city. If this is indeed the case (and circumstantial evidence lends support to it), *La Estrella* must clearly be seen as a vitriolic attack on the philandering of Spain's monarch, his abuse of regal power, and the connivance at this of Olivares.

There are a number of plays by Calderón which deal with more or less the same theme. The earliest of these would appear to be *Amor, honor y poder*, which was first staged in the royal palace by Acacio Bernal's company in 1623.[8] That the King who attempts to abuse his power is Edward III of England links the play with the visit of the Prince of Wales, although the implication of the theme must have made the compliment a dubious one. The King's attempt virtually to bribe Estela and her family, his appointing them to palace posts to ensure that Estela be within the King's power, the frustration of the King's initial attempt to seduce Estela after entering her room, even the disguised Infanta's visit to Enrico in his prison clearly resemble situations found in *La Estrella*. The names of the heroines of the two plays are also virtually the same. The play is, of course, a comedy, and the wish that the Prince of Wales and the Spanish Princess be happily married is reflected in the ending.

The theme recurs in *Saber del mal y del bien*, though the King's attempt to make Hipólita buy her brother's life by surrendering to him is subordinated to the main theme of the hazards of the *privado*'s life. Hipólita's refusal to believe that the King could abuse his power in this way seems to be an echo of *La Estrella*. But in Calderón's play, the King is not painted in black colours, nor is there any intention of passing judgment on him. The Conde states explicitly in Act I (perhaps this is Calderón's anticipation of criticism):

> Que es soberana justicia
> el Rey; y aunque yerre, vos
> no lo habéis de remediar;
> porque nadie ha de juzgar
> a los Reyes, sino Dios.[9]

At the same time, the King must awaken to his obligations:

[REY:]   porque más quiere
quien llega a querer de veras
el honor de lo que ama,
que el fin de lo que desea.

                              (III. p. 138b.)

A little tag in Act II of *Saber del mal y del bien*, García's accusation of Álvaro: "¿Alcahuetico me sois?", leads us on to a third play of Calderón's,

El secreto a voces.[10] In Act III of this latter play, also, Fabio, hidden under the table, eavesdrops on Federico and Enrique, and exclaims in an aside: "¡Oigan, oigan! / ¿Alcahuetico es mi amo?" According to E. Cotarelo, this play can be assigned to 1642.[11] This date is rather late for my immediate purpose, which is to draw attention to the fact that a number of plays, all dealing with the theme of the abuse of power, can reasonably be assigned to the period 1623 to 1631. But there are a number of points to which it would be useful to draw attention. Calderón's play, as has been pointed out, is a *refundición* of Tirso's *Amar por arte mayor.*[12] In typical Calderonian fashion, Tirso's double intrigue has been reduced to a single one (the number of characters being correspondingly reduced), the Duchess Flérida is the one who tries to abuse her situation (she obviously corresponds to Blanca in Tirso's play), and the key to the lovers' code (the production of a handkerchief) is introduced quite early on in the play; such a code is promised at the end of Act I, and we know what it is to be early in Act II. This simplification is, of course, much better suited to Calderón's linear or syllogistic plot-construction, whereas the more complex intrigue is admirably suited to Tirso's "telescopic" structure. The use of a secret code by the lovers and the outrageous *burla* practised on Flérida are the vital features Calderón adopts from Tirso's play. Calderón's light-hearted treatment of the theme, with its tragic overtones, also recalls Tirso's play.

All the same, it is perhaps significant that Calderón was interested in this play of Tirso's to the extent that he re-cast it. *Amar por arte mayor*, we remember, was first published in Tirso's *Quinta parte* (Madrid, 1636) and is the first play in that collection. This *parte* is interesting in that it bears an *aprobación* by Calderón himself, dated 16th July, 1635. In it, he states: "hay en ellas [i.e., the *comedias*] mucha erudición y exemplar doctrina por la moralidad que tienen encerrada en su honesto y apacible entretenimiento." E. M. Wilson has commented with his usual insight on this *aprobación*:

The tribute to Tirso, when Calderón was only 35, is more important. Here charm-ingly enough is a young man's homage to an elderly master, whom he praises for his religion and morality as well as for his art. The delicate acknowledgment of Tirso's leadership ("los que más deseamos imitarle") and the implied challenge to the ecclesiastical opponents of the popular theatre by the claim that Tirso's plays are religious, moral and exemplary are both noteworthy. In so far as he attempted to follow the older man's example, his plays would have, the readers would suspect, the same aim.[13]

My superficial comparison of *Amar por arte mayor* with *El secreto a voces* supports this view fully. Calderón's homage to Tirso was thus carried a step further in 1642 when he wrote *El secreto a voces*. That homage is made even more explicit in Arnesto's speech in Act III:

> Los cuerdos amigos son
> el libro más entendido
> de la vida, sí, porque
> deleitan aprovechando.[14]

The technical influence of Tirso's play is obvious. Nor are the moral and exemplary aspects of the theme ignored. But, we suspect, Calderón's play is less "dangerously" presented than Tirso's. I shall return to this point presently.

But first I should like to refer briefly to three of Lope's plays. C. E. Aníbal, in his article, draws attention to two of them. As he says, there is a striking resemblance between Lope's *Servir con mala estrella* and *La Estrella de Sevilla*. Furthermore, a similar situation is to be found in Lope's *El poder en el discreto* (8th May, 1623), which is reflected in Calderón's *Amor, honor y poder* (staged 29th June, 1623). Finally, there is the curious case of *El castigo sin venganza* (1631), which was withdrawn after its first performance. It is supposed that the Duke's association with "mujercillas viles" may have been taken as an indirect allusion to Philip's philandering.[15]

The above points may be helpful in dating *Amar por arte mayor*. Doña Blanca de los Ríos assigns the play to 1635.[16] In the actual text of the introduction, however, she adduces no evidence which can point to later than 1630–1631. G. E. Wade has suggested that it is unlikely that Tirso wrote any plays after 1631.[17] A. K. G. Paterson has also suggested that by this date Tirso's own statements indicate that he was moving away from the theatre to other literary forms.[18] These, it is true, are only tentative suggestions adduced on the basis of circumstantial evidence, but they may be borne in mind as we consider some other, more suggestive points.

The tone of the first two acts of Tirso's play is comparatively sombre, especially in view of the generally light-hearted third act. It is interesting to examine the criticism contained in some of the speeches in these acts. Most of the attacking passages deal with the theme of the abuse of royal power. Tello describes Sancho's polite threat to Lope thus:

> [TELLO:]   y si celos son gigantes
> en pretendientes humildes,
> ¿qué serán en pechos reales?
> Llamó a don Lope su primo,

y declarándole aparte
sentimientos de su ofensa,
más que severo amigable,
le pidió que desistiese
de deseos principiantes,
sin competir con coronas
jubiladas de rivales.
(I.i. pp. 1167b–1168a.)

Lope's jealous outburst seems to hint at more than Elvira's social ambitions. (One is inclined to suspect that one of Tirso's reasons for making Lope easily jealous was that such criticism could be more natural and more extreme.)

[LOPE:] ¿No os pareció muy bizarro?
Pero ¿qué príncipe hay feo?
¿No es su discreción notable?
Pero ¿cuándo un rey fue necio?
No hay llaves que no falseen
coronas; y según esto,
poco importó el advertirle
tenerle cerrado el pecho.
Alojábame en él yo
confiado y indiscreto;
halléle en mi compañía;
es rey, túvele respeto;
despejéle la posada,
porque en lugar tan estrecho,
no saliendo el uno, ¿cómo
un vasallo y rey cabremos?
(I.viii. p. 1177a.)

The *gracioso* is more outspoken when he finds himself in prison:

BERMUDO: ¿Qué quieres? allá van leyes
Et caetera. Estrellas son;
naciste en oposición
de las damas y los reyes.
El leonés te tiene preso
por dar gusto al navarrisco,
y a su infanta basilisco
cuyo amor le quita el seso.
(II.i. p. 1181a.)

Lope corrects Bermudo's analysis of Ordoño's motives:

[LOPE:]   Celos que tiene de mí
                         le abrasan el corazón,
                         y ocasionan mi prisión.
                                              (II.i. p. 1181a.)

Lope, too, complains that the egoism of kings leads to the violation of
human rights:

[LOPE:]   Hame el rey favorecido,
                         amor, porque más me enciendas
                         mientras con celos me ofendas;
                         que ya, atropellando leyes,
                         interesables los reyes,
                         si fían, es sobre prendas.
                                              (II.iv. p. 1182b.)

Elvira comments on the tyranny of Ordoño:

[ELVIRA:]   Celos, si no tiranías
                         de Ordoño, le tienen preso [a Lope]
                         . . . .
                         cuantos le temen, me avisan
                         que el poder, si injusto, real,
                         le intenta quitar la vida.
                                              (II.v. p. 1184a.)

This is all the result of hubris:

[ELVIRA:]   No sufre la majestad
                         por la lisonja aplaudida,
                         inobediencias amantes;
                         que es sol y fácil se eclipsa.
                                              (II.v. p. 1184a.)

But if the self-conceit of kings is fattened on flattery, flattery can be
deceitful, and it is by pretending to surrender to the demands of Ordoño
and Blanca that Elvira and Lope can live in safety and preserve their love.
The criticism of the abuse of kingly power is clearly expressed. With this
goes an equally clearly declared intention of resisting tyranny. Ordoño
may think that his power and status give him illimitable rights (III.vii.
p. 1201b). But Elvira affirms from the very beginning that the individual
has certain inalienable rights, one of which is the right to love the person
of one's choice: the King's jurisdiction cannot be extended to cover one's
will and emotions:

[ELVIRA:]   Reine Ordoño allá, que yo

dentro de mí misma reino
tanto más majestuosa
cuanto mayor considero
la jurisdicción de un alma
cuyas potencias gobierno,
mejor que él aduladores,
ya nobles, o ya plebeyos.

(I.viii. p. 1178a.)

She maintains this attitude to the very end, and, in her letter to Lope, encourages him to resist, for the ultimate victory will be his (III.viii. p. 1203b).

It is clear why the overwhelming majority of the *comedias* seem to centre around apparently frivolous love-affairs. There is something more to it than the intrinsic interest they provide. Drama can be said to deal primarily with relationships: the ways in which individuals, members of society, social groups communicate or fail to communicate with one another. The couple, a man and woman, form, of course, the basic social unit. The nature of their relationship may remain on the personal and private plane. But these individuals are also members of society, and an examination of their relationship can be a springboard for the discussion of larger problems. When C interferes with a system of communication set up by A and B, we get a "simple" case of love and jealousy. However, when C is King and A and B are his subjects, the whole question of social relationships arises, and this, as we have seen, happens in this play. The duty of the King to respect the rights of his subjects (in this case, the right to love and marriage) and his moral obligation not to abuse the power which is his for the purpose of protecting his subjects' rights by violating those very rights in order to satisfy his selfish desires are the problems treated in Tirso's play. But the tone of the play, it must be emphasised, is not wholly grave: serious ideas are adorned in pleasing garb. I shall now try to show that in this play Tirso does not seem to be stating general principles only; he is apparently criticising an existing state of affairs as well.

There is a curious passage in Bermudo's speech in which he reproaches Elvira for her apparent fickleness and ingratitude:

[BERMUDO:]   Por ella olvidó a Isabela,
la mujer más resabida,
más discreta, más hermosa,
más gentilhombra, más rica
que una abadesa en las Huelgas,

> que una condesa en su villa,
> y una dama de teatros,
> que es más que todas las dichas;
> quien tal hace, que tal pague.
>
> (II.v. p. 1183b.)

Our attention is drawn to it by the unusual comparisons Bermudo makes, which are apparently irrelevant to the context, if, indeed, not wholly pointless. However, the triple combination is too conspicuous not to arouse our suspicions, and it seems, in fact, that these references are to actual persons.

Fortunately enough, it appears reasonably easy to identify the "abadesa en las Huelgas" as Ana de Austria (1567?–163. . . ?). On page 206 of the first volume of the *Diccionario de Historia de España* (Madrid, 1952), we are given an account of her life, from which the following extracts are taken:

Doña Ana de Austria era hija natural de don Juan de Austria y doña María de Mendoza, dama de honor de la princesa doña Juana de Austria. . . . desde el primer momento, se hizo cargo de la niña doña Magdalena de Ulloa, que con tanto amor había cuidado de don Juan durante su niñez. Abandonó doña Magdalena la corte y se retiró a su palacio de Villagarcía de Campos para consagrar por entero su vida a criar y educar a la niña. Cuando doña Ana cumplió siete años de edad, fué colocada en el convento de Agustinas de Madrigal, donde más tarde profesó. . . .

Hacia 1591, la vida sencilla y apartada de doña Ana sufrió una fugaz transformación con motivo de haber tomado parte inocente en las tramas del *Sebastianismo*. . . . Descubierta la trama por la justicia real, . . . doña Ana fué trasladada al monasterio de Ávila, se la castigó a reclusión en su celda durante cuatro años y a ayunar todos los viernes a pan y agua, perdiendo además el tratamiento de "excelencia." Pero al poco tiempo se levantó el castigo; doña Ana fué llevada al monasterio de las Huelgas de Burgos, donde fué elegida abadesa perpetua.

En 1615 doña Ana recibió en el monasterio a Isabel de Borbón, que llegó en visita acompañada de Felipe III y de su futuro esposo el príncipe Felipe [IV]; . . . Se sabe que doña Ana aún vivía en 1625, pues Baltasar Porreño le dedicó su *Vida de Juan de Austria* en dicho año.

The exact date of her death has apparently not yet been established, but the unlucky lady was still alive on the 20th of June, 1627, for, in the *Noticias de Madrid*, we read among the entries for that day the following passage:

Este día llegó nueva de Burgos, que pasando por aquella Ciudad mi Señora la Marquesa de Charela y sus hijas, salió a recebirlas el Arzobispo, con grande ostentación, y con orden secreta que tenía de su Majestad so color que visitasen a la Señora Doña Ana de Austria, Abadesa perpetua de las Huelgas. Estando dentro, mostró el Arzobispo la orden de su Majestad para que una de las hijas que tenía mi Señora la Marquesa, que tenía título de Princesa, se quedase en depósito en aquel convento hasta que su Majestad mandase otra cosa y así se hizo, despidiéndose de ella su madre con muchas lágrimas.[19]

The entry is enigmatic, but perhaps not excessively so. G. Marañon elucidates the difficulty for us:

En la Biblioteca Nacional hay copia de una carta, muy probablemente auténtica, de la Marquesa de Charela, dirigida al Conde-Duque, que da a entender el rigor con que el ministro trató a esta señora. Es interesante, por tratarse de la madre de una amante famosa de Felipe IV, madre, a su vez, de uno de los hijos bastardos de éste, Don Fernando Francisco de Austria, al que llamaban "el Charelo," que a poco murió; la que, según se dice, dió lugar a la fundación del convento de las Calatravas, cuya cuya iglesia aun existe, con este nombre, en Madrid. . . . La Marquesa madre negocia en esta carta, con poca dignidad, mercedes para su marido, en premio de que su hija "haya asegurado la sucesión del Rey con un hijo." Se queja al Conde de no ser atendida: "Acuérdese V. E.—le dice—de que pedí las Galeras y me propuso la Caballería [para su marido], que jamás me contenté con ella ni el Marqués la quiere." Asegura que no son ciertas las voces que han corrido de que ella trataba de engañar a Olivares, y las llama "chismes insubstanciales," atribuyéndolos al P. Salazar. Estos Charela eran gente alborotada. Un hermano de la Marquesa, don Alonso Enríquez, murió en Flandes, en 1634, en un desafío con un Conde francés, cuyo criado, que era por cierto español, atravesó por la espalda, con un estoque, a Don Alonso. La infeliz amante del Rey, "que tenía título de Princesa," fue enclaustrada en las Huelgas, de Burgos.[20]

It seems probable, then, that Tirso's "condesa en su villa" is, in fact, La Charela. The juxtaposition of the "condesa" and the "abadesa en las Huelgas" is far too obvious. The affair with La Charela seems to have been the first known affair of Philip's. Deleito y Pinuela gives the following information:

El primer amor extralegal de Felipe IV, conocido, parece que fue la hija del conde de Chirel, dama de afamada beldad, allá hacia 1625, cuando el rey frisaba en los veinte años, aunque antes comenzaran sus fugaces aventuras.

Como su familia era de ilustre prosapia, emparentada con el almirante de Castilla, para facilitar aquella relación se alejó de la corte al padre de la joven (que era casi una niña), dándole mando en las galeras de Italia. La madre sí fué sabedora del suceso. Coronamiento natural de él fué que naciese al siguiente año un vástago, el primero de los bastardos reales, al que se llamó don Fernando Francisco de Austria, y que falleció prematuramente.[21]

Fernando Francisco, then, was born in 1626,[22] and, as we have seen, just a year later his mother was immured in Las Huelgas, although the *Cartas de los Jesuitas* seem to indicate that she was in Italy in 1634 (was she set free or exiled?). The encloistering of royal mistresses and bastards seems to have been normal procedure of the period, but there was probably an additional reason for La Charela's sudden and obviously unexpected immurement.

Perhaps the most famous of Philip's mistresses was "La Calderona." Tirso's "dama de teatros / que es más que todas las dichas" seems to be La Calderona herself. It is well known that Philip's passion for her was more than a superficial and passing attraction. When this affair with La Calderona started has not been exactly determined, but, as A. G. Amezúa has pointed out, La Calderona's son, the second Don Juan de Austria, was born on the 7th April, 1629, and must thus have been conceived in July, 1628.[23] Deleito has stated, however, that Don Juan was born two years after the beginning of the affair,[24] which can thus be put back by a further year. Now, Amezúa has pointed out that La Calderona worked in the company of Andrés de la Vega along with the latter's wife, Amarilis, during the period of 1627–1629. In 1626, Vega's company performed before the King and Queen in Aranjuez. Amarilis was there and Amezúa thinks La Calderona may possibly have been there too. In November of the following year, 1627, Amarilis acted in a performance of *Las paredes oyen* by her husband's company before the King. La Calderona probably took part in this performance. The company returned to Aranjuez in 1628 at the command of the Infante D. Carlos. Amezúa points out that Amarilis and La Calderona must have worked in the *corrales* in Madrid during the summer of 1628. Andrés de la Vega's company played in Valencia from the 24th September to the 29th December of that same year. La Calderona went to Valencia, but seems to have returned soon afterwards to Madrid because of her pregnancy, which she revealed to the Duke of Medina de las Torres, who, according to Amezúa, "hizo volver a la cómica a Madrid, aposentándola en las casas de un tal Ferroche, sitas en la calle de Leganitos."

In the light of the preceding information it seems reasonable to suppose that the immurement of La Charela was due to Philip's incipient passion for La Calderona. It is one of those grotesque and ironical twists of fate that the natural daughter of the first Don Juan de Austria should have played a part, albeit an incidental one, in clearing the stage for Philip's new affair, which was to lead to the birth of the second Juan de Austria. To complete the ironical circle, Amezúa quotes the following entry from page 644 of the *Genealogía, origen y noticias de los comediantes de España*

(B.N.M.Ms. 12918).

Calderon. Esta fue (sin auerse podido aueriguar el nombre ni con quien casó) la madre del Sr. don Juan de Austria, y luego que pario la puso en un combento de vn lugar de la Alcarria el Rey Phelipe IV en donde murio abadesa, y al tiempo que estava preñada estubo representando en Valencia.

If the above identifications are accurate, the *gracioso*'s speech quoted earlier is an obvious reference to events during the years 1627–1628.

Before passing on to my next main point, I should like to mention, *en passant*, two curious details which arise from the preceding paragraphs. The first is Deleito's statement concerning the father of La Charela: "para facilitar aquella relación se alejó de la corte al padre de la joven . . . dándole mando en las galeras de Italia."[25] What is obvious here is the bestowal of an honour which simultaneously paves the way for subsequent dishonour. The case of Peribáñez immediately comes to mind, but such equivocal honours are granted in the plays which I have been discussing, e.g., those given to Busto in *La Estrella* and to Lope in *Amar por arte mayor*. Perhaps even more repulsive is the character of the Marquesa de la Charela who, as Marañón makes clear, sought to exploit her daughter's dishonour in order to obtain further honours for her husband. The second detail is an even more curious one, and provides an example of the coincidence of art and the popular imagination (although there may be more to it than this). The situation in *Amar por arte mayor* in which the King and Princess are deceived is not only ingeniously contrived, but also a very suggestive one. Lope and Elvira continue to love each other, but pretend to love Blanca and Ordoño respectively. Now, rumour has it that the first lover of La Calderona was Olivares' son-in-law, the Duque de Medina de las Torres, who, afraid of losing the King's favour, surrendered La Calderona to Philip. Amezúa gives Mme. D'Aulnoy's version of the story:

Un día Felipe IV—sigue relatando la fantástica Condesa—sorprende juntos a los dos amantes, y en el arrebato de su cólera, saca un puñal para matar a su rival; pero entonces ella se interpone y se ofrece como vítima propiciatoria y salva al Duque. El Rey destierra a éste; pero los dos amantes continúan comunicándose por cartas. Entonces el Monarca obliga a la Calderona a que se encierre en un monasterio, como era costumbre con las favoritas regias cuando dejaban de serlo, recibiendo el velo de religiosa de manos del Nuncio de España.

Deleito y Piñuela agrees that this may be all pure gossip. Marañón dismisses the story out of hand as a complete fabrication:

Todo es, sin duda, invención. Baste considerar que la aventura de *la Calderona* ocurrió en 1627, pocos meses después de morir la hija de don Gaspar, la dulce María, dejando a su viudo, el Duque, sumido en un desconsuelo no muy largo, pero no tan corto que haga verosímil la sospecha de su enredo con la cómica; y a su padre el Conde-Duque, apartado para siempre de toda liviandad. (p. 33)

Finally, we may consider briefly Doña Blanca de los Ríos' two main arguments for assigning the play to 1630 or later. She claims that Tirso satirises Lope in this play because in 1630 Tirso

había recibido de Lope dos grandes ofensas: el indisculpable desdén con que le trata en *El laurel de Apolo* y la carta en que comenta pérfidamente *El Chitón de las tarabillas*, sangrienta sátira de Quevedo contra Téllez. Esta evidente hostilidad entre Lope y Tirso explica la lluvia de sátiras que Tirso disparó desde esta comedia contra las perfidias y agresiones del *Fénix*, siempre aquejado de celos estéticos contra Fray Gabriel.[26]

Now, in the first place, it is hard to see how Tirso could know what the contents of Lope's letter to Sesa were. Secondly, as Ruth L. Kennedy has pointed out, relations between Tirso and Lope were strained as early as 1623.[27] Thirdly, Doña Blanca gives no examples of anti-Lopean satire in the play and such satire, in fact, seems non-existent.

Secondly, Doña Blanca takes Blanca's complaint:

> Triste cosa es que hayan dado
> las coronas soberanas
> en desterrar sus hermanas
> por sola razón de estado
>
> (I.ii. p. 1170a.)

as an "evidente alusión al casamiento de la infanta Doña María, hermana de Felipe IV, con el rey de Hungría" (p. 1164). As Doña Blanca points out, the Hungarian ambassador arrived in Madrid on the 3rd October, 1629, and the new Queen left at the beginning of 1630. On the other hand, the marriage contract was signed in September, 1628, and the marriage was effected by proxy on the 25th April, 1629. The ambassador arrived with presents in October, 1629.[28] Thus any public protest could have been made as early as the latter part of 1628. But there is little evidence that public feeling against this marriage was great.

We may recall, however, that there was violent opposition to the earlier attempt to marry the same Princess to the Prince of Wales in 1623. Such a marriage would have been regarded as a real *destierro*, because of the difference of religion, whereas the King of Hungary was Catholic and belonged to the House of Austria. It is possible, then, that the passage refers to the negotiations of 1623. (If this play was a *particular* or intended for performance at court, this hypothesis would be considerably strengthened.) One other detail would seem to indicate that the reference is to the earlier courtship of 1623. Doña Blanca, taking 1630 as the *terminus a quo* for the date of composition, supposed, from the mention of Oviedo and León, that Tirso had visited those places at some time during the period 25th July, 1630 to 18th November, 1631. This, of course, is quite possible, but there is another detail which merits consideration. In I.iv, Bermudo advises Lope to flee:

> Gijón es fin de la tierra
> de Europa, y de Inglaterra
> huele el puerto y besa el mar;
> una nave de Plemúa
> aguarda, las vergas altas;
> si su plaza de armas saltas,
> y calles de golfos rúa,
> trocando españolas cortes,
> sus soplones desmentimos;
> y si aquí príncipes fuimos,
> seremos allá milortes.
>
> (I.iv. p. 1171a.)

Now, Tirso's love of the exotic is obvious. (In *Esto sí que es negociar*, e.g., we are introduced to a Scottish Duchess). But this reference to England would seem gratuitous, especially as Lope and Bermudo are in prison at the beginning of Act II. It seems probable, then, that there is an allusion to the events of 1623 in the play.

There are two possibilities here. The earlier speech of Bermudo may have been inserted into the play during a revision in 1627–1629. That is, the play may have been written c. 1623 and revised some five years later. There is a reference to the secret preparations made for Blanca's marriage to the Duke:

> [SANCHA:]   y en León nos alegramos
> de que a pesar del secreto
> que amor hasta aquí ha tenido
> (si es posible que en él le haya)
> viene el duque de Vizcaya.
>
> (I.ii. p. 1169b.)

This may be an allusion to the secrecy which attended the Prince of Wales' visit to Madrid to court María. Alternatively, the play may have been written after the failure of the negotiations in 1623. A small point seems to support this. Blanca, we note, does not marry the Duque de Vizcaya, who is too busy fighting the French, but King Sancho of Navarre. (This may be an allusion to her marriage to the King of Hungary.) And, as I have suggested, there seem to be echoes of *La Estrella* (1624?) in this play.

To end, I shall sum up a few of the points made above. Internal evidence seems to suggest that the play was perhaps written (or revised) not later than 1630, and possibly some time during the period of 1627–1629. If it was intended to be performed at court and the allusions are to the Infanta, the play must have been written and staged before her departure from Madrid early in 1630. But the next point raises difficulties. The play seems to be an attack on Philip IV, or, at least, could have been so interpreted at the time. (Is the opening scene in which the King is shown hunting an indirect reference to Philip, whose skill with the gun was notorious?) By virtue of its theme, it seems to belong to a group of plays, almost all apparently written between 1623 and 1631, which are bound together by the theme of the abuse of royal power for the satisfaction of passion. From this, two points arise. In 1625, Tirso was censured by the Junta de Reformación for writing immoral plays and ordered to be exiled. The real motive behind the decree of the Junta, Olivares' brainchild, has been a matter for conjecture. The theory that Tirso came into conflict with the authorities because of his outspoken political criticism seems to find support in this analysis of *Amar por arte mayor*, which indicates that the events of 1625 had not muzzled Tirso. (If the play was written before 1625, it would, of course, contribute towards these events.) In the second place, the sequence of events during the years 1620 to 1625 appears to offer an intriguing pattern. R. L. Kennedy has recently shown that Lope's friendship for Tirso began in late 1621 and lasted for only about two years. In 1623, Tirso's complaints against Lope's attitude begin to appear, as, e.g., in *Antona García*. Tirso's embarrassing defence of Lope in *La fingida Arcadia* (1622) must have hastened their estrangement. At this time Lope was courting Olivares and resentful of the fact that the Conde-Duque favoured Vélez de Guevara. In 1623, the surprise visit of the Prince of Wales caused a great stir in Spain. The *fiestas* in his honour, Aníbal argues, found an echo in *La Estrella de Sevilla*, written in late 1623, or, as I have suggested, early 1624. In 1625 we meet the edict of the Junta de Reformación. Now, Leavitt has suggested that some of the scenes in *La Estrella* may have been influenced by some of Tirso's plays. Ruth L. Kennedy has also pointed out other details which *La*

Estrella and some of Tirso's plays have in common.[29] Lope's wooing of Olivares would add further weight to the evidence against his being the author of *La Estrella*. Vélez's favour with the Conde-Duque would seem to weigh against Aníbal's suggestion that he may have had a hand in its composition. Tirso, around this time, was attacking Lope, Vélez and the Conde-Duque.[30] *Amar por arte mayor* bears, as we have seen, a thematic similarity to *La Estrella*, and other probable echoes of the latter in Tirso's comedy have also been mentioned. Tirso's play furthermore seems to contain additional criticism of Philip. Could Tirso have had a hand in the writing or planning of *La Estrella*? And could this have any connexion with the Junta de Reformación's edict in 1625?

This is a question which I cannot pursue here. To end, I can only repeat that, in this play, Tirso's disapproval of the high-handed attitudes and actions of the upper nobility and even the King is clearly indicated.

NOTES

1 First published in Tirso's *Quinta parte* (Madrid, 1636).

2 All references to *Amar por arte mayor* are by Act, scene and page to *Tirso de Molina. Obras dramáticas completas*, III, ed. B. de los Ríos (Madrid, 1958).

3 See, e.g., H. Thomas's introduction to his translation of the play, *The Star of Seville* (Oxford, 1950), pp. ix–x, and the introduction by Hill to *La Estrella de Sevilla*, eds. Reed, Dixon and Hill (Boston, 1939), pp. xxx–xxxiv.

4 A certain amount of confusion attends the story of Philip's designs on the Duchess of Albuquerque. Mme. D'Aulnoy, in her *Relation du voyage d'Espagne*, tells us that the lady in question was the above Duchess. Bertaut, in his *Journal d'un voyage*, names the lady as the Duquesa de Veragua (who was the sister of the Duquesa de Alburquerque). It is possible that both references are to the same incident, though there is some difference in details. For details, see J. Deleito y Piñuela, *El rey se divierte* (2nd ed., Madrid, 1955), pp. 21ff. G. Marañón agrees that there may be some truth in the rumour: *El Conde-Duque de Olivares* (3rd ed., Madrid, 1952), p. 39.

5 "Observaciones on *La Estrella de Sevilla*," *HR*, II (1934), 1–38. According to Morley and Bruerton (*The Chronology of Lope de Vegas's 'Comedias'* [New York, 1940], pp. 241–42), the play may have been written between 1604 and 1608, probably between 1604 and 1606.

6 *The 'Estrella de Sevilla' and Claramonte* (Harvard, 1931), pp. 19ff.

7 For an account of this trip, see J. Deleito y Piñuela, *op. cit.*, section LXXXI ("El Rey en Sevilla").

8 See the introduction to the play in *Don Pedro Calderón de la Barca. Obras completas*, II, ed. A. Valbuena Briones (Madrid, 1956), pp. 51–56. The dating

of this play and also of *Saber del mal y del bien*, to which I refer later, is supported in N. D. Shergold and J. E. Varey: "Some Early Calderón Dates," *BHS*, XXXVIII (1961), 274–86.

9 Act I, p. 115b. All references are to the ed. of A. Valbuena Briones: *Calderón. Obras completas* I, (Madrid, 1959).

10 This play is included in the 2nd vol. of Valbuena Briones' ed. of Calderón (already referred to), pp. 1204–43. References are by Act and page. The accusation levelled at Álvaro is curious. He is the King's *privado* and we know that Olivares, Philip's *privado*, was popularly supposed to be his *alcahuete*.

11 *Ensayo sobre la vida y obras de D. Pedro Calderón de la Barca* (Madrid, 1924), p. 235n.

12 See E. Cotarelo: *Tirso de Molina: Investigaciones bio-bibliográficas* (Madrid, 1893), p. 168. Also, Valbuena Briones, in his introduction to the play, *loc. cit.*, p. 1203.

13 "Seven *Aprobaciones* by Don Pedro Calderón de la Barca," in *Homenaje a Dámaso Alonso*, III (Madrid, 1963), pp. 605–618.

14 Act III, p. 1237a. Tirso's *Deleytar aprovechando* was published in Madrid in 1635, in the same year, that is as his *Quinta parte*. See E. Cotarelo, *Comedias de Tirso de Molina*, I (Madrid, 1906), pp. xlviii–liii.

15 See p. 3 of the introduction to C. A. Jones' ed. of this play (Oxford, 1966).

16 In her introduction to the play in *Tirso de Molina. Obras dramáticas completas*, III (Madrid, 1958), pp. 1163–66.

17 "Notes on Tirso de Molina," *HR*, VII (1939), 69–72.

18 *Tirso de Molina. An Edition of 'La venganza de Tamar' with bibliographical, textual and Literary Criticism*. Ph.D. thesis, Cambridge, 1965. I am grateful to Dr. Paterson for having allowed me to consult his copy of his thesis.

19 *Noticias de Madrid. 1621–1627*, ed. A. González Palencia (Madrid, 1942), pp. 161–162.

20 G. Marañón, note 22, pp. 175–6. The letter in the Biblioteca Nacional is given as Mss. 954, f. l. 430.

21 Deleito y Piñuela, p. 19. As will be realised, Deleito has erred with respect to the name of the parent, which should, in fact, be the "Marquesa de Charela." According to an editor's note to one of the letters of the Jesuits (*Memorial histórico español*, XIV [Madrid, 1862], p. 8, note 1): "D. Antonio Manrique estuvo casado con una señora siciliana, que fue marquesa de Ciarella." The death of the King's bastard son is recorded in the *Cartas de los jesuitas* (*M.H.E.*, XIII, Madrid, 1861) pp. 30 and 51.

22 See Deleito y Piñuela, *op. cit.*, in which a section is devoted to "Los bastardos reales."

23 "Unas notas sobre la Calderona," *Estudios Hispánicos. Homenaje a Archer M. Huntington* (Wellesley, Mass., 1952), pp. 15–37.

24 *Op. cit.*, pp. 27ff.

25 *Op. cit.*, p. 19. There would seem to be a contradiction here with Marañón's

account and a possible inaccuracy on Deleito's part if the "mercedes" the Marquesa pleads for in her letter are the "galeras."

26 On p. 1166 of her introduction to the play.

27 "A Reappraisal of Tirso's Relations to Lope and his Theatre," contains a valuable summary of earlier work on this topic by Ruth L. Kennedy.

28 For details, see Deleito, p. 40.

29 "Studies for the Chronology of Tirso's Theatre," *HR*, XI (1943), 17–46.

30 See R. L. Kennedy, "A Reappraisal. . . ," and also "Literary an Political Satire in Tirso's *La fingida Arcadia*," in *The Renaissance Reconsidered. Smith College Studies in History*, XLIV (1964), pp. 91–110.

CHAPTER VII

Mari-Hernández la gallega.
The Re-Structuring of Society (I)

With the next two plays, *Mari-Hernández la gallega* and *Antona García*, we come full circle back to the *mujer varonil*. There are, however, some significant differences between the treatment of this figure here and that in the plays examined in the first three chapters of this book. The stress here is rather on the masculinity of the protagonists (which, however, does not detract from their basic femininity—if the paradox is not too violent) than on male disguise, although disguise does play some part in *Mari-Hernández la gallega*. More important, however, is the conspicuous social element in these two plays. They thus contain a fusion of the principal elements of the plays analysed in the preceding chapters of this book. In other words, to the element of the *disfrazada de hombre* and its accompanying theme of personal relationships is united the theme of inter-class relationships.

The story of *Mari-Hernández* is simple enough.[1] Don Álvaro is forced to flee from Portugal for political reasons. Moved by jealousy, he falls in love with the peasant-girl, María, on the rebound, so to speak, and woos her in an idyllic Galician pastoral valley. When Doña Beatriz, his first love, reappears with adequate explanations (which are really unnecessary), he abandons María, who, offended, swears revenge. She succeeds in persuading the King to force Álvaro to marry her and not Beatriz.

This story, simple though it is, contains a number of interesting features. The marriage between Álvaro and María is an inter-class union, the partners coming from virtually opposite ends of the social scale: he is a count, she a peasant-girl.

Secondly, the marriage raises an elementary question of justice. It may be argued with some justification that Beatriz, whose claims are just as strong as María's—perhaps even more so, since Álvaro loved her first and she is his social equal—, is unfairly treated. But it is clear that, on the other hand, the marriage ensures justice for María. As I shall argue, this marriage is important for Tirso's basic thesis.

Álvaro must marry María, not only because the King orders him to do so, but because his treatment of María was irresponsible (as was his treatment of Beatriz). It is this theme of personal and social responsibility which underlies the play. A lack of a sense of responsibility among the members of one class towards those of another produces social disharmony, which it is the aim of the action of the play to resolve.

But social harmony is clearly only one aspect of an overall, larger context of disharmony in which the action of the play is situated. This is, on the international level, the state of hostility between Castile and Portugal.[2] Curiously enough, in this opposition between Castile and Portugal, Portugal is presented in an unfavourable light. It is Castile and the Castilians, the Reyes Católicos and the Conde de Monterrey who are the repositories of justice, legal and social, and true nobility. Persecuted Portuguese nobles seek refuge in Castile (I.i. p. 66a). Álvaro and Beatriz, too, flee to Galicia. And in II.iii–vii, the generosity, nobility, courtesy, and affability of the Conde de Monterrey are emphasised. Consider, for example, the comments of the peasants:

[MARÍA:]	¡Qué apacible!		
GARCÍA:		¡Qué llano!	
MARÍA:	Es conde.		
GARCÍA:		Es Acebedo.	
DOMINGA:			Es castellano.
			(II.iv. p. 83a.)

The international disharmony of the Castilian-Portuguese opposition is reflected in the national, internal conflict in Portugal between the King and the nobles. John II's policy of crushing the power of the nobles is, of course, a historical fact. So the bloody events narrated by Álvaro in I.i have some justification in history. But there are gruesome details in Álvaro's speech (also historically true) which suggest wilful, gratuitous, and vindictive cruelty on the part of the King. Compare, for example, this detail:

[ÁLVARO:]   Al Conde de Montemor,
                su hermano, y gran condestable
                de Portugal, aunque ausente,
                ha mandado el Rey sacarle
                su estatua, y en la villa
                y plaza mayor de Abrantes

> la espada y banda le quita
> cuadrada, que es degradarle
> de condestable y marqués,
> y luego degollar hace
> el simulacro funesto,
> saliendo (¡rigor notable!)
> sangre fingida del cuello
> de la inanimada imagen.
>
> (I.i. p. 66a.)

Obviously the King is not merely excessively severe. However, what make his actions more culpable are his lack of judgment, his willingness to listen to traitors, and his readiness to act on the information they give him.

These are, of course, evil advisers, which lifts a little of the blame from the King's shoulders. At the head of this band of traitors to the state, who, devoid of civic responsibility, seek only their own advancement, is Don Egas, the evil genius of the play. He remains in the background for most of the time, but he is not any less culpable. Since he, in a sense, is the person who is ultimately responsible for the disharmony of the play, it is he who is punished by death towards the end. His presence is convenient for two main reasons: he, rather than the King, is overtly punished; and since he is the one who wrongly advised the King, the latter can be presented in a more favourable light towards the end.

The presence of these traitors, symbolised by Don Egas, does not, however, absolve the King of all blame. The picture Álvaro paints of him in I.i is none too flattering (although we must bear in mind that Álvaro is an interested party and also that he himself is not a model of responsibility). The King is precipitate in his actions, and his judgment is blinded by his passions: he is all too ready to jump to conclusions:

> [ÁLVARO:]   Verosímiles indicios
> no admiten en pechos reales,
> cuando la pasión los ciega,
> argumentos disculpables.
>
> (I.i. p. 65b.)

(It is this tendency in the King to be convinced by a superficially plausible case which allows him to be taken by María's lie in III.ii—and so execute justice). All this implies that the King's attitude towards the nobles, his subjects, is unfair and unjust.

A specific example of this injustice is his treatment of Álvaro. The latter, being a noble, is also threatened by the King's wrath:

[ÁLVARO:]   Yo que, como primo suyo,
                     soy también participante,
                     si no en ıa culpa, en la pena,
                     para que también alcance,
                     estoy dado por traidor
                     . . . .
                                              (I.i. p. 66a)

But there is more to his persecution of Álvaro.

The King is Álvaro's rival for Beatriz's affection. What makes his persecution of Álvaro more than an abuse of royal power is the fact that he is already married. In I.iii, the King makes a surprise visit to Beatriz at night—to inform her that he intends to marry her to Egas. He seems to have realised his folly:

[REY:]   constante habéis resistido
                     mi poder y voluntad,
                     porque mienta la experiencia
                     que afirma no hay resistencia
                     contra un gusto majestad;
                     y yo también, vuelto en mí,
                     cuerdo he juzgado a vergüenza
                     que una mujer reyes venza,
                     y un rey no se venza a sí.
                                              (I.iii. p. 68b.)

At the same time, it is clear that the king has not ceased to love Beatriz. One is led to suspect that his attempt to marry her to his *privado*, Egas, is simply a convenient way of making her his mistress, apart from preventing her from marrying Álvaro, which he could not allow from the point of view of honour. Álvaro manages to excape to Galicia, but she is imprisoned on the King's orders.

It is this interference by the King in the relationship between Beatriz and Álvaro which leads to the latter's flight to Galicia and his wooing of Mari-Hernández. Galicia is presented as a haven, where innocence and simplicity dwell:

ÁLVARO: Caldeira, esta es Galicia.
                     No vive en estas tierras la malicia
                     de envidias y traiciones,
                     de lisonjas, engaños y ambiciones.
                     Los que en mi busca vienen,

aquí jurisdicción ni ayuda tienen.

(I.vii. p. 73b.)

Here dwells, too, the pastoral shepherdess, María, whose beauty Álvaro finds so striking. The pastoral context is emphasised:

ÁLVARO: Bien haya aquesta aspereza,
            que os puede ver cada día,
            este arroyo y fuente fría,
            cristal de vuestra belleza.
            Las aves que os lisonjean,
            el prado que os rinde flores,
            el pastor que os dice amores,
            las almas que en vos se emplean,
            el gusto que en vos se hechiza,
            la libertad presa en vos,
            y yo que os he visto . . .

(I.x. p. 77b.)

The pastoral aspect of María is also evident from the start. When she first appears (I.ix), she is culling flowers with her companion, Dominga, for her birthday party. Her concern for her beauty reveals the coquette, but also has Neo-Platonic overtones:

MARÍA: ¿Hay más aborrecible cosa
            que una vieja que fue hermosa,
            la cara llena de pliegues
            y aojando con la vista?
            Dominga, morir me agrada
            moza, y de todos llorada,
            mejor que vieja y malquista.

(I.ix. p. 75a.)

It is this rustic beauty whom Álvaro regards as an antidote for his love for Beatriz, a love which he mistakenly thinks no longer exists (I.x. p. 79a).

María, too, falls in love with Álvaro at first sight. But she is not entirely sure of his love for her. In an intensely lyrical scene, she voices her fears:

[MARÍA:]   Dejaréis en vuesa tierra
            la memoria y voluntá;
            trairéis las sobras acá
            para que a mí me hagan guerra.
            Pues también los de la sierra
            son personas, lisonjero.

(II.xi. p. 88b.)

These words are, of course, a part of María's coquetry: she wants Álvaro to affirm his love and thus reassure her. But they are, ironically, much nearer the truth than she thinks. She is afraid he will abandon her:

MARÍA: Ni en mí el dudar
                          que quien se olvida y ausenta,
                          haciendo de su amor venta,
                          querrá comer y picar.
                                        (II.xii. pp. 88b–89a.)

Álvaro reassures her: "Tú sola eres mi querida" (II.xii. p. 89a). He even goes further:

MARÍA: Pues jurad, si sentís eso,
                          sobre esta cruz.
ÁLVARO: Juro y beso.
                                        (II.xii. p. 89a.)

It is precisely at this point that, ironically, Beatriz enters. The bitter puns and sarcasm of her words reveal her anger and jealousy:

BEATRIZ: Marquesa soy,
                          que a marcar agravios vengo,
                          en vez de marcos de amor.
                          Quien tan bien penas divierte,
                          y con tanta prevención
                          a enfermedades de ausencia
                          tan presto antídoto halló,
                          no morirá malogrado.
                          ¡Qué cortesano que sois!
                          Besamanos dais cumplidos;
                          que hasta aquí pensaba yo
                          que se daban de palabra,
                          mas puestos por obra no;
                          si no es que le dais el pulso
                          vos enfermo, ella dotor.
                          ¡Bien pagáis obligaciones
                          de quien desprecia por vos
                          créditos que, ya fallidos,
                          pone el vulgo en opinión!
                                        (II.xiii. p. 89b.)

Explanations follow in II.xvi, and Álvaro apologises.

With this reconciliation, María's earlier fears are realised. Álvaro, in an off-hand way, tells María that their romance is over, and, adding insult to injury, gives her a ring as a souvenir (II.xviii. p. 92b–93a). So Álvaro's wooing and promises were little more than irresponsible trifling with María's affections. His moral irresponsibility is clearly linked to social arrogance. For Álvaro, María is not a "persona" (compare her words in II.xi: "Pues también los de la sierra / son personas, lisonjero"), but a mere instrument of pleasure and amusement, to be taken up or cast away at will. María is furious at such treatment and determines to seek vengeance.

First, by means of a lie (technically), she gets the King to promise to compel Álvaro to marry her. This suits the King perfectly. Anything is acceptable, so long as Álvaro and Beatriz do not marry (III.ii. p. 96a). Dominga has scruples of conscience over María's lie, but María basing herself (unconsciously perhaps) on Biblical and religious arguments, defends her actions. The Biblical overtones of this passage are obvious:

DOMINGA: ¿No es pecado levantar
                testimonios y mentiras
                a don Álvaro?
MARÍA: ¿Yo en qué?
DOMINGA: En que al Rey Don Juan le digas
                que te gozó.
MARÍA: La mujer
                que de un hombre fue querida,
                ya es gozada en el deseo,
                y la afrenta si la olvida.
                        (III.vii. p. 98a–b.)

Now, this is a witty justification on María's part. As such, it is comic. But it is simultaneously a very serious point: the biblical overtones not only ensure the comic effect, but also underline how serious María is. Her attitude, one may object, is much too serious, when one considers that Álvaro was merely flirting with her. But that is precisely the point. Álvaro's casual attitude, which is fully within the literary conventions of the time, is morally wrong. That is why there is a criticism in the play both of this literary, conventional attitude and Álvaro's behaviour.

But before I discuss that more fully, I must refer to María's second step in securing her vengeance. This is concerned with the social problem of class. Álvaro has treated María badly because she is only a peasant-girl, and, as such, hardly a person to be taken seriously. The undermining of the attitude of those nobles who pride themselves on their blue blood and look down on the lower classes is effected humorously.

To be sure, the King in III.ii promises to make María a Marchioness (i.e., make her the equal to Beatriz). This is what happens at the end of the play, of course. But Tirso has a point to prove before that.

As so often in Tirso, the point is proved with rigorous logic in a comic scene.[3] In III.v, María, dressed as a man, presents herself before the Conde de Monterrey, claiming to be a blood relation. Juan García de Morrazos' father was cook to the Count's father. Therefore they ate the same food. So, María continues:

MARÍA:	Das comidas ¿non se faz
	o sangue con que se crían
	os corpos?
CONDE:	¿Quién duda deso?
MARÍA:	Pois si a comer ambos viñan
	día e noite d'hum manjar,
	craro está que ambos dois tiñan
	hum sangue mismo em dois corpos,
	sendo ansí, bem se averigua
	que descemdemos d'hum sangue
	eu, e vossa señoría,
	e que sendo seu parente
	me ha de facer cortesía.
CONDE:	No puedo negar el deudo;
	que es la prueba peregrina
	bastante a ejecutoriarse
	en cualquier chancillería.

(III.v. p. 97a–b.)

Álvaro is immensely tickled:

ÁLVARO:	Que, ocasionando la risa,
	viene un cocinero a ser
	el más noble de Castilla.

(III.v. p. 97b.)

But the point has been made.

Morrazos, having proved his nobility, is now content to enjoy the rights accruing to him:

MARÍA:	Os pes
	me dai, nom porque vos sirva
	(que non sirven os Morrazos),
	mas porque desde hoje viva
	a vossa custa em descanso.

(III.v. p. 97b.)

On the comic level of the thesis of the play, this parasitic attitude has not a little in common with that of nobles such as Álvaro who consider that their status confers nobility on them which exonerates them from responsibility. But on the level of the plot, María is thus enabled to live in the Count's palace, where she can thwart Álvaro's plans.

This she does easily in III.xv. Álvaro has just promised to marry Beatriz and is explaining that she has no grounds for fear or jealousy of María:

> [ÁLVARO:] ¿Cómo os puede a vos dar celos
> una pastora grosera
> ignorante en facultades
> de amor, que estima agudezas?
> ¿Qué hermosura ha de tener
> una tosca montañesa,
> que adornan sayales pobres,
> y soles y aires afeitan?
> ¿Tan mal gusto tengo yo,
> que permita competencias
> de una villana, vos noble?
> ¿De una simple, vos discreta?
>
> (III.xv. p. 104a.)

María's challenge underlines Álvaro's unworthy behaviour:

> [MARÍA:] Vos sí que el villano sois,
> pues que por no pagar deudas
> de quien de esposa os dio mano,
> ponéis en su honor la lengua.
>
> (III.xv. p. 104a)

Beatriz withdraws, offended. In the duel scene (III.xix), María, on seeing Álvaro threatened, attacks his attackers and wounds Egas mortally.

There are two important points to be noted here. Álvaro now owes his life to María's noble action. Secondly, there is the obvious justice of Egas' death at María's hands. The implications of the noble peasant-woman killing the ignoble nobleman are not to be missed. María, morally noble, is elevated to the ranks of the nobility by the King.

The movement towards reconciliation, set in motion from the beginning of the play, is now completed. Egas' confession of his crimes and sins and his death lead to reconciliation. On the international level, Castile and Portugal are now at peace: war is brought to a halt by the exercise of generosity. On the civil level, Egas' death implies the end of the persecution of the nobles and their reconciliation with the King. The marriage of María to Álvaro is symbolic of moral and social harmony.

I should now like to take up the point made earlier that Álvaro's behaviour can be seen in terms of a literary convention and that both are
criticised in the play. The overall theme of the play is that of responsibility in social and personal relationships. This is connected with various
aspects of the play's structure.

I have already mentioned the lyricism of II.xi–xii, but it actually begins
in II.x. I cannot here undertake a close analysis of the style of this section.
A few brief remarks must suffice. The verse-forms are the *romance* and,
later, the *redondilla*. There is a slightly archaic flavour to the ballad which
opens this cuadro:

DOMINGA: Mal segura zagaleja,
                la de los lindos ojuelos,
                grave honor de los azules,
                dulce afrenta de los negros.
                ¿Qué tienes de ayer acá,
                que a lo que colijo dellos,
                desveladas inquietudes
                les tiranizan el sueño?

                                        (II.x. p. 86a.)

The setting is, appropriately, the woods. But note how the words are
chosen for effect: "mal segura," the archaising "mal" rather than "no" or
"poco," and the litotes, produced by the negating of the positive "segura."
The diminutives "zagaleja" (instead of "zagala") and "ojuelos." This *romance*, as Doña Blanca points out in her introduction, is "culto" and not
traditional. Tirso's decision to use it to open this scene was certainly
an *acierto*. The wistful, bitter-sweet flavour pervades the scene: sweet
because there is love; bitter because there is deceit. But perhaps what
contributes most to the lyrical effect is the rhythm of these lines and their
soft, feminine cadences. That is why the irruption of Beatriz into this idyllic scene is so violent and brutal. The octosyllables are preserved, but how
jarring is the sudden switch from *redondillas* to Beatriz's *romances* with
their masculine endings and harsh assonance in "o," their bitter punning
and sarcasm! This is not to say that this brutal irruption is not foreshadowed. It is in the wistful air pervading the love-scene and in the flashes
of burlesque in the midst of the most intense lyricism. Consider the effect
in these lines:

[DOMINGA:]   Aojado te han, mi serrana:
                mucho lloras; mal te han hecho.

¡Pregue a Dios que no te opilen
pensamientos indigestos!

(II.x. p. 86a–b.)

The last two lines effectively prevent sentiment from degenerating into sentimentality. A similar effect is produced with Dominga's words:

¿Hásete antojado algo?
Que diz que en aquestos tiempos
hay doncellas con antojos.
¿Has comido barro o yeso?

(II.x. p. 86b.)

The pastoral setting and mood coincide. But it is important to remember that this is literary and artificial. The style is *culto*. This is quite evident in Álvaro's opening speech in II.xi p. 88a. Secondly, this idyllic episode is an interlude, clearly framed by the tone and the incidents of the enclosing scenes. The change in tone with Beatriz's entrance is no less definite than the change in tone from the *romances* with assonance in "i – a" in II.ix to the softer assonance in "e – o" in II.x. But the whole episode which starts with II.x and ends with the reconciliation of Álvaro and Beatriz forms a larger unit which is framed by the Conde's departure to see the bear (II.vii) and his return (II.xvii).

In the interval between these two points in the action, Álvaro has moved, I suggest, from play-acting (his wooing of María) to real-life actions (his reconciliation with Beatriz). María was only a dream-like episode in his life. When he awakes, he is re-integrated into life and society, and bids his dream farewell: "Adiós, graciosa serrana" (II.xviii. p. 93).

My interpretation of this episode as a pseudo-dream and a literary device seems to be supported by an earlier scene in the play where the hint is more explicit. Our first view of María is as a pastoral shepherdess, as I have already remarked. But this is unreal. Real shepherds and mountain-dwellers have appeared earlier in I.v–vi. Their preoccupations are not with death and beauty, as are María's, but with more worldly things: "OTERO: No hay sino matar y comer." (I.v. p. 70b). They are concerned with hunting animals—and Jews. Their love for the beautiful María is neither Platonic nor courtly:

OTERO:	Par Dios, que cuando la veo
	de manera me emberrincho,
	que como rocín relincho.
CARRASCO:	¡Mas harre allá!

MARTÍN: Yo babeo
                         siempre que la llego a habrar.
                                        (I.vi. p. 72b.)

This bit of pastoral realism has, of course, burlesque overtones. Its factual
realism is anti-pastoral. But these *serranos* are also clearly burlesque
knights-errant. Benito, "Yo que só / gala desta serranía" (I.vi. p. 72b),
will not allow Otero to aspire to María's hand any more than the King
will tolerate Álvaro as a rival in love. So the two shepherds decide to
have a duel. But, uncourtly as they are, instead of arming themselves to
do battle, they undress to have a tussle. The winner's reward is not to be
a love-token, but a goat.

María's initial appearance in I.ix, therefore, is, in part, unreal. And this
is so, I suggest, because, from one point of view, she can be regarded as
a literary creation of Álvaro's dream. Note that Álvaro has just arrived in
Galicia, to him a refuge, a place of safety, and falls asleep in I.viii. He is
assimilated into the rustic setting when he dons, along with Caldeira, the
garb of the shepherds. But this assimilation is only partial. As is the case
with all pastoral shepherds, his courtly dress can be discerned beneath his
rustic clothes:

[MARÍA:]   Desde la cintura arriba
                  es pastor, y lo que queda
                  está vestido de seda.

                                        (I.x. p. 75b.)

The symbolic significance of this is clear enough. What one must remember is that this dress is only a temporary disguise, which is abandoned
when Beatriz re-appears.

But, to return to the scene under discussion, soon flashes of burlesque
appear. There is an inter-play between dream and reality as María the
shepherdess is transformed suddenly into María, the *mujer varonil*, a real-
life *serrana* who is not averse to killing Jews for the good of her soul and
the Church (the thematic link with the earlier scene with the shepherds is
obvious):

[MARÍA:]   Este será algún judío
                  de los que andan a prender
                  porque no quieren comer
                  tocino. ¡Qué devarío!
                  Yo quiero dar hoy venganzas
                  a la igreja y sus denuestos;
                  que quien mata alguno destos

diz que gana perdonanzas.
Esta media lancha tomo.

(I.x. p. 75b.)

Like María Sarmiento, in *Antona García*, she is about to hurl this boulder on to Álvaro, "y a nuestro jodío ahorro / de dotor, cura y entierro" (I.x. p. 75b), but is smitten by a sudden love for him. Don Álvaro awakes, and, as if in a dream, begins to court María. His dream ends, as we have seen, with his reconciliation with Beatriz.

The fact that some of the crucial scenes in the play are thus framed-in appears significant. They can be said to represent one view of life (idealistic and literary) which contrasts with the view of life present in the framing-scenes (a realistic one). The idealistic, literary view, the play argues, when transposed into real life produces irresponsible actions. The resultant chaos is in no way different from that which ensues when man attempts to act out his dreams in real life.[4] Álvaro, in wooing María, is playing a game, acting out a dream. For him, this courtship is a sort of therapeutic psychiatric treatment: María is an instrument, not a person. That he is insensitive to the consequences of his actions is due to his particular way of viewing the members of the lower classes.

For María, however, all this is not a dream.[5] That is why we get glimpses of the grotesque in the midst of the idealisation of the country. María is transformed from a shepherdess into a *mujer varonil* and then into a normal peasant-girl who falls in love with the handsome stranger. At the end, it is the *varonil* aspect of María which is exploited in order to restore harmony and order to a disturbed world.

It is clear now why Álvaro is made to marry María and not Beatriz. It is vital for the thesis of the play. But Beatriz, too, contributes to the ending. Her behaviour in II.xiii is anything but dignified. Under the stress of jealousy and anger (intensified by her recent experiences), she loses her self-control. The duel between her and María is an inversion of the motif of the earlier fight between Otero and Benito. The burlesque of the chivalresque convention is carried a step further: we see two women fighting over a man.[6] What makes the scene more grotesque is the fact that one of them is actually a Marchioness. The idea that love is a leveller of ranks is given a new twist here. The weapons used in this duel are not heroic either: they are a dagger and a sling. (Is this intended to be an echo of David fighting Goliath?)

The burlesque of conventions is continued in the sub-plot, which contains the parallel love-affair between Caldeira and Dominga. In the true tradition of the *gracioso*, Caldeira satirises Álvaro's behaviour by imitation and amplification. The love of Caldeira and Dominga for each other also provides a cynical comment on the tradition of pastoral love.

In II.i, Dominga proposes a sound, business-like attitude as the basis for their marriage:

> [DOMINGA:] . . . cinco ducados gano.
> Siete da a cada vaquero;
> si él os recibe y conoce,
> siete y cinco serán doce.
> Juntaremos el dinero;
> . . . .
> y los diez años pasados,
> podrá envidiarnos, casados,
> el conde de Monterrey.
>
> (II.i. p. 80a–b.)

The basis of this marriage is clearly *interés*. Nor does Caldeira seem unduly worried over Dominga's supposed promiscuity. The financial and social benefits which would accrue from their marriage would be an adequate compensation.

In II.xviii, Caldeira reflects and amplifies Álvaro's treatment of María in his own treatment of Dominga. The cynicism is further amplified later:

> con la mondonga, me avisa
> el sábado mondongar,
> y con Domingo, mudar
> cada domingo camisa.
>
> (III.viii. p. 100a.)

But even here, as in II.xviii, Caldeira still affirms his determination to marry Dominga; in this he shows a shadow of the decency which Álvaro lacks. Here we have satire by contrast and parody. The parallelism between the sub-plot and main plot is systematically maintained, but the point I wish to make is, I think, clear enough.[7]

To sum up, the play can be said to contain a criticism of an irresponsible attitude towards life. Such irresponsibility is associated with and illustrated through certain literary conventions, which are also shown to be false. Literary and social satire, then, are united in this play, as they are in the next.

NOTES

1 This play was first published in Tirso's *Primera Parte* (Seville and Madrid, 1627). Doña Blanca de los Ríos assigns it to 1610 or 1611 in her introduction in *Tirso de Molina. Obras dramáticas completas*, vol. II (2nd ed., Madrid, 1962), pp. 53–64.

2 The play is set in the aftermath of the "Guerra de la Beltraneja." Peace has not been established completely: there are still border skirmishes. An attempt is being made to ensure lasting peace by a marriage between the Portuguese Prince and the Infanta of Castille. This is what the Conde alludes to in III.xxiv., p. 107b.

3 A. K. G. Paterson has drawn attention to the fact that Tirso's characters are often arguing a case (in his Ph.D. thesis, *Tirso de Molina. An Edition of "La venganza de Tamar," with bibliographical, textual and literary criticism*, Cambridge, 1965).

4 Cf. the situations in *Don Quijote* and *La vida es sueño*. In this interpretation of *Don Quijote*, I follow that put forward by A. A. Parker in his article: "El concepto de la verdad en el Quijote," *RFE*, XXXII (1948), 287–305.

5 Hartzenbusch observes that in her lie to the King, "Miente demasiado bien María, porque el espectador la cree" (on p. 227 of his *Examen* of this play: *Teatro escogido de Fray Gabriel Téllez*, vol. IV, Madrid, 1839).

6 This episode is most likely a deliberate reminiscence of the duel between Bradamante and Marfisa in Canto XXXVI of Ariosto's *Orlando Furioso*.

7 The close and systematic parody of the main plot in the sub-plot has been noted by E. Gijón in her book: *El humor en Tirso de Molina* (Madrid, 1959), pp. 128–32.

CHAPTER VIII

Antona García.
The Re-Structuring of Society (II)

Antona García, a "historical" play, first published in Tirso's *Parte cuarta* (1635), is episodic in structure.[1] The story itself deals with incidents in the "Guerra de la Beltraneja." Two factors give a sense of direction to the incidents. The first is that they centre around the capture of Toro. The second, and perhaps more interesting and important, is the progress of the love-affair between Antona and the Conde of Penamacor. Other formal aspects help to ensure structural unity. The most obvious is the insertion of one conflict into a larger one, which in turn is inserted into an even larger one, forming a structural pattern similar to the ones already noted in *Mari-Hernández la gallega*, *Amar por arte mayor*, and *Don Gil*. The Castilian-Portuguese conflict is reflected in the more local conflict between the peasants and nobility of Toro, and this, in turn, is reflected on the individual level, on the one hand, in the conflict between Antona and María, and, on the other, on the much more attenuated initial tension between Antona and Penamacor which finally resolves into an implied union, which echoes the larger reconciliation and forgiveness with which the play ends. Other, smaller factors also contribute towards structural unity. Such are the deliberate and frequent use of parallelisms and contrasts (the behaviour of Antona and that of the Conde; that of Antona and María; the resemblances between Antona and Isabel; and so on), the use of connecting thematic motifs within the body of the play (e.g., Bartolo's grotesque courting of Gila, narrated in I.iii, foreshadows the Conde's flirtation with Antona in I.vi), and the recurrence of the opening motifs at the end: Toro is captured; the Reyes Católicos are on stage with Antona, etc. But what is perhaps the central feature of the play is the presence of three *mujeres varoniles*, the most important of them being, as the title implies, Antona García. It is in the comparison and contrast of these women that the central interest of the play lies.

While, as I shall argue, the presence of Isabel and María in the play serves to draw attention to Antona through her being compared and contrasted with them, the portrayal of Antona herself has been regarded as a problem. I. L. MacClelland, in her sensitive analysis of the dramatic realism of the mob scene in the play, has some interesting remarks to make about the heroine. She draws attention to Antona's femininity, her maternal instinct drawn out by the Ventera, the strength of her personality, the skilful way in which she can handle the mob, and, of course, her masculinity: "the disconcerting fact about Antona," says McClelland, "is that sometimes she has a man's might and a woman's mind, and sometimes a man's might and a man's mind too."[2] This constitutes a dramatic weakness, according to McClelland: ". . . the dramatist . . . failed in this instance to portray Antona compositely" (p. 70). The specific weakness in portrayal are pointed out: ". . . instead of showing combined, or even convincingly at variance, in her peasant nature the masculine qualities of leadership and a feminine intuitiveness—or possibly a strong maternal instinct—she is disintegrated; and not all the dramatist's amendments nor all the spectator's goodwill can put her tidily together" (p. 70). McClelland suggests that the imperfection may be attributed to Tirso's carelesness, and that there is no unified picture of the heroine as a result, she has to be seen in bits and pieces: ". . . Tirso never stopped to imagine her as a whole and therefore never supplied all the clues to her hypothetical completeness. She is best appreciated in part—that is, in each of her characteristics separately; and, had she existed for the 'mob' scene alone, she would still have been among the most promising of Tirso's creations" (p. 73). As will be realised, this is a serious criticism of Tirso's dramatic technique. It cannot be denied that there are contradictory and conflicting sides to Antona's character. But these, perhaps, do not necessarily need to be attributed to a faulty dramatic technique.

Margaret Wilson offers a different interpretation of Antona's character. Antona is "*desmesurada*, larger than life . . . She is alive, just as Don Juan is alive; but in both cases it is the exaggerated, quintessential life of the artistic creation, rather than a convincing verisimilitude. It is easier to believe in Laurencia (of *Fuenteovejuna*) as a real woman, but Antona is a more compelling work of art" (p. xxi). As is evident, Wilson concentrates on the artistry of the portrayal and the exaggeration which is an inherent part of it. These are, I think, important factors in any just assessment of Antona.

The element of artistic exaggeration which Wilson points to, is stressed even more strongly by A. Soons.[3] He sees Tirso as a mannerist dramatist:

"By a process familiar from our knowledge of the plastic arts of the triumphant period of *manierismo* he has allowed his emulation of previous works to stop at an ingenious 'disposition of materials'; Lope's skilful 'invention' of a theme is ignored. In *Antona García* Tirso has recurred to what has been assented to by the spectators of his age, and dramatic means have become confused with ends." As a result of this approach, Soons argues, Tirso seems to create a drama which one may describe as parasitic: "This adherence to proven practice rather than to what his predecessors have venerated allows the dramatist to create plays out of his own and others' 'stock.'" But, adds Soons, "He also needs to convey his impression of life poetically, if only to reject other authors' efforts as absurd—or even to reject as absurd human efforts in general—and for this reason Tirso floods his play with unserious and parodistic features. His own series of 'strong' women-characters are travestied in *Antona García*; peasants are stage-peasants; a Portuguese will have to be a stage Portuguese; a stirring fable of heroism, once the source of local patriotic pride, will be converted into burlesque by a succession of facetious situations. Tirso is apparently repudiating previous drama on serious subjects. . . ." Soons, I think, is right in calling attention to the absurdity of some aspects of the play and the burlesque nature of the characters, but, for reasons which I shall make clear, I think that he perhaps overstates his case, especially in the conclusions he draws. I am not sure that I properly grasp the point Soons is making, but insofar as his argument implies that Tirso is more questioning than Lope, it is a suggestive one.[4]

What I shall try to do in this analysis is bring together and develop points which have been made by these critics. I shall suggest that the apparent inconsistency in Antona's portrayal, noted by McClelland, is deliberate, part of the "desmesurada" Antona who is a creation of Tirso's artistic vision. The exaggeration, however, is part idealisation (as Magaret Wilson implies) and part burlesque (as Soons suggests). Again, as Soons seems to imply (if I understand him correctly), this technique can be related to Tirso's questioning attitude. But I should also suggest (and here my view differs somewhat from Soons') that this attitude is not wholly negative. It is not, it seems to me, primarily in the "conflict of legalities" (to use Soons' phrase) that Tirso is interested in this play. He is interested in Antona. And the appeal is not to legality, justice, or philosophy, but to morality (and, therefore, religion). In other words, I shall argue that Antona's grotesque portrayal is an aspect of the literary satire of the play, and that this is linked to a social thesis which is, at bottom, the same as is present in *Mari-Hernández la gallega* and, in general, in the plays examined in the second half of this book.

The exaltation of Antona is central to the play. It is about her, above all else. There are two basic reasons for this. The first is historical and extra-literary. The play is probably connected with the lawsuit conducted by Antona García's descendants, as R. L. Kennedy has pointed out. It was therefore of topical interest. But the exaltation of a worthy peasant is a theme dear to Tirso's heart, as we have seen, although it appears frequently enough in other authors. Thus, as in the case of Sixtus V, history provides poetry with its material. This is certainly the second reason for the writing of this play.

Comparison and contrast, i.e., the exploitation of the harmonic structure, are the fundamental technical features in Tirso's portrayal of Antona. Parallelisms are established between Antona, on the one hand, and Isabel and María on the other. Secondly, there are parallelisms between the actions of Antona and those of the Conde de Penamacor. These are especially important in view of the implications of the love-intrigue.

First, I shall discuss the three *mujeres varoniles* who form the central core of the play. Isabel and María are connected directly with the basic, historical story of the play, while Penamacor, whom I shall discuss subsequently, is more important for the love-intrigue, and, consequently, although a Portuguese nobleman, is not wholly identified with the side represented by María. Antona is compared and contrasted with the two women, and the portrait which thus emerges is all the more striking. The fact that three *mujeres varoniles* are presented (María indirectly) right at the beginning of this play is itself grotesque. It is an embarrassment of riches, and it is significant.

The grotesque is often a sign of the satirical, and grotesque details are evident in *Antona García*. An excellent instance is the method, invented by the eighth Castilian, of dying eyes black (III.iii), which is a *reductio ad absurdum* of a well-established joke, and a satirical comment on the fashion of the day, which would even defy nature. There is an obvious connexion between this joke and one of the central problems in the play, which hinges on the urge to social conformity. If we examine the portrayal of Antona García, too, we can easily see that she is a grotesque creature. One way in which Tirso hints at this is by contrasting Antona with an authentic *mujer varonil*, Isabel. In Antona, we get, to a certain extent, a disfiguration of Isabel.

The Queen may be regarded as the authentic warlike woman. That she is in military garb is made clear from Antona's words: "tan apuesta y guerreadora" (I.ii. p. 411a). By appearing at the very opening of the play, she fixes herself in our minds as the standard by which Antona and María may be measured. Her harangue to the troops opens the play and reveals her as warlike, imperious, and not lacking in valour. As Margaret Wilson says, she shows a "spirited resistance even when the outlook is black" (p. xvii). It is not her femininity with which we are primarily impressed: the Almirante refers to "esa virtud atractiva" (I.i. p. 409b) with an awesome admiration. Her military ambitions make her in a way the rival of Fernando, her husband. We see her half hoping that Fernando will delay long enough to enable her to have the glory of taking Zamora, as Margaret Wilson points out: "y si se tarda, gozaré la gloria / yo sola desta hazaña" (II.iv. p. 427b). In the same scene, she reveals that she even aspires to the Portuguese crown (p. 427a). It is no surprise that the Almirante's admiration finds expression in the words: "¡Valor de la Semíramis de España!" (II.iv. p. 427b).

But her ardour for war is not all: she is a well-balanced character:

> Lícito es en los trabajos
> buscar honestos alivios,
> que un pecho real es tan ancho
> que pueden caber en él
> aprietos y desenfados.
> Gocemos la villanesca.
>
> (I.i. p. 410a.)

She is a gracious Queen, and her conduct towards her followers and her subjects reveals this. She is also generous to her defeated enemies, and issues a general pardon at the end. But the most human side of her character is revealed in her affection for Antona.

Isabel is, too, an embodiment of decorum. She advises Antona to renounce her warlike nature:

> No hagáis de hazañas alarde
> porque el mismo inconveniente
> hallo en la mujer valiente
> que en el marido cobarde.
>
> (I.ii. p. 412a.)

This is the decorum of the sexes. A woman should be womanly, and be subordinate to man (and here we can guess how hard Isabel must strive to subordinate herself to Fernando):

> No os preciéis de pelear,
> que el honor de la mujer

> consiste en obedecer,
> como en el hombre el mandar,
> y vedme cuando entre en Toro.
>
> (I.ii. p. 412b.)

And not even Isabel is spared Tirso's irony, as the last line reveals. This irony is underlined: Isabel condemns María in her opening speech:

> Doña María Sarmiento,
> su mujer, vituperando
> su misma naturaleza,
> en el acero templado
> trueca galas mujeriles;
> plaza de armas es su estrado,
> sus visitas, centinelas,
> y sus doncellas, soldados.
>
> (I.i. p. 408b.)

But Isabel is conscious of what is proper, and in the antepenultimate scene of the play (III.ix), she constrains herself to follow Fernando's lead, suppressing her own desire to punish the rebels.

Finally, it is important to note the parallel that Tirso establishes between Isabel and Antona. Margaret Wilson has referred to this: "Isabel advises Antona at her wedding to settle down and become a submissive housewife; but she does not practise what she preaches, and nor can Antona resign herself to domesticity." Both Isabel and Antona are described as "Semíramis." "This reflection of the Queen in the local heroine," says Margaret Wilson, "is obviously meant as a measure of the latter's importance" (p. xviii).

The relationship between the two women is reinforced. Antona and Isabel are both beautiful and warlike. Margaret Wilson notes that Antona "describes the Queen's beauty unashamedly to her face in such rustic terms of comparison as parsley, wheat, milk, onions and garlic" (p. xv). This point can be taken further. Just as the Queen is described in rustic terms, Antona is praised by the villagers thus: "Más valeis vos, Antona, / que la corte toda" (I.ii. p. 410b). And the parallelism is carried to details. Antona is praised in more or less *culto* terms:

> OTRO: Sois ojiesmeralda,
>   sois carirredonda,
>   y, en fin, sois de cuerpo
>   la más gentilhombra.
>   No hay quien vos semeje,

> reinas ni señoras,
> porque sois más linda.
>
> (I.ii. pp. 410b–411a.)

But in Antona's praise of Isabel, the latter, also, we learn, has green eyes—"vuesos dos ojos parecen / dos matas de perejil" (I.ii. p. 411a)—and she, too, is "cariharta." That this parallel is deliberate and symbolic is perhaps suggested by the fact that the Conde refers to Antona's "dulces ojos morenos"—which we may safely regard as a more accurate and factual description. It is obvious, then, that we are invited to compare and contrast Antona and Isabel. The importance of this will become obvious when I discuss the social thesis of the play. On a purely literary level, it will be clear that the grotesque aspect of the heroine's portrayal is stressed in this way.

Doña María Sarmiento, "vituperando / su misma naturaleza," constitutes our second *mujer varonil*. In Margaret Wilson's words, she is the "hard, vicious villainess he [Tirso] needs as a worthy antagonist for Antona" (p. xvii). Bartolo's judgment only confirms this:

> un dimuño de moger
> llamada Doña María
> Sarmiento, de una ventana
> medio tabique arrojó
> con que en la cholla la dio
> ¡hazaña, pardiez, villana!
>
> (II.v. p. 428b.)

It will be noted that, just as Antona is referred to in courtly terms and compared with the Queen, María is here likened to a "villana"—her action was a base one. She was the only one to have recourse to the most primitive of weapons, a stone, or, rather, a rock (which was more in keeping with her Titanic character—even the peasants used agricultural implements: "¿No hay palas, bieldos, / trancas, arados?" asks Antona, [II.iii. p. 425a])—, and her attack was a treacherous one. This is significant, for María, of all the characters, is the most contemptuous of the peasants: her speech in II.ii expresses her scorn for the lower classes, whom she regards as inferior in every respect and whom she is prepared to bring to heel by the use of force if necessary, if bribes cannot tempt them. She berates the Conde for loving Antona:

> Eclipsa su sangre clara
> quien como vos se enamora
> de una rústica villana.

(II.ix. p. 432b.)

I shall discuss this point again later, but it is clear that María is an interesting study in her own right, since she serves as a contrast to two other variants of the *mujer varonil* type. She, unlike Isabel, is a one-sided character, driven, as Isabel puts it, by "la pasión y el interés" (I.i. p. 408b), and this is more a pathological than an artistic defect.

María is more of a demagogue than her husband. Her speech, though insulting to the peasants, almost cows them into surrender. Arguments, proofs, abuse follow in torrential flow; a bribe is bolstered with a sinister threat of force. But her judgment is prejudiced: in fact, her speech and her actions verge on the hysterical. She acts on prejudice: the *villanos* are inferior because they are *villanos*; the nobles are superior, therefore the nobles are right; in addition, the *letrados* support the nobles. Therefore, when she comes up against Antona, her fury does not allow her to think clearly, for Antona's arguments are as subtle as any *letrado* can produce. María is moved by envy to the verge of madness: "mi envidia vos tiene loca," says Antona to her, and this is revealed in her relentless pursuit of the wounded peasant woman. She is obsessed by one thought—the need to kill Antona, who is an obstacle in her way, and, after her treacherous attack, urges the soldiers to finish her off: "Acabalda de matar" (II.iii. p. 426a). Face to face with Antona at the end of Act II, María panics: all she can do is shout for help and flee when the Conde opposes Antona, although only a moment before she was urging him to kill the peasant woman.

So the last we see of María is a clean pair of heels—most unbecoming in a *mujer heroica-guerrera*. Her influence does not end here, however, since Antona's desire to be revenged on her is a further and delightful motive behind Antona's actions; the latter's hatred of María reveals a very feminine aspect of her character. To see a feud existing between two Amazons is not unamusing.

To sum up, María is an anti-*mujer varonil*. As a psychological study, she borders on the pathological: she is ruled by prejudice, hate and envy; her obsession with the need for Antona's death—prophetic, as she herself declares—reveals her unsettled mental state. Her hysterical outpourings can cow a mob, even though Antona can sway and lead them better. For María is, in short, a deformed character: her lack of virtues and feelings makes her almost inhuman.

Antona, our third *mujer varonil*, is a "prodigio." She is not deformed in the way María is: she is not dominated by one obsession. She is a more fully drawn character than Isabel. Margaret Wilson has accurately described her as "desmesurada." On the other hand, she does not conform to the ideal type of the *mujer heroica-guerrera*, notwithstanding the parallel established between her and Isabel: "la sarta que al cuello llevo / nos encadena a los dos" (I.ii. p. 412b). She is very much larger than life, but is also exaggerated to the point of caricature.

The first thing we notice is a tension between Antona as a woman and Antona as a *mujer varonil*. She is an extremely beautiful woman with a woman's feelings and sensitivities. I. L. McClelland, though unhappy over what she regards as Tirso's artistic inconsistency, rightly sees at the bottom of Antona's portrayal "an idealistic peasant woman with a dominating personality, strong as a man, sometimes both mentally and physically so; a woman with insight and something of a sense of humour" (p. 69). This is quite accurate. The Conde is witness to her strength and beauty. Her sense of humour is evident when she offers to make Penamacor "Conde del rastrillo" (I.vi. p. 418b). Her woman's feelings are revealed when the *Ventera* gets her to confess her love for her daughter. At other times, too, we catch glimpses of a sensitive nature. Margaret Wilson has observed how Antona's sorrow for her dead husband expresses itself as a sudden outburst of hatred for the Conde. The fact that she immediately turns her mind to thoughts of vengeance does not prevent her from expressing in surprisingly restrained and effective language the nature of the relationship between her dead husband and herself: "De que era, en fin, dueño mío, / no le imagino llorar" (II.vii. p. 431a).

But Antona is of a practical nature, and she is, says Pero Alonso, a "mujer de digo y hago" (III.viii. p. 448b). She is not devoid of feelings, although her practical nature leads her to suppress them, or rather channel their energies into action:

> lágrimas trueque el pesar
> en venganzas, que yo fío
> que mi mudo sentimiento
> por su muerte, ha de encender
> a Toro, aunque soy mujer.
>
> (II.vii. p. 431a.)

This is one aspect of her *varonil* character. She explains to the Count that she is "a la guerra inclinada" (I.vi. p. 417a). She therefore consciously and deliberately plays a part for which she is fitted by nature; but because this aspect of her nature conflicts with the truly feminine one (and this dual aspect is surely characteristic of any well-developed human being), she exaggerates the masculine aspect of her nature, of which she is too conscious. Therefore, while she parallels the prototype of the *mujer heroico-guerrera*, Isabel, she at the same time tries to out-Semiramis Semiramis. Thus, when Tirso, as I. L. McClelland says, "obstinately recalls her at every turn to a strong-man exhibition" (p. 69), he is not guilty of an inconsistency, but rather faithfully represents the inner tension of an exceptional character.

The integrity of Antona's character is evident. She is not to be suborned. In her counter-speech to the mob, she combats María's arguments, subtly countering each reason with a counter-reason—even though she insists she is no more than an ordinary peasant woman. The three speeches of Isabel, María and Antona help to bring out the resemblances and differences of the three women.

Her sense of decorum equals her Queen's. She realises her duties as a married woman: "que yo hago lo que debo" (I.iv. p. 414b). She recognises the need for social decorum: "que como al reye la lanza / honra a la mujer el huso" (I.iv. p. 414b). And she reminds the Conde of the social difference between them. She observes the rules of marital decorum: she rejects the advances of the Count and forbids amorous conversation; she will not enter into any irregular liaison:

> Porque pretender de mí
> lo que el bien querer procura,
> si no es por mano del cura,
> es, ya lo veis, frenesí.
>
> (II.vii. p. 431a.)

Her self-control reflects Isabel's, although only up to a point: she regrets the death of her comrades, but ". . . aunque en el alma los lloro, / los disimulo en la cara" (III.i. p. 434a). She makes an effort to restrain herself when the Portuguese chaff her in the inn. But the parallel with Isabel inevitably breaks down, as it must if Antona is to be other than a mere reproduction of Isabel. She must go beyond the conventional ideal type—and thus enter the realm of the grotesque.

David Worcester, discussing grotesque satire, observes that often the grotesque enters into character-drawing of the most delicate order. The tendency of burlesque satire is to particularize, and the detail chosen is unusual and eccentric. Worcester refers to its "pursuit of the odd, macabre and eccentric," in which it is fantastic rather than realistic. It is satire by description. "A clash of ideas is implicit in the process of creating a scale of values at variance with the common standards of mankind."[5]

This is surely the point behind Tirso's unusual portrayal of Antona. She is a burlesque *mujer varonil*, and the details Tirso chooses to exaggerate reveal this. In the portrayal of Antona we note the consistent use of exaggeration and violent contrast. Antona differs from the traditional line of *mujeres heroico-guerreras* in being a peasant woman rather than a queen or noblewoman. The anecdotes which introduce her indirectly strike a grotesque note. She is not only strong but incredibly so: "[ANTONIO:] Tira a la barra y al canto / con el labrador más diestro." (I.i. p. 410a.) She is, in fact, something of a champion athlete. She apparently does not always agree with the law, as she shows when she rescues her cousin from its clutches:

[ANTONIO]:   cogió al jumento y al hombre,
       y llevándolo en los brazos,
       como si de paja fueran,
       los metió en la iglesia a entrambos.

           (I.i. p. 410b.)

She does not hesitate to shut up troublesome soldiers in the *corral*.

Yet, when we first meet her, she enters as a bride, and later on carries on what almost amounts to a mild flirtation with the Conde. But we are not allowed to forget the *mujer varonil*. Her conversation is punctuated with a violent war-cry: "Reine Isabel" and ends with her crushing the Conde's hand. The behaviour is, to say the least, highly eccentric, more so in a woman occupied with domestic tasks. These she executes with a characteristic *brío* and seems to enjoy her position as a housewife. Far from trying to escape her femininity, she marries, becomes a widow, and, before promising to marry for the second time, she has twins almost on the stage—in an almost heroic manner; not quite, however, for she finds her labour pains hard to bear, and realises that she is, after all, only a woman in some respects. Nevertheless, in the famous scene at the inn, where we see her tired and hungry—human, to say the least, and a woman (now a *viuda varonil*)—and witness her discomfort, she continues her strong-man act. She beats up four Portuguese with a bench, though having confessed to being tired and hungry; announces *a secas* to the Ventera: "Sabed que preñada estó" (III.iv. p. 441b)—and few things can be more grotesque in a *mujer varonil*, especially under the circumstances; is delivered of a child, delivers the Conde from his captors, forcibly ejecting them from the inn; reluctantly tears herself away from the Conde's interesting account of the war in order to be delivered of another child, and straightway returns to hear the rest of the story, only to see that she must sling her twins over her shoulders and set off. The *mujer varonil* is obviously reduced to absurdity. This grotesque alternation is constant throughout the play. Antona turns from a fervent admiration of the Queen to an enthusiastic application to her household duties, from which she hurls herself into battle for the Queen (II.v. p. 428b). For this is the one duty which overrides all other considerations.

The above remarks make it plain that Antona is an obvious caricature of the *mujer heroico-guerrera*, ideally represented in the play by Isabel. In the first place, we note that Isabel and Antona are both opposed to María. The Queen and Antona are on the same side politically, and, being of similar natures, feel a mutual admiration and friendship. María, by her base actions, shows up the nobility of the peasant woman and also emphasises the true nobility of the Queen. The parallelism between the Queen's opening speech and María's in II.ii emphasises the contrast between them. María is thus an important character foil to these two and drives them closer together.

But this very affinity, carefully eked out by stylistic parallels, leads us to compare and contrast Isabel and Antona. It will be noticed that the aspects of Antona's character which are grossly exaggerated are precisely those which are not consonant with our idea of a *mujer varonil*. This tends to emphasise the grotesque aspect of her portrayal. Antona is subject to love from the very beginning. Unlike Isabel, she is a housewife full of zest. She lacks Isabel's absolute self-control. She is impetuous. She agrees to submit to her husband's authority, but will fight for Isabel if the need arises.

On the other hand, her warlike nature makes continual irruptions into her emotional life: she speaks of war to the Conde when he would court her; beats up the Portuguese and frees the Count during her confinement; and her woman's hatred for María is one of the reasons for her eagerness to lead the surprise attack on Toro. Antona's is a grotesque portrayal: she is a woman who wants to be both man and woman. Tirso is obviously stretching this figure as far as it can go: a basic and realistic psychological tension is exaggerated out of all proportion, for he is satirising a literary type.

This, of course, can be linked with the definitive appearance of a realistic literary trend at the beginning of the seventeenth century.[6] The female warrior was essentially a creation of idealistic literature. While the existence of the *mujer varonil* in real life is not to be doubted, she is the exception rather than the rule. If Antona is ridiculed in this play, one reason for it is that she is trying to act like an essentially literary type.

The tensions between her artificial *persona* as a *mujer varonil* and her "real" feminine nature produces a grotesque character. In this rejection of a "literary" approach to life, *Antona García* and *Mari-Hernández* possess a factor in common.

If, in the figure of Antona García, Tirso has compared a literary convention with reality and found it absurd, on the social level he compares an aspect of seventeenth-century reality with an ideal and finds it equally absurd. Antona García is an absurd character because she is unnatural; a petrified social structure is absurd because it, too, is unnatural. And María is the representative of such a structure.

I have already drawn attention to the parallel established between Antona and Isabel—a parallel in character, supported by parallels in imagery and situations. Tirso's intention is obviously to point out the affinity between these two characters. In opposition to them stands María, who is presented, morally, as the real *villana*. Antona, the peasant woman, acts nobly. María's real dramatic function (apart from being a political and personal enemy to Antona and, consequently, one of the motivating elements of the action) is to serve as a character foil to Antona. But these two details are only part of a larger pattern. María represents the attitude of the nobles who are hostile to Isabel and Fernando and who support the Portuguese. Her attitude towards the Castilian lower classes is one of contempt and this is why she is the enemy of Antona and berates the Conde for loving her.

The love-affair between Antona and Penamacor, a conventional element of the *comedia*, is a integral part of the theme. The love turns from a mild flirtation in I.vi to a promise of marriage in III.viii. The unusual nature of this proposed marriage is evident, as Margaret Wilson observes: ". . . great emphasis is laid on Antona's social status" (p. xv); she "repeatedly tells the Count she can never marry him because of the difference in rank between them" (p. xv). "Yet," continues Margaret Wilson, "at the end this barrier is disregarded and there is a hint of possible union between the peasant woman and the noble. Here too we have a typically Tirsian trait, a 'desenlace' which unites 'cayados con cetros,' 'seda con sayal'" (p. xv). Margaret Wilson goes on to comment: "His relative indifference to social distinctions clearly divides Tirso from his master Lope de Vega, who always retained a strictly hierarchical view of society. . . . Tirso's nobles are often genuinely in love with women of lower rank and end by making them their wives. This is virtually the case in *Antona García*; to be sure, Antona jokingly imposes an impossible condition to her acceptance of the Count, and Tirso thus cleverly safeguards historical truth, for of course, no such marriage ever took place; but to all intents and purposes the play may be said to lead up to it, and thus the class struggle is resolved" (pp. xv–xvi).

In fact, right through the play there is a stress on social decorum. Isabel advises Antona to subordinate herself to her husband in I.ii and Antona comments: "Mande y rija mi marido, / pues Dios su yugo me ha puesto" (I.ii. p. 412b). Isabel herself does the same: "El rey, mi señor, podrá / hacer lo que sea servido" (III.ix. p. 449b). She thus forgoes her desire for vengeance. Antona stresses in I.iv, when she sends Bartolo off to guard the flock, that social duties must be conscientiously fulfilled. Ulloa's speech to the peasants affirms that the duty and function of the nobles are to guide the lower classes. Let them submit to their rulers:

> Hombres buenos, reducíos;
> y lo que no os pertenece
> dejad a quien tiene el cargo.
>
> (II.i. p. 423a.)

Antona repeatedly points out to the Conde that social barriers are an obstacle to their marriage:

> la seda junto al sayal,
> fuerza es que parezca mal,
> porque ni pega, ni cuaja.
>
> (II.vii. p. 431a.)

Now, the theoretical arguments advanced are fundamentally right, because they ensure the smooth working of society. But there are other arguments put forward in the play which, though they may seem to develop logically from the above, are really instruments of social injustice and oppression. In I.vii, Don Basco gives his opinion of the *villanos*: "pero pecheros *villanos* / de poca importancia son" (I.vii. p. 422a). Their only use is to pay taxes; their opinion regarding government is not wanted. María's speech in II.ii is full of abuse for the peasants. They are "bárbaros," blind and unlettered; she believes that they can be suborned or, if they prove recalcitrant, intimidated. Again, the Conde's love for Antona is, from María's point of view, degrading. The two points that emerge from all this are, first, the assumption of the innate inferiority of the *villanos* because of their social status, and, secondly, the insistence on keeping the different social classes rigidly separate (to ensure, of course, that the economic burden of the country should fall on the *villanos*, and that the nobility maintain their privileged position.)

Against this unjust attitude stands Antona. As a representative of the people she is set on par with the nobility: "Más valéis vos, Antona, / que la corte toda." She is in no way an inferior person, but treated as a friend by the Queen. Her speech is a vigorous defence and even an exaltation of the *villanos*. She opposes her rustic, honest common-sense, clear and unprejudiced, to the "arguciones" of suborned "*letrados*." She sees facts and is not interested in legalistic niceties; she prefers certainty ("una hermana con certeza") to doubt ("una hija . . . en duda") (II.iii. p. 424b.). Moreover, "voz del puebro es voz de Dios" (p. 424b), and no judge can argue against that. It is therefore no surprise that the definitive triumph of the Reyes Católicos is associated with a popular movement, or that María, D. Basco and the Portuguese are eventually defeated.

The point Tirso is making is clear enough. If the existing social conventions produce a state of affairs in which the socially noble are morally unworthy, then those conventions must be modified so that society can be re-structured. This re-structuring of society is what is implied in the love and courtship of Antona and the Conde.

The progress of their courtship is parallel with the various stages in the taking of Toro. There are various obstacles in the way of their love. At the beginning of the play Antona is presented as being near the top of her class. She is rich, and of unadulterated blood, proud of her status. Her marriage to Juan brings her fulfilment, and thus we can see her as the perfect, contented housewife in I.vi. But she is worthy of a higher status. This is symbolised by Penamacor, and she must show herself worthy of being his wife. There are two main aspects concerning her rise, and it will be helpful to discuss them separately.

Antona rises above her social status by surpassing herself. She models herself on Isabel, and being exceptional herself, easily proves her moral superiority to María. (That Antona is never really allowed to demonstrate her physical superiority over María, although this is clearly suggested, while María's treacherous act causes Antona severe physical injury may be significant: it is morality, nobility of soul Tirso is interested in, not brute force.) At the same time, she is the natural leader of the peasants (i.e., she is at the top of her social class), and fights on behalf of the Reyes Católicos. By this action she at once goes beyond her social as well as sexual sphere of action, i.e., she acts as a member of the noble or fighting class, and as a man. As she proves her worth, the obstacles to her union with Penamacor are removed. Thus Monroy's death can be seen as symbolical. Having fulfilled the duties of her class and exceeded them, Antona can now rise. She, like Penamacor, (but for different reasons) can be regarded as an exception to her class.

The Conde, we must remember, is himself an important character in the play and much more than the conventional, love-sick Portuguese Soons sees. Since he is a Portuguese, he is Antona's political enemy. But he is also truly noble; his actions are worthy of his status; he is just—impartially so, for he saves Antona from María and María from Antona; he has a strong sense of duty and his political loyalty is firm; he is compassionate. In short, he is the true nobleman, as opposed to the María Sarmiento type. He sees in Antona qualities which fit her to be his wife, and, instead of choosing a wife of the María type, he subordinates political and social differences to love.

The extent to which Antona has risen is underlined by the parallelism of the scenes in which she and Penamacor appear. At first (I.vi), their basic equality as human beings is evident. Antona is a match for Penamacor: she can discourse on war, keep Penamacor under control. But the social inequality is still there. This is also stressed when in II.iii Penamacor protects her and saves her from the vindictive hatred of María and the Portuguese soldiers. Penamacor's nobility of soul is evident. But Antona cannot long be his captive: she breaks loose. In her assent upwards, it is emphasied that her masculinity is not a negation of her femininity (hence the birth-scene). In the midst of her labour, literally and symbolically, she rescues Penamacor from his Castilian captors, the parallel with the earlier scene being reinforced verbally:

ANTONA:	¿Acordáisos cuando herida
	me defendisteis en Toro
	de aquella Doña María
	y de todos sus parientes?
PENAMACOR:	Pendiendo de vos mi vida
	no hice mucho, si era fuerza
	morir yo sin vos.
ANTONA:	No olvidan
	deudas de tanta importancia
	las que son agradecidas.
	Soldados, o lo que son,
	vuélvanse a Zamora y digan
	al Don Álvaro que lleva
	al Conde Antona García,
	que ella dará cuenta de él.

(III.vi. p. 444b.)

Antona stresses that she is repaying a debt to the Count (which implies their social equality):

ANTONA: Si los avisan
                    que es Antona quien lo manda,
                    y que así se desobriga
                    de otro tanto que hizo el conde
                    por ella y que queda viva
                    y a su servicio como antes,
                    daráles buenas albricias.

                                    (III.vi. p. 445a.)

It is at this point that Penamacor repeats his offer of marriage which, as Margaret Wilson says, is accepted by Antona, but with an impossible condition attached to her acceptance:

PENAMACOR: En fin, ¿prometéis ser mía?
ANTONA: Sí, con una condicion.
PENAMACOR: ¿Y es?
ANTONA: ¿Juráis vos de cumplirla?
PENAMACOR: Claro está.
ANTONA: Que vos paráis
                    los hijos y yo las hijas.

                                    (III.viii. p. 449b.)

Antona is thus, at the end, raised up to be the Conde's wife and so her elevation to the top of Toro's battlements is clearly symbolical. For when the hereditary nobility have become degenerate, the only true regeneration can be effected by introducing fresh, healthy blood from the lower classes where it runs red but true. Considered within this context, Antona's parting joke to the Count opens to reveal a sublimely beautiful symbolism for all its outward grotesqueness: "Que vos paráis / los hijos y yo las hijas." This, surely, is the theme of the play. That is why I am inclined to offer a different interpretation to Soons'; for if this process (by which the civilised elements receive and sublimate the tremendous powers of nature, which though noble are uncontrolled—hence the dichotomy of Antona's character) is not archetypal, one would be at a loss to say what is.

The second point concerning the elevation of Antona is the grotesque nature of her portrayal. I have already suggested above one reason for the dichotomy in her character. But there are others, which become clearer if we consider the conventions of the literary context in which Golden Age plays were written.

In the play, two peasants, Antona and Bartolo, rise socially. Both are treated grotesquely in the course of the play, but both are "redeemed" at the end. Now, if we hark back to the three women in the play, we shall see that their simultaneous presence is one of its key features. They represent three different social classes and are treated in three different ways. Isabel, despite the ironical touches we notice, is treated nobly. María is condemned, but we feel sorry for her: the essence of her plight is that her values are the wrong ones: she is concerned only with the accidents of her social status, and consequently, of life. Antona is ultimately to marry a Count, and she gains the glory of the capture of Toro (whereas Isabel had to be content with entering Zamora with Fernando) and she wins our hearts, for she is *simpática* and her character is truly noble. But, like Bartolo, she is treated grotesquely.

Here we have, of course, the threefold division of styles—high, mixed, and low—in Isabel, María, and Antona.[7] This, as Auerbach has made clear, was a stylistic convention based on literary and, ultimately, social prejudices. From this point of view, Antona is treated grotesquely because, first, she is a member of the lower classes; secondly, she is "wrong" in being a *mujer varonil* (Isabel—not even María—can be *varonil*, for she is Queen and ruler, and that only when Fernando is absent) and thus "wrong" in usurping the social functions of men: she fights, leads the villagers, carries the standard; and thirdly, she is "wrong" in usurping the political duties of the upper classes, the nobility.

But, at times, two wrongs can make a right. The real nobility have forgotten their social functions and duties: this is what María's attitude signifies. They are, in fact, degenerate. The "mixed" style is a debasement here, for it looks downwards instead of upwards.

To whom, then, is one to turn to effect a regeneration of the nobility but the peasantry? Antona symbolises all that is noble in human nature: she saves the Conde, for example, from his Castilian captors as he had saved her from her Portuguese enemies. Her nobility shines out through all the grotesque trappings.

Tirso points to Antona's redemption from her grotesqueness by her coming marriage to Penamacor, and this welds together the literary and social aspects of the play, strengthening its organic unity. The final vision we have of Penamacor and Antona walking hand in hand into marriage, this symbolic union of the highest and lowest rungs of society, reveals, in one brilliant flash, Tirso the idealist behind Tirso the satirist. Thus the fact that the play is unfinished can be considered a positive virtue, since we are left with the feeling that the achievement is within grasp. (But do we, at the same time, see the pessimistic scepticism of the practical idealist? Despite the optimistic ending of the play, we know that historically the ending was otherwise.) Yet, it is this vision of Tirso's which enables us to see a bit more clearly Tirso the man: the vision of the nobility producing worthy sons of the country (and, on this symbolic level, there is no absurdity in Antona's condition to the Count) who will turn to the daughters of the earth and, by lifting them up and not despising them, will themselves be renewed and reinvigorated, supported and enriched in a full and active social harmony.

NOTES

1 Ruth L. Kennedy has argued that the play was written or revised in February or early March, 1623, in her article: "On the Date of Five Plays by Tirso de Molina," *HR*, X (1942), 183–214. Margaret Wilson, on p. ix of the introduction to her ed. of the play (Manchester Univ. Press, 1957), suggests that revision may have taken place as late as 1625. Doña Blanca de los Ríos assigns the play to the year 1622, seeing in it reflections of Tirso's quarrel with Lope. See her introduction to the play in *Tirso de Molina. Obras dramáticas completas*, III (Madrid, 1958). Doña Blanca did not live to complete the introduction, so her commentary is not as extensive as is usual with her. My quotations, by Act, scene, and line, refer to this ed.

2 *Tirso de Molina: Studies in Dramatic Realism* (Liverpool, 1948), Chap. III, pp. 69–70.

3 "Two Historical *Comedias* and the Question of *Manierismo*," *RF*, LXXIII (1961), 339–346. This article, translated into Spanish, is reprinted in his book *Ficción y comedia en el siglo de oro* (Madrid, 1967).

4 It does not, however, appear to be wholly valid. Consider the implications for the social structure of Lope's *El villano en su rincón* and *El perro del hortelano*.

5 *The Art of Satire* (Cambridge, Mass., 1940), Chapter III, section V: "Grotesque Satire."

6 This has been discussed by A. A. Parker in his book *Literature and the Delinquent* (Edinburgh Univ. Press, 1967).

7 For a discussion of the division of styles, see E. Auerbach's *Mimesis* (New York, Anchor Books, 1957; 1st ed., 1946). See also E. C. Riley, *Cervantes's Theory of the Novel* (Oxford U.P., 1964; 1st published, 1962), and in particular, Chap. IV, section 2: "Style and Decorum."

Conclusion

In my introduction, I stated that critics, with some exceptions, have traditionally argued that the morality of Tirso's comedies is suspect and his technique primitive, if not carelessly incompetent.

In this book, I set out to examine the validity of these judgements by analysing closely a number of his comedies. The hypothesis I simultaneously put forward was this: that if the comedies are seen as satirically conceived, the traditional view must be modified. In my attempt to test this hypothesis, I examined plays in which the satire of social and/or literary conventions plays a crucial role.

This general hypothesis seems to have been confirmed. I have shown that, if we see Tirso's comedy as satiric comedy, our response to it must differ from the traditional one. The two main points established are these: first, that the plays are concerned with exploring moral and social problems; and secondly, that they are by no means technically unsatisfactory.

As regards the morality of Tirso's comedies, I have tried to show that there is a fundamental concern with personal and social relationships and, especially, the attitudes and values on which these are based. For Tirso, the ultimate foundation on which these relationships are to be built is the morality which is grounded in religion.

This means that, within the context of seventeenth-century society in particular, and human life in general, the assertion of moral values as the touchstone of valid and genuine actions and attitudes leads to a challenging of the conventions and assumptions which often in practice govern personal as well as social relationships. Quite often Tirso supports a violation of existing conventions and what may appear at first glance to be a violation of morality in order to affirm deeper, genuine moral values.

This makes it clear that Tirso is not suggesting that the existing social structure should be bodily inverted or destroyed. If people were guided by moral values, Tirso would, we feel, have no quarrel with the traditional social structure. But, in that case, we should also have to grant, the structure would be different, and similar to the one proposed by Tirso. What he advocates is a more radical re-structuring of society on the basis of criteria moral and religious, and not secular and worldly. Within this proposed structure, each individual would be accorded the position he truly deserved. This is probably the basic reason why the figure of the illegitimate son or the *segundón* occurs so often in Tirso's plays: they are individuals who have to prove their worth, since they do not automatically inherit a safe niche in society. By showing how they attain their positions in the social structure, Tirso puts forward his own views on society.

Ultimately, Tirso is advocating a flexible approach to life. That is why he concentrates on the nature of a particular situation and the appropriate response of the individual to it. This, perhaps, is the explanation for his use of extreme or highly ambiguous situations, where the automatic, conventional response proves to be invalid. Thus any petrification in social conventions or in the personal response to life is the butt of his satire.

The implications of this view of Tirso's comedies for the theories of comedy which I have considered in relation to the plays analysed will be evident. I am not convinced that the application of the theory of the comic catharsis to Tirso's plays is wholly valid. There would seem to be a socially subversive element in Tirsian (and Golden Age) comedy mainly because the Christian way of life is socially subversive. The analyses of plays in which Tirso suggests that social barriers are not inviolable seem to imply that Lope's *El perro del hortelano* makes the same point. Tirsian comedy (and therefore Golden Age literature in so far as Tirso's comedy is representative of it) is problematic and, ultimately, serious.

Perhaps the most serious point Tirso's comedy makes concerns the absurdity of life. This pervades Tirso's drama and is the view to which all the merriment leads. This, in a way, is a pessimistic view of life. In this, Tirso's comedy supports Kerr's theory.

But it would be wrong to conclude that Tirso makes his point with puritanical righteousness and severity. Tirso's view of life is more balanced and humane, and takes into account human weakness and needs. It has been argued that satire and comedy are irreconcilable, and that one crucial difference between the two is the entirely subjective viewpoint of the satirist. That, I suggest, is taking too narrow a view of the term "satire."

In so far as Tirso's comedies criticise certain aspects of life and art by ridiculing them, they can be regarded as satirical. But Tirso is not a didactic, moralising playwright, burning with righteous indignation against the crimes and sins of mankind, and with a message for humanity which they must heed if they would not perish. He is, first of all, a superb writer of comedy. His satire can, if we so wish, be seen simply as basic material out of which he builds his comedies. But I think that we can go further than this and see his own view of life reflected in his work. His comedies aim to show how absurd man and his follies can be. Thus, Tirso has a standpoint outside himself. This is seem most clearly in his ironical attitude, which produces an extremely subtle form of comedy.

Tirso's sense of the absurd, reinforced by his ironic attitude towards his creations and his audience, seems to me to be the real distinguishing feature of his comedy. It is this which tempts one to regard his plays as examples of comedy of the absurd, using this term, however, without its modern, existentialist overtones. I shall return to this presently, but first I should like to discuss some more specific aspects of Tirso's comedies.

As regards Tirso's dramatic art, it is clear that a central aspect is the satire of literary conventions, which parallels the satire of the social conventions. Here, again, it is the petrification of dramatic devices into automatic dramatic conventions which is ridiculed. But it is precisely this ridicule which re-invests these conventions with new life.

The conventions Tirso satirises are varied: they include conventional literary and dramatic types and figures, the conventional use of figures and situations, and the burlesque of the causal dramatic structure.

This seems to point to the following conclusion: that Tirso's plays can, on the one hand, be regarded as conscious experiments in dramatic structure. This explains the use of unusual structural forms, which hitherto had been regarded as haphazard, make-shift constructions. Such experimentations means that some brilliant solutions are found, but, also, that some experiments do not progress beyond mere explorations of possibilities.

Tirso's experimentation means that he uses a looser dramatic structure than does Calderón. On the one hand, this looseness is part of the Lopean heritage: Lope has fixed the form of the *comedia*, but the structure is not yet fixed. The theatrical conventions of the time, whereby plays were written with specific companies in mind, also contribute to this looseness in structure. On the other hand Tirso turns this fault into a virtue. The interplay of ideas, characteristic of wit, needs ample room, and the structuring element in Tirso's plays is predominantly wit. It is this which links causally unrelated scenes, incidents and episodes. The harmonic structure, therefore, is of crucial importance in Tirso. It is used, of course, by Calderón, but in conjunction with a causal structure. Tirso's main contribution in the historical evolution of the structure of the *comedia* is the perfecting of the dramatic structure of wit.

Another characteristic of Tirso's comic art is his sense of the absurd. The experimenting, questioning, critical approach noted implies a highly intellectual form of drama. Here it may be convenient to recall Alan

Paterson's observation that Tirso's characters often seem to be arguing a case. The proliferation of miniature debates (conducted according to formal rules and using formal terminology, although in a burlesque manner) is adequate proof of this. Quite often, it has been noted, the point is couched in a humorous, if not absurd, form and is intended to expose an absurdity. A clear feature of the later Tirso is the complex use of irony which points the absurdity of a situation.

The shift from a simple to a more complex use of irony reflects what is a characteristic feature of Tirso's art, namely, his developing technique. By this, I mean his tendency to develop in what appear to be later plays situations which occur in embryonic form in earlier ones, i.e., a kind of *refundición*, though of his own plays, not those of other writers. This developing technique covers not only situations and figures but also structures, themes and styles. This aspect of Tirso's technique, of which his so-called "self-plagiarism" is one manifestation, is of some help in establishing a relationship between various plays of Tirso's, and also a rough chronological order of certain plays. But much more work needs to be done on the way in which Tirso's technique develops before definite conclusions can be drawn.

One aspect of Tirso's art in which this development can be traced is his style. From any point of view, the question of style is a crucial one in the study of Tirso's theatre. Attention has already been drawn to his argumentative style, used constantly in establishing a point.

But there is also the more properly "poetic" use of style: the structural function of images; the use of imagery to embody implicit comments on characters, etc. There is, finally, the development from an early freer style to a more Calderonian style in Tirso's late manner.

This point brings us to Tirso's position in the historical development of the *comedia*. He, of course, always acknowledged his debt to the great master, Lope. The latter, however, did not regard Tirso's successes graciously. This is perhaps indicative of the fact that Lope recognised Tirso's genius and realised that he was no mere second-rate imitator of himself.

This is indeed true. Tirso is already striking out in various new directions. Several of them lead to Calderón. At various places in this book, I have pointed out features of Tirso's art which anticipate Calderón. Some of the problems Tirso examines are later explored by the younger writer—the father-child relationship, the question of authority and obedience, etc. What is particularly interesting, however, is the extent to which Tirso foreshadows various formal and structural aspects of Calderonian drama. There is, above all, the artificiality of Tirso's plays; in tone, the ironical, self-conscious attitude towards conventional dramatic situations; in structure, the systematic use of parallelisms and symmetry; in style, the structural use of imagery (already present to some extent in Lope), and the development of a more artificial, courtly style.

In Tirso, in short, we can discern a movement away from Lope towards Calderón. Tirso's experiments allow Calderón to perfect one of the possible forms into which the structure of the *comedia* could have crystallised. There are other potential forms, however, which are not developed. It is perhaps the rigour of logic, anticipating the more rigid conventions of the latter part of the seventeenth century, which imposes itself on the *comedia* with Calderón. After him, it leads into that petrification against which Tirso constantly fought. Tirso belonged to a freer age: his was a freer mind; his a freer art-form. It is in this freedom, reflected in his flexible, happy approach to life and art (even in their most serious aspects), that the source of his essential originality lies. It was the loss of this freedom for Tirso and, ultimately for Spain, which the Junta de Reformación's decree of 1625 symbolised.

Bibliography

Abrams, F. "Pedro Noriz and Tirso de Molina in the Enchanted Head Episode of the *Quijote*," *RoN*, X (1968), no. 1, 122–8.

_____ . "Tirso de Molina Alias Sancho Panza and a New Cervantine Etymology for Barataria," *RoN*, IX (1967), no. 2, 281–6.

Adams, N. B. "Siglo de Oro Plays in Madrid, 1820–1850," *HR*, IV (1936), 342–57.

Alborg, J. L. *Historia de la literatura española*. 2 vols. (Madrid, 1966–7).

Alemany y Selfa, B. *Vocabulario de las obras de don Luis de Góngora y Argote* (Madrid, 1930).

Allain, M. " 'El burlador burlado': Tirso de Molina's Don Juan," *MLQ*, XXVII (1966), 174–84.

Alonso, D. *Poesía española* (5th ed., Madrid, 1966).

Alonso, D. and Bousoño, C. *Seis calas en la expresión literaria española* (Madrid, 1963).

Alonso, M. *Enciclopedia del idioma*, 3 vols. (Madrid, 1958).

Alpern, H. "Jealousy as a Dramatic Motive in the Spanish *comedia*," *RR*, XIV (1923), 276–85.

Amezúa, A. G. de. "Unas notas sobre la Calderona," in *Estudios hispánicos. Homenaje a Archer M. Huntington* (Wellesley, Mass., 1952), pp. 15–37.

Amorós, A. "Dos libros sobre Tirso de Molina," *CHA*, LXV (1966), no. 194, 362–5.

Anderson, M. J. (ed.). *Classical Drama and its Influence. Essays Presented to H. D. F. Kitto* (London, 1965).

Aníbal, C. E. "Observations on *La Estrella de Sevilla*," *HR*, II (1934), 1–38.

_____ . "Tirso de Molina," *HBalt*, XII (1929), 325–7.

Anonymous. "De la biografía de Zumel, por Tirso de Molina," *Est*, V (1949), 337–40.

_____ . "Notas sobre el convento grande de la Merced de Madrid, donde vivió Fray Gabriel Téllez," *Est*, V (1949), 777–9.

_____ . "Tirso de Molina (nacido en Madrid en 1585 y muerto en Soria en 1648)," *Atenea*, LXXXIX (1948), no. 274, 1–3.

Arco y Garay, R. del. "Más sobre Tirso de Molina y el medio social," *BRAE*, XXXIII (1953), 19–72, 243–93.

_____ . "La sociedad española en Tirso de Molina," *Revista internacional de sociología*, II (1944), no. 8, 175–90; III (1945), no. 10, 459–77, nos. 11–12, 335–59.

Argensola, B. L. de. "Del estilo propio de la sátira," in L. and B. L. de Argensola: *Obras sueltas* (Madrid, 1889).

Aristotle. *On the Art of Poetry* (Translated by I. Bywater with a preface by Gilbert Murray. Oxford, 1962).

Arjona, J. H. "Una nota a *El burlador de Sevilla*," *HR*, XXVIII (1960), 150–1.

Artiles Rodríguez, J. "La partida bautismal de Tirso de Molina," *RABM*, V (1928), 402–11.

Ashcom, B. B. "By the Altitude of a Chopine," in *Homenaje a Rodríguez-Moñino*, I (Madrid, 1966), pp. 17–27.

—————— . "Concerning *la mujer en hábito de hombre* in the *comedia*," *HR*, XXVIII (1960), 43–62.

—————— . "The First Builder of Boats in *El burlador*," *HR*, XI (1943), 328–33.

Aubouin, E. *Technique et psychologie du comique* (Paris, 1948).

Aubrun, C. V. "La comedia doctrinale et ses histoires de brigands. *El condenado por desconfiado*," *BH*, LIX (1957), 137–51.

—————— . *La comédie espagnole, 1600–1680* (Paris, 1966).

—————— . "Le Don Juan de Tirso de Molina, Essai d'interprétation," *BH*, LIX (1957), 26–61.

—————— . *Histoire du Théâtre Espagnol* (Paris, 1965).

Auerbach, E. *Mimesis: the Representation of Reality in Western Literature* (English translation: Princeton, 1953, and Anchor Books, New York, 1957. 1st published, 1946).

Avrett, R. "Tirso and the Ducal House of Osuna," *RR*, XXX, (1939), 125–32.

Ayala, F. "Erotismo y juego teatral en Tirso," *Ínsula*, XIX (Sept., 1964), no. 214, pp. 1, 7.

Baquero Goyanes, M. "Perspectivismo y sátira en *El criticón*," *Homenaje a Baltasar Gracián* (Zaragoza, 1958), pp. 27–56.

Barber, C. L. *Shakespeare's Festive Comedy* (Princeton Univ. Press, 1959. Reprinted, Cleveland and New York, 1968).

Bataillon, M. "Don Rodrigo Calderón Anversois," *Bulletin de l'Académie Royale de Belgique (Classe des Lettres)*, 5e série, XLV (1959), no. 12, 595–616.

—————— . " 'La picaresca.' A propos de *La pícara Justina*," *Wort und Text. Festschrift für Fritz Schalk* (Frankfurt am Main, 1963), pp. 233–50.

—————— . "*El villano en su rincón*," *BH*, LI (1949), 5–38, LII (1950), 397. Reprinted in *Varia lección de clásicos españoles* (Madrid, 1964), 329–72.

Bell, A. F. G. "The Authorship of *La Estrella de Sevilla*," *MLR*, XXVI (1931), 97–8.

—————— . *Castilian Literature* (Oxford, 1938).

—————— . "Some Notes on Tirso de Molina," *BSS*, XVII (1940), 172–203.

Bentley, E. *The Life of the Drama* (London, 1965).

Bergson, H. and Meredith, G. *Comedy. "Laughter." "An essay on Comedy"* with an intro. and appendix by W. Sypher, (Anchor Books, New York, 1956).

Berne, E. *Games People Play* (Penguin Books, 1968. 1st published, 1964).

Bihler, H. "Más detalles sobre ironía, simetría y simbolismo en *El burlador de Sevilla* de Tirso de Molina," in *Actas del primer congreso internacional de hispanistas* (Oxford, 1964), pp. 213–18.

Bomli, P. W. *La femme dans l'Espagne du siècle d'or* (La Haye, 1950).

Bradbrook, M. C. *English Dramatic Form* (London, 1965).

——————. *The Growth and Structure of Elizabethan Comedy* (Peregrine Books, 1963. 1st ed. 1955).

——————. *Themes and Conventions of Elizabethan Tragedy* (Cambridge, 1966. 1st ed., London, 1935).

——————. "Virtue is the True Nobility: A Study of the Structure of *All's Well That Ends Well*," in *Shakespeare. The Comedies*, ed. K. Muir (Englewood Cliffs, N.J., 1965), pp. 119–32.

Bravo-Villasante, C. *La mujer vestida de hombre en el teatro español de los siglos XVI–XVII* (Madrid, 1955).

Brenan, G. *The Literature of the Spanish People* (Cambridge, 1951. 2nd ed. 1953).

Brooks, H. "Themes and Structure in *The Comedy of Errors*," in *Shakespeare. The Comedies* (Englewood Cliffs, N.J., 1965). pp. 11–25.

Brooks, J. L. "*La estrella de Sevilla*: 'admirable y famosa tragedia,' " *BHS*, XXXII (1955), 8–20.

Brown, J. R. *Shakespeare and his Comedies* (2nd ed., 1962, reprinted, London, 1968. 1st ed., 1957).

Bruerton, C. "*La Ninfa del cielo*, *La serrana de la Vera* and related plays," in *Estudios hispánicos. Homenaje a Archer M. Huntington* (Wellesley, Mass., 1952), pp. 61–97.

——————. "*La quinta de Florencia*, fuente de *Peribáñez*," *NRFH*, IV (1950), 25–39.

——————. "Three Notes on *El burlador de Sevilla*," *HR*, XI (1943), 162–3.

——————. "A Critique of *Tirso de Molina. Studies in Dramatic Realism* by I. L. McClelland," *HR*, XVII (1949), 343–7.

Buchanan, M. A. "Notes on the Spanish Drama: Was Tirso one of the authors of *El caballero de Olmedo*?," *MLN*, XXII (1907), 215–8.

Burke, K. *Counter-Statement* (2nd ed. Los Altos, California, 1953).

Bushee, A. H. *Three Centuries of Tirso de Molina* (Univ. of Pennsylvania Press, 1939).

Bushee, A. H. and J. Millé Giménez. "Un estudio sobre Tirso traducido por Millé," *Est*, VI (1950), 120–50.

Calderà, E. "Un motivo delle commedie 'de enredo': l'elaborazione de *El melancólico*," in *Studi tirsiani* (Milan, 1958), pp. 95–110.

Campbell, O. J. *Shakespeare's Satire* (New York, O.U.P., 1943).

Cantel, R. "Le Portugal dans l'œuvre de Tirso de Molina," in *Mélanges d'études portugaises offerts à M. Georges le Gentil* (Paris and Chartres, 1949), pp. 131–53.

Casalduero, J. "Acotaciones a *El Burlador de Sevilla* de Tirso de Molina," *Die neueren Sprachen*, XXXVIII (1929), 594–98.

——————. "Contribución al estudio del tema de Don Juan en el teatro español," *Smith College Studies in Modern Languages*, XIX (Northampton, Mass., 1938), nos. 3–4.

——————. "El desenlace de *El Burlador de Sevilla*," in *Studia philologica et litteraria in honorem L. Spitzer* (Berne, 1958), pp. 111–22.

——————. *Estudios sobre el teatro español* (Madrid, 1962).

——————. "Sentido y forma de *El vergonzoso en palacio*," *NRFH*. XV (1961), 198–216.

Castañeda, J. A. "El impacto del culteranismo en el teatro de la edad de oro," in *Hispanic Studies in Honor of Nicholson B. Adams* (Chapel Hill, Univ. of North Carolina Press, 1966), pp. 25–36.

Castro Leal, A. *Juan Ruiz de Alarcón: su vida y su obra* (Mexico, 1943).

Castro Seoane, Fr. J. "La merced de Santo Domingo, provincia adoptiva del Maestro Tirso de Molina." *Est*, V (1949), 699–724.

Catholic Encyclopaedia, vol. XIV (New York, 1912).

Chambers's Encyclopaedia, vol. XII (New ed., London, 1959).

Charlton, H. B. *Shakespearean Comedy* (Reprinted, London 1967. 1st published, 1938).

Chasles, P. "Tirso de Molina," in *Italie et Espagne. Voyages d'un critique à travers la vie et les livres*, II (2nd ed., Paris, 1869), pp. 337–50.

Chaunu, P. "La société espagnole au XVIIe siècle. Sur un refus collectif de mobilité," *BH*, LXVIII (1966), 104–15.

Chaytor, H. J. (ed). *Dramatic Theory in Spain* (Cambridge, 1925).

Cioranescu, A. "La biographie de Tirso de Molina. Points de repère et points de vue," *BH*, LXIV (1962), 157–92.

Claudio Rosales, J. "Un problema de métrica en *Don Gil de las calzas verdes*," *Atenea*, LXXXIX (1948), 388–97.

Coe, A. M. "Un estudio sobre Tirso traducido por Millé," *Est*, VI (1950), 119–50.

Coghill, N. "The Basis of Shakespearean Comedy," *Essays and Studies of the English Association, New Series*, III (1950), 1–28.

Corominas, J. *Diccionario crítico etimológico de la lengua castellana*, 4 vols. (Berne, 1954–1957).

Cotarelo y Mori, E. *Bibliografía de las controversias sobre la licitud del teatro en España* (Madrid, 1904).

——————. *Ensayo sobre la vida y obras de Don Pedro Calderón de la Barca* (Madrid, 1924).

——————. "Examen de una conferencia acerca de Tirso de Molina," *RABM*, 3a época, X (1906), tomo 14, números 4 y 5, 394–401.

——————. *Tirso de Molina. Investigaciones bio-bibliográficas* (Madrid, 1893).

——————. "Ultimos estudios acerca de *El Burlador de Sevilla*," *RABM*, XVIII (1908), 75–86.

Covarrubias, S. de. *Tesoro de la lengua castellana o española*, ed. M. de Riquer (Barcelona, 1943).

Crawford, W. *Spanish Drama before Lope de Vega* (Univ. of Pensylvania Press, 1937).

Deleito y Piñuela, J. *El declinar de la monarquía española* (2nd. ed., Madrid, 1947).

——————. *La mala vida en la España de Felipe IV* (3rd ed., Madrid, 1959)

——————. *La mujer, la casa y la moda en la España del Rey Poeta* (Madrid, 1946).

——————. *El rey se divierte* (2nd ed., Madrid, 1955).

——————. *Sólo Madrid es corte* (Madrid, 1942).

——————. *También se divierte el pueblo* (Madrid, 1944).

——————. *La vida religiosa española bajo el cuarto Felipe* (Madrid, 1952).

Delgado Varela, J. M. "Psicología y teología de la conversión en Tirso," *Est*, V (1949), 341–77.

Dellepiane de Martina, A. B. "Ficción e historia en la *Trilogía de los Pizarros de Tirso*," *Fi*, IV (1952–53), 49–168.

Delpy, G. "Réflexions sur *El burlador de Sevilla*," *BH*, L (1948). 463–71.

Diccionario de Autoridades (Facsimile ed., Madrid, 1963. 1st ed., 1726).

Diccionario de Historia de España (Madrid, 1952).

Diccionario de literatura española (3rd ed., Madrid, 1964).

Dieulafoy, M. *Le théâtre édifiant. Cervantes, Tirso de Molina, Calderón* (Paris, 1907).

Domínguez Ortiz, A. *La sociedad española en el siglo XVIII*, I (Madrid, 1963).

Doran, M. *Endeavors of Art* (Univ. of Wisconsin Press, 1954. Reprinted, 1964).

Durán, A. "Apuntes biográficos sobre el Maestro Tirso de Molina," ed. J. E. Hartzenbusch (Madrid, 1848), pp. xi–xvi.

——————. "Examen de *El condenado por desconfiado*," in *Comedias escogidas de Tirso de Molina*, ed. J. E. Hartzenbusch (Madrid, 1848), pp. 720–4.

Eliot, T. S. "A Dialogue on Dramatic Poetry," in *Selected Essays* (3rd ed., London, 1963), pp. 43–58.

——————. *Elizabethan Dramatists* (London, 1968).

——————. *The Use of Poetry and the Use of Criticism* (London, 1964. 1st published, 1933).

Elliott, J. H. *Imperial Spain. 1469–1716* (London, 1963).

Elliott, R. C. *The Power of Satire* (Princeton Univ. Press, 1960. 3rd printing, 1966).

Ellis-Fermor, U. *The Frontiers of Drama* (2nd ed., London, 1964).

Empson, W. *Seven Types of Ambiguity* (3rd ed., London, 1963).

Enciclopedia universal. Espasa-Calpe, vol. LVI (Madrid, 1927).

Encyclopaedia Britannica, vol. XX (London, 1962).

Entrambasaguas, J. de. "La convivencia coetánea de Lope de Vega y Tirso de Molina," *Est*, XVIII (1962), 387–97.

Escudero, A. M. "Tirso, novelista," *Atenea*, LXXXIX (1948), no. 276, 420–35.

Esslin, M. *The Theatre of the Absurd* (Revised ed., Penguin Books, 1968).

Evans, B. *Shakespeare's Comedies* (O.U.P., 1967).

Fichter, W. L. "Color Symbolism in Lope de Vega," *RR*, XVIII (1927), 220–31.

Fichter, W. L. and Sánchez Escribano, F. "Una anécdota folklórica del *Tan largo me lo fiais* no notada hasta la fecha," *RFH*, IV (1942), 70–3.

Fitzmaurice-Kelly, J. *A New History of Spanish Literature* (O.U.P., 1926).

Flores García, F. *La corte del rey-poeta* (Madrid, 1916).

Ford, J. D. M. *Main Currents of Spanish Literature* (New York, 1919).

Freeburg, V. O. *Disguise Plots in Elizabethan Drama* (New York, 1915).

Froldi, R. "Il *Deleitar aprovechando* nella poetica tirsiana," in *Studi tirsiani* (Milan, 1958).

Frye, N. "The Argument of Comedy," *English Institute Essays (1948)* (New York, 1949), 58–73.

——————. *A Natural Perspective. The Development of Shakespearean Comedy and Romance* (Columbia Univ. Press, 1965).

Fucilla, J. G. "*El convidado de piedra* in Naples in 1625," *BC*, X (1958), no. 1, 5–6.

——————. "The Ismael Episode in Tirso's *La prudencia en la mujer*," *BC*, XIII (1961), no. 1, 3–5.

——————. "On the Mirror Symbols in Tirso's *El Aquiles*," *BC*, IX (1957), no. 1, 4–5.

Gabriel y Ramírez de Cartagena, A. de. *Alrededor de Tirso de Molina* (Madrid, 1950).

García Blanco, M. "Algunos elementos populares en el teatro de Tirso de Molina," *BRAE*, XXIX (1949), 413–42.

——————. "Una curiosa utilización del romancero en el teatro de Tirso de Molina," *Est*, V (1949), 295–301.

——————. "Regacho: 'lacayuelo.' Un pretendido aragonesismo de Tirso de Molina," *Fi*, III (1951), 207–11.

——————. "Tirso de Molina y América," *CHA*, VI (1950), 243–58.

García López, J. *Historia de la literatura española* (8th ed., Barcelona, 1964).

Gardner, H. "*As You Like It*," in *Shakespeare. The Comedies*, ed. K. Muir (Englewood Cliffs, N.J., 1965), pp. 58–71.

Gatti, J. F. (ed.) *El teatro de Lope de Vega. Artículos y estudios* (Buenos Aires, 1962).

Gicovate, B. "Observations on the Dramatic Art of Tirso de Molina," *HBalt*, XLIII (1960), 328–37.

Gijón, E. "Concepto del honor y de la mujer en Tirso de Molina," *Est*, V (1949), 479–655.

——————. *El humor en Tirso de Molina* (Madrid, 1959).

Gil de Zárate, A. Article on Tirso in *Comedias escogidas de Tirso de Molina*, ed. J. E. Hartzenbusch (Madrid, 1848), pp. xxxi–xxxv.

Glaser, E. "*La mejor espigadora* de Tirso de Molina," *LR*, XIV (1960), 199–218.

_____ . "Referencias antisemitas en la literatura peninsular de la edad de oro," *NRFH*, VIII (1954), 39–62.

Glenn, R. F. "Disguises and Masquerades in Tirso's *El vergonzoso en palacio*," *BC*, XVII (1965), no. 2, 16–22.

Gómez de Baquero, E. "El teatro religioso en España. *El condenado por desconfiado*," in *De Gallardo a Unamuno* (Madrid, 1926), pp. 161–85.

González López, E. *Historia de la literatura española. Edad Media y siglo de oro* (New York, 1962).

González Palencia, C. A. ed. *Noticias de Madrid, 1621–1627* (Madrid, 1942).

_____ . "Quevedo, Tirso y las comedias ante la junta de reformación," *BRAE*, XXV (1946), 43–84.

Goodman, P. *The Structure of Literature* (Phoenix Books, Univ. of Chicago Press, 1962. 1st ed., 1954).

Green, O. H. *Courtly Love in Quevedo* (Univ. of Colorado Studies in Language and Literature, no. 3, 1952).

_____ . "Courtly Love in the Spanish *Cancioneros*," *PMLA*, LXIV (1949), 247–301.

_____ . "Notes on the Pizarro Trilogy of Tirso de Molina," *HR*, IV (1936), 201–25.

_____ . *Spain and the Western Tradition*, 4 vols. (Univ. of Wisconsin Press, 1963–1966).

_____ . "A Hispanist's Thoughts on *The Anatomy of Satire*," *RPh*, XVII (1963), 123–33.

_____ . "New Light on Don Juan: A Review Article," *HR*, VII (1939), 117–24.

Groult, P. "Tirso de Molina et le Portugal," *LR*, V (1951), 57–8.

Guastavino Gallent, G. "Notas tirsianas," *RABM*, LXVII (1959), 677–96.

_____ . "Notas tirsianas (II)," *RABM*, LXIX (1961), 817–60.

_____ . "Notas tirsianas (III)," *RABM*, LXX (1962), 121–39.

_____ . "Sobre *La elección por la virtud* de Tirso," *Revista de Literatura*, XXVII (1965), 51–63.

Gunckel, H. L. "La admiración de Tirso de Molina por Chile y los araucanos," *Est*, V (1949), 199–204.

Hall, E. T. *The Silent Language* (Garden City, New York, 1959).

Halstead, F. G. "The Attitude of Tirso de Molina toward Astrology," *HR*, IX (1941), 417–39.

_____ . "The Optics of Love: Notes on a Concept of Atomistic Philosophy in the Theatre of Tirso de Molina," *PMLA*, LVIII (1943), 108–21.

Hamilton, G. H. "Political Satire in the Seventeenth Century," *BSS*, VIII (1931), 150–7.

Hamilton, T. E. "Spoken Letters in the *Comedias* of Alarcón, Tirso and Lope," *PMLA*, LXII (1947), 62–75.

Hatzfeld, H. *Estudios sobre el barroco* (Madrid, 1964).

Hayes, F. C. "The Use of Proverbs as Titles and Motives in the *Siglo de Oro* Drama: Tirso de Molina," *HR*, VII (1939), 310–23.

Hazard, P. *La crise de la conscience européenne* (Paris, 1963).

Heathcote, A. A. *The Portrayal of Women Characters in the Religious Plays of Tirso de Molina*, M.A. thesis (Manchester, 1954).

Henríquez Ureña, P. "Tirso de Molina," in *Obra Crítica* (Mexico, 1960), pp. 546–7.

Herrero García, M. *Ideas de los españoles del siglo XVII* (2nd ed., Madrid, 1966).

Herrick, M. T. *Comic Theory in the Sixteenth Century* (Urbana, 1950).

Hesse, E. W. "Catálogo bibliográfico de Tirso de Molina," *Est*, V (1949), 781–889. Supplements in *Est* as follows: no. 1 in VII (1951); no. 2 in VIII (1952); No. 3 in IX (1953); no. 4 in X (1954); no. 5 in XI (1955); no. 6 in XII (1956); no. 7 in XVI (1960).

——————. "The Incest Motif in Tirso's *La venganza de Tamar*," *HBalt*, XLVII (1964), 268–76.

——————. "The Nature of the Complexity in Tirso's *Don Gil*," *HBalt*, XLV (1962), 389–94.

Hesse, E. W. and MacCrary, W. C. "La balanza subjetiva-objetiva en el teatro de Tirso: ensayo sobre contenido y forma barrocos," *HispI*, no. 3 (1958), 1–11.

——————. "The Mars-Venus Struggle in Tirso's *El Aquiles*,"*BHS*, XXXIII (1956), 138–51.

Highet, G. *The Anatomy of Satire* (Princeton Univ. Press, 1962).

Hodgart, M. *Satire* (London, 1969).

House, H. *Aristotle's Poetics* (London, 1961).

Huarte de San Juan, J. *Examen de ingenios para las ciencias* (Austral, Buenos Aires, 1946).

Huerta, E. "Tirso el vergonzoso," *Atenea*, LXXXIX (1948), 371–86.

Hume, M. *The Court of Philip IV* (London, 1907).

Hurtado, J. y González Palencia, A. *Historia de la literatura española* (5th ed., Madrid, 1943).

Iriarte, M. de. *El doctor Huarte de San Juan y su examen de ingenios: contribución a la historia de la psicología diferencial* (3rd ed., Madrid, 1948).

Jacquot, J. (ed.). *Le lieu théâtral à la Renaissance* (Paris, 1964).

Javier de Burgos, F. Article on Tirso in *Comedias escogidas* de Tirso de Molina, ed. J. E. Hartzenbusch (Madrid, 1848), pp. xxvi–xxx.

Jesuits. *Cartas de algunos padres de la compañía de Jesús sobre los sucesos de la monarquía entre los años de 1634 y 1648*, 7 vols., in *Memorial histórico español*, vols. XIII–XIX (Madrid, 1861–1865).

Jones, R. O. "Ariosto and Garcilaso," *BHS*, XXXIX (1962), 153–64.

——————. "Góngora and Neoplatonism Again," *BHS*, XLIII (1966), 117–20.

——————. "Neoplatonism and the *Soledades*," *BHS*, XL (1963), 1–16.

——————. "*El perro del hortelano* y la visión de Lope," *Fi*, X (1964), 135–42.

_____ . "The Poetic Unity of the *Soledades* of Góngora," *BHS*, XXXI (1954), 189–204.

Juliá Martínez, E. "Rectificaciones bibliográficas. *Adversa fortuna de don Alvaro de Luna,*" *Revista de bibliografía nacional*, IV (1943), 147–50.

Keeble, T. W. "Some Mythological Figures in Golden Age Satire and Burlesque," *BHS*, XXV (1948), 238–46.

Kennedy, R. L. "Attacks on Lope and his Theatre, 1617–1621," in *Hispanic Studies in Honor of Nicholson B. Adams,* eds. J. E. Keller and K. L. Selig (Univ. of North Carolina Press, 1966).

_____ . "Certain Phases of the Sumptuary Decrees of 1623 and their Relation to Tirso's Theatre," *HR*, X (1942), 91–115.

_____ . "Contemporary Satire Against Ruiz de Alarcón as Lover," *HR*, XIII (1945), 145–65.

_____ . "Escarramán and Glimpses of the Spanish Court in 1637–38," *HR*, IX (1941).

_____ . "Literary and Political Satire in Tirso's *La fingida Arcadia,*" in *The* ʳ *.aissance Reconsidered. Smith College Studies in History*, XLIV (Northampton, Mass., 1964), pp. 91–110.

_____ . "The Madrid of 1617–25. Certain Aspects of Social, Moral and Educational Values," in *Estudios hispánicos. Homenaje a Archer M. Huntington,* I (Wellesley, Mass., 1952), pp. 275–309.

_____ . "The New Plaza Mayor of 1620 and the Reflection in the Literature of the Time," *HR*, XII (1944), 49–57.

_____ . "Notes on two interrelated plays of Tirso: *El amor y el amistad* and *Ventura te dé Dios, hijo,*" *HR*, XXVIII (1960), 189–214.

_____ . "On the Date of Five Plays by Tirso de Molina," *HR*, X (1942), 183–214.

_____ . "*La prudencia en la mujer* and the Ambient that Brought it Forth," *PMLA*, LXIII (1948), 1131–90.

_____ . "A Reappraisal of Tirso's Relations to Lope and his Theatre," *BC*, XVII (1965), no. 2, 23–34; XVIII (1966), no. 1, 1–13.

_____ . "Studies for the Chronology of Tirso's Theatre," *HR*, XI (1943), 17–46.

_____ . "Tirso's *No hay peor sordo*: Its Date and Place of Composition," in *Homenaje a Rodríguez-Moñino,* I (Madrid, 1966), pp. 261–78.

_____ . "Tirso's Satire of Ruiz de Alarcón," *BC*, XVI (1964), no. 2, 1–12.

Kenyon, H. A. "Color Symbolism in Early Spanish Ballads," *RR*, VI (1915), 327–40.

Kerr, R. J. A. "Plot-Structure in *La prudencia en la mujer,*" *El Clarín*, no. 25 (1958), 1–3.

Kerr, W. *Tragedy and Comedy* (London, 1968).

Kitto, H. D. F. *Form and Meaning in Drama* (London, 1968. 1st published, 1956; 2nd ed., 1964).

Knight, G. W. "Helena," in *Shakespeare. The Comedies*, ed. K. Muir (Englewood Cliffs, N.J., 1965), pp. 133–51.

Knights, L. C. *Drama and Society in the Age of Jonson* (Peregrine Books, 1962. 1st ed. 1937).

Kott, J. *Shakespeare Our Contemporary* (2nd ed., London, 1967).

La Joie, R. G. "La singularidad de los dos errores de la *Segunda parte* de las comedias del Maestro Tirso de Molina," *BH*, LVII (1955), 416–20.

Langer, S. *Feeling and Form. A Theory of Art Developed from Philosophy in a New Key* (New York, 1953).

Lauter, P. *Theories of Comedy* (New York, 1964).

Lawrence, W. W. *Shakespeare's Problem Comedies* (Penguin Books, 1969. 1st published, 1931. Revised ed., 1960).

Leavitt, S. E. *The "Estrella de Sevilla" and Claramonte* (Cambridge, Mass., 1931).

——————. "A Note on the *Burlador de Sevilla*," *RR*, XX (1929), 157–9.

——————. "Strip-tease in Golden Age Drama," in *Homenaje a Rodríguez-Moñino*, I (Madrid, 1966), pp. 305–10.

Leech, C. *"Twelfth Night" and Shakespearian Comedy* (Univ. of Toronto Press, 1965. Reprinted, 1968).

Lerner, L. (ed.) *Shakespeare's Comedies. An Anthology of Modern Criticism* (Penguin Books, 1967).

Lessing, G. E. *Hamburgische Dramaturgie* (1767–1769. English transl. by H. Zimmern, London, 1879. Reprinted, New York, 1962).

Lewis, C. S. *The Allegory of Love* (O.U.P., New York, 1963. 1st ed., 1936).

Ley, C. D. *El gracioso en el teatro de la península (siglos XVI y XVII)* (Madrid, 1954).

Lida de Malkiel, M. R. "Sobre la prioridad de ¿*Tan largo me lo fiáis?*: Notas al *Isidro* y a *El burlador de Sevilla*," *HR*, XXX (1962), 275–95.

Lista, A. Article on Tirso in *Comedias escogidas de Tirso de Molina*, ed. J. E. Hartzenbusch (Madrid, 1848), pp. xxii–xxvii.

——————. "*La beata enamorada o Marta la piadosa*. Comedia de Tirso de Molina, refundida en cinco actos," *El Censor*, X (1821), 449–53.

——————. "*La celosa de sí misma*: comedia en tres actos, de Tirso de Molina," *El Censor*, IX (1821), 99–109.

——————. "*Pruebas de amor y amistad*. Comedia en tres actos de Tirso de Molina," *El Censor*, X (1821), 271–80.

——————. "Reflexiones sobre la dramática española en los siglos XVI y XVII," *El Censor*, VII (1821), 138–9.

——————. "*El vergonzoso en palacio*," *El Censor*, VI (1821), 423.

Livermore, H. V. *A History of Portugal* (Cambridge, 1947).

López, Alfonso. "La Sagrada Biblia en las obras de Tirso," *Est*, V (1949), 381–414.

López, Angel. *El cancionero popular en el teatro de Tirso de Molina* (Madrid, 1958).

López Estrada, E. "*La Arcadia* de Lope en la escena de Tirso. Nota para el estudio del tema pastoril en Tirso de Molina," *Est*, V (1949), 303–20.

López Navío, J. "Una comedia de Tirso que no está perdida," *Est*, XVI (1960), 331–47.

López Tascón, J. "*El condenado por desconfiado* y Fray Alonso Remón," *BBMP*, XVI (1934), 533–46; XVII (1935), 14–29, 144–71, 273–93; XVIII (1936), 35–82, 133–82.

McClelland, I. L. *Tirso de Molina. Studies in Dramatic Realism* (Liverpool, 1948).

McCrary, W. C. "The Authorship of *Próspera* and *Adversa fortuna de Don Álvaro de Luna*," *BHS*, XXXV (1958), 38–40.

————— . "La elaboración de una escena simbológica: Ensayo sobre contenido y forma barrocos. II," *HispI*, no. 13 (1961), 23–32.

McCready, W. C. *Bibliografía temática de estudios sobre el teatro español antiguo* (Toronto, 1966).

Macedo Soares, J. C. de. "Tirso de Molina," *Est*, V (1949), 671–85.

Maeztu, R. de. *Don Quijote, don Juan y Celestina: Ensayos de simpatía* (Madrid, 1926).

Mahood, M. M. *Shakespeare's Wordplay* (London, 1968. 1st published, 1957).

Malinowski, B. *The Language of Magic and Gardening. (Coral Gardens and their Magic, vol. II)* (2nd ed., London, 1966).

Malvezzi, V. *Historia de los primeros años del reinado de Felipe IV*, ed. D. L. Shaw (London, 1968).

Mancini, G. "Caratteri e problemi del teatro di Tirso," in *Studi tirsiani* (Milan, 1958), pp. 11–89.

Marañón, G. *El conde-duque de Olivares* (3rd ed., Madrid, 1952).

————— . *Don Juan* (Austral. 9th ed., Madrid, 1960).

Marín, D. *La intriga secundaria en el teatro de Lope de Vega* (México, 1958).

Marni, A. "Did Tirso employ counterpassion in his *Burlador de Sevilla*?," *HR*, XX (1952), 123–33.

Martínez de Azagra, A. "Almazán en tiempo de Tirso de Molina," *Est*, V (1949), 157–83.

Martínez de la Rosa, F. Article on Tirso in *Comedias escogidas de Tirso de Molina*, ed. J. E. Hartzenbusch (Madrid, 1848), pp. xxx–xxxi.

Mas, A. *La caricature de la femme, du mariage et de l'amour dans l'œuvre de Quevedo* (Paris, 1957).

Matulka, B. "The Feminist Theme in the Drama of the Siglo de Oro," *RR*, XXVI (1935), 191–231.

May, T. E. "*El condenado por desconfiado*. 1. The Enigmas. 2. Anareto," *BHS*, XXXV (1958), 138–56.

Menéndez Pelayo, M. "Tirso de Molina," in *Estudios y discursos de crítica histórica y literaria*, III (Madrid, 1941), pp. 47–81.

Menéndez Pidal, R. "El arte nuevo y la nueva biografía," *RFE*, XXII (1935).

————— . *España y su historia*, vol. II (Madrid, 1957).

_____ . *Estudios literarios* (Buenos Aires, 1939).

Mérimée, E. *A History of Spanish Literature*, transl. by S. G. Morley (London, 1931).

Mesonero Romanos, R. Article on Tirso in *Comedias escogidas de Tirso de Molina*, ed. J. E. Hartzenbusch (Madrid, 1848), pp. xvi–xxii.

Metford, J. C. J. "The Enemies of the Theatre in the Golden Age," *BHS*, XXVIII (1951), 76–92.

_____ . "Tirso de Molina and the Conde-Duque de Olivares." *BHS*, XXXVI (1959), 15–27.

_____ . "Tirso de Molina's Old Testament Plays," *BHS*, XXVII (1950), 149–63.

Moir, D. "The Classical Tradition in Spanish Dramatic Theory and Practice in the Seventeenth Century," in *Classical Drama and Its Influence*, ed. M. J. Anderson (London, 1965), pp. 191–228.

Molina, J. "Un Tirso de crónicas y viajes," *Atenea*, LXXXIX (1948), no. 276, 436–57.

Montesinos, J. F. "Una cuestión de amor en comedias antiguas españolas," *RFE*, XIII (1926), 280–3.

Montoto, S. "Una comedia de Tirso que no es de Tirso," *Archivo Hispalense*, 2a época, VII (1946), 99–107.

Morby, E. S. "Portugal and Galicia in the Plays of Tirso de Molina," *HR*, IX (1941), 266–74.

Morel-Fatio, A. *La comedia espagnole du XVIIe siècle* (2nd ed., Paris, 1923).

_____ . "Les défenseurs de la comedia," *BH*, IV (1902).

_____ . "Études sur le théâtre de Tirso de Molina, I: *La prudencia en la mujer*," *BH*, II (1900), 1–109, 178–203.

_____ . "La prudence chez la femme, drame historique de Tirso de Molina," in *Études sur l'Espagne*, 3e série (Paris, 1904), pp. 25–72.

_____ . *Le théâtre espagnol. (Bibliographie)* (Paris, 1900).

Moreno García, C. "Las mujeres y Tirso," *Revista contemporánea*, CI (Madrid, 1896), 418–27.

Morley, S. G. "Character Names in Tirso de Molina," *HR*, XXVII (1959), 222–7.

_____ . "Color Symbolism in Tirso de Molina," *RR*, VIII (1917), 77–81.

_____ . "*Fuente Ovejuna* and Its Theme Parallels," *HR*, IV (1936), 303–11.

_____ . "The Use of verse-forms (strophes) by Tirso de Molina," *BH*, VII (1905), 387–408.

_____ . "El uso de las combinaciones métricas en las comedias de Tirso de Molina," *BH*, XVI (1914), 177–208.

Morley, S. G. and Bruerton, C. "Addenda to the Chronology of Lope's *Comedias*," *HR*, XV (1947).

_____ . *The Chronology of Lope de Vega's Comedias* (New York, 1940).

Morris, C. B. "Metaphor in *El burlador de Sevilla*," *RR*, LV (1964), 248–55.

Muir, K. (ed.) *Shakespeare: The Comedies. A Collection of Critical Essays* (Englewood Cliffs, N.J., c 1965).

Muñoz, V. "Zumel y el molinismo," *Est*, IX (1953), 345–86.

Muñoz Peña, P. *El teatro del Maestro Tirso de Molina. Estudio crítico literario* (Valladolid, 1889).

Nicoll, A. *The Theory of Drama* (London, 1931).

——————. *World Drama* (London, 1949).

Nolasco Pérez, P. "Tirso de Molina pasajero a Indias," *Est*, V (1949), 185–97.

Nomland, J. B. "A Laughter Analysis of Three Comedias of Tirso de Molina," *MLF*, XXXI (1946), 25–40.

Northup, G. T. "*El dómine Lucas* of Lope de Vega and Some Related Plays," *MLR*, IV (1908–09), 462–73.

Nougué, A. "A propos de l'auto-imitation dans le théâtre de Tirso de Molina," *BH*, LXIV (2) (1962), 559–66.

——————. *L'Œuvre en prose de Tirso de Molina. "Los cigarrales de Toledo" et "Deleytar aprovechando"* (Paris, 1962).

——————. "Le thème de l'aberration des sens dans le théâtre de Tirso de Molina. Une source possible," *BH*, LVIII (1956), 23–35.

——————. " 'La venta de las Pavas' chez Tirso de Molina," *BH*, LXII (1960), 326–30.

Oñate, M. del Pilar. *El feminismo en la literatura española* (Madrid, 1938).

Ortúzar, M. "*El condenado por desconfiado* depende teológicamente de Zumel," *Est*, IV (1948), 7–41.

——————. "Nueva aclaración," *Est*, V (1949), 321–36.

Palomo, Ma. del Pilar. "Nota de cronología tirsista: *El caballero de Gracia*," *Segis*, II (1966), 121–4.

Parker, A. A. *The Approach to the Spanish Drama of the Golden Age* (London, 1957).

——————. "El concepto de la verdad en el *Quijote*," *RFE*, XXXII (1948), 287–305.

——————. "The Father-Son Conflict in the Drama of Calderón," *FMLS*, II (1966), 99–113.

——————. "Fielding and the Structure of *Don Quixote*," *BHS*, XXXIII (1956), 1–16.

——————. "History and Poetry: the Coriolanus Theme in Calderón," in *Hipanic Studies in Honour of González Llubera* (Oxford, 1959), pp. 211–24.

——————. *Literature and the Delinquent. The Picaresque Novel in Spain and Europe 1599–1753* (Edinburgh Univ. Press, 1967).

——————. "Metáfora y símbolo en la interpretación de Calderón," in *Actas del primer congreso internacional de hispanistas* (Oxford, 1964), pp. 141–60.

——————. "Reflections on a New Definition of 'Baroque' Drama," *BHS*, XXX (1953), 142–51.

——————. "Towards a Definition of Calderonian Tragedy," *BHS*, XXXIX (1962), 222–37.

Parker, J. H. *Breve historia del teatro español* (Mexico, 1957).

——————— . "Lope de Vega's *Arte nuevo de hacer comedias*: Post-Centenary Reflections," in *Hispanic Studies in Honor of Nicholson B. Adams*, (Chapel Hill, Univ. of North Carolina Press, 1966), pp. 113–30.

——————— . "Tirso de Molina, defensor de la comedia nueva," *Revista Universidad de San Carlos*, XII (1948), 39–48.

Paterson, A. K. G. "The Textual History of Tirso's *La venganza de Tamar*," *MLR*, LXIII (1968), 381–91.

——————— . *Tirso de Molina: An Edition of "La venganza de Tamar"* with *bibliographical, textual and literary criticism*, Ph.D. thesis (Cambridge, 1965).

——————— . "Tirso de Molina: Two Bibliographical Studies," *HR*, XXXV (1967), 43–68.

Peacock, R. *The Art of Drama* (2nd printing, London, 1960).

Penedo Rey, Fray M. "Almazán y Madrid en la biografía de Tirso," *Est*, I (1945), 172–5.

——————— . "Ampliación al trabajo del Rev. P. Fr. Miguel L. Ríos 'Tirso no es bastardo,'" *Est*, V (1949) 14–8.

——————— . "Documentos para la biografía de Tirso de Molina," *Est*, V (1949), 725–76.

——————— . "El fraile músico de los *Cigarrales de Toledo* de Tirso de Molina," *Est*, III (1947), 383–90.

——————— . "Investigaciones tirsistas en Guadalajara," *BC*, III (1951), no. 2, 1.

——————— . "Muerte documentada de Fray Gabriel Téllez en Almazán," *Est*, I (1945), 192–206.

——————— . "Noviciado y profesión de 'Tirso de Molina,' ¿1600?–1601," *Est*, I (1945), 82–98.

——————— . "Para la *Santa Juana* de Tirso de Molina," *Est*, VIII (1952), 581–7.

——————— . "Por las fuentes de la dramática de Tirso de Molina," *Est*, IX (1953), 285–331.

——————— . "La primera firma de Tirso de Molina. Guadalajara, 1603. Glosas y documentos," *Est*, VIII (1952), 115–30.

——————— . "Tirso de Molina: Aportaciones biográficas," *Est*, V (1949), 19–122.

——————— . "Tirso de Molina en Soria," *Est*, I (1945), 179–80.

——————— . "La dramática de Tirso de Molina vista por doña Blanca de los Ríos," *Est*, III (1947), 277–84.

——————— . "Exaltación de la Hispanidad en Tirso de Molina," *Est*, I (1945), 176–8.

Penna, M. *Don Giovanni e il mistero di Tirso* (Turin, 1958).

Pérez, C. A. "Verosimilitud psicológica de *El condenado por desconfiado*," *HispI*, no. 27 (1966), 1–21.

Peristiany, J. G. *Honour and Shame. The Values of Mediterranean Society* (London, 1965).

Peyton, M. A. "Some Baroque Aspects of Tirso de Molina," *RR*, XXXVI (1945), 43–69.

Pfandl, L. *Cultura y costumbres del siglo de oro* (Barcelona, n.d.).

——————. *Historia de la literatura nacional española en la edad de oro* (Spanish transl., 2nd ed., Barcelona, 1952).

Piddington, R. *The Psychology of Laughter. A Study in Social Adaptation* (2nd ed., New York, 1963).

Pijoán, J. "Acerca de las fuentes populares de *El condenado por desconfiado*," *HBalt*, VI (1923), 109–14.

Placer, Fray G. "Algo sobre las monjas en las comedias de Tirso de Molina," *Est*, XVI (1960), 319–30.

——————. "Biografía del Ilmo. Fray Marcos Salmerón," *Est*, IV (1948), 554–60.

——————. "Biografía del P. Alonso Remón, clásico español," *Est*, I (1945), 59–90.

——————. "Los curas en las comedias de Tirso de Molina," *Est*, XV (1959), 435–65.

——————. "Los lacayos de las comedias de Tirso de Molina," *Est*, II (1946), 59–115.

——————. "Un nuevo retrato de Tirso," *Est*, V (1949), 721–4.

——————. "Nuevos datos acerca de Fray Gabriel Téllez," *Est*, VI (1950), 339–52.

——————. "Los sacristanes de Tirso de Molina," *Est*, XV (1959), 117–26.

——————. "Tirso en Galicia," *Est*, V (1949), 415–78.

Potts, L. J. *Comedy* (4th impression, London, 1966).

Radoff, M. L. and Salley, W. C. "Notes on the *Burlador*," *MLN*, XLV (1930), 239–44.

Raynor, H. "A Play on Love Regardless of Sex," *The Times*, 18th Sept., 1967.

Read, H. *Poetry and Experience* (London, 1967).

Rennert, H. A. *The Spanish Stage in the Time of Lope de Vega* (New York, 1909).

——————. "Tirso de Molina's *El condenado por desconfiado*," *MLN*, XVIII (1903), 136–9.

Reynolds, J. J. "An Anecdote in *El condenado por desconfiado*," *BC*, VIII (1956), no. 1, 13–4.

Ridler, A. (compiler) *Shakespeare Criticism 1919–1935* (O.U.P., 1965, 1st published, 1936).

Righter, W. *Logic and Criticism* (2nd impression, 1965).

Riley, E. C. *Cervantes's Theory of the Novel* (O.U.P., 1964. 1st published, 1962).

Río, A. del. *Historia de la literatura española*, 2 vols, (Revised ed., New York, 1963).

Ríos, M. L. "Tirso de Molina no es bastardo," *Est*, V (1949), 1–13.

Ríos, M. L. and Núñez Barbosa, J. "La hipótesis de doña Blanca de los Ríos de Lampérez sobre la fe de nacimiento de Tirso de Molina," *Atenea*, XC (1948),

299–314.

Ríos de Lampérez, B. de los. *Del siglo de oro* (Madrid, 1910).

—————. *El enigma biográfico de Tirso de Molina* (Madrid, 1928).

Robles Pazos, J. "Sobre la fecha de *Fuenteovejuna*," *MLN*, L (1935), 179–82.

Rogers, D. "Fearful Symmetry: The Ending of *El burlador de Sevilla*," *BHS*, XLI (1963), 141–59.

Rogers, P. P. "Spanish Influence on the Literature of France," *HBalt*, IX (1926), 205–35.

Romera, A. R. "Tirso de Molina y su secreto," *Atenea*, LXXXIX (1948), no. 276, 460–9.

Romera-Navarro, M. "Las disfrazadas de varón en la comedia," *HR*, II (1934), 269–86.

—————. *Historia de la literatura española* (Boston, 1928).

—————. "El humorismo y la sátira de Gracián," *HR*, X (1942), 126–46.

Rosselli, F. "Su *La fingida Arcadia*," in *Studi tirsiani* (Milan, 1958).

Roux, L. "Quelques aperçus sur la mise en scène de la *comedia de santos* au XVIIe siècle," in *Le lieu théâtral à la Renaissance*, ed. J. Jacquot (Paris, 1964), pp. 235–52.

Salomon, N. "Simple remarque à propos du problème de la date de *Peribáñez y el Comendador de Ocaña*," *BH*, LXIII (1961), 251–8.

—————. "Toujours la date de *Peribáñez y el Comendador de Ocaña*, 'tragicomedia' de Lope de Vega," *BH*, LXIV (1962), 613–43.

Salvadorini, V. "Don Álvaro de Luna nell'interpretazione di Tirso," in *Studi tirsiani* (Milan, 1958).

Samonà, C. "L'esperienza cultista nel teatro dell'età di Lope: appunti ed esempi," in *Studi di letteratura spagnola*, ed. C. Samonà (Rome, 1964), pp. 99–168.

—————. "Premesse ad uno studio de *La prudencia en la mujer*," in *Studi tirsiani* (Milan, 1958).

Sánchez Escribano, F. "El Burlador de Sevilla, hombre sin nombre," *BC*, VII (1955), no. 1, 9.

Sancho de San Román, R. *La medicina y los médicos en la obra de Tirso de Molina* (Salamanca, 1960).

Sanz y Díaz, J. *Tirso de Molina* (Madrid, 1964).

Schack, A. F. *Geschichte der dramatischen Literatur und Kunst in Spanien* (Berlin, 1845–6; 2nd ed., Frankfurt am Main, 1854, Spanish transl., Madrid, 1885–7)).

Schalk, F. "Melancholie im Theater von Tirso de Molina," in *Ideen und Formen. Festschrift für Hugo Friedrich zum 24. xxi. 1964*, ed. F. Schalk (Frankfurt am Main, 1965), pp. 215–38.

Schanzer, E. "A Midsummer-Night's Dream," in *Shakespeare. The Comedies*, ed. K. Muir (Englewood Cliffs, N. J., 1965), pp. 26–31.

Schücking, L. L. "Direct Self-Explanation," in *Shakespeare Criticism 1919–1935*, compiled by A. Ridler (O.U.P., 1965), pp. 152–79.

Sedgwick, F. B. "On the Meaning of Catalinón," *BC*, VI (1954) no. 2, 4–6.

Serratosa, Fr. R. "El padre y maestro fray Gabriel Téllez como religioso," *Est*, V (1949), 687–97.

Shepard, S. *El Pinciano y las teorías literarias del siglo de oro* (Madrid, 1962).

Shergold, N. D. *A History of the Spanish Stage* (O.U.P., 1967).

Shergold, N. D. and Varey, J. E. "Some Early Calderón Dates," *BHS*, XXXVIII (1961), 274–86.

——————— . "Some Palace Performances of Seventeenth Century Plays," *BHS*, XL (1963), 212–44.

Silva Tapia, W. "Cercanía de Tirso de Molina en *El condenado por desconfiado*," *Atenea*, LXXXIX (1948), 400–19.

Sloman, A. E. "The Two Versions of *El burlador de Sevilla*," *BHS*, XLII (1965), 18–33.

Solá-Solé, J. M. "Dos notas sobre la génesis del tema de don Juan," *REH*, II (1968), 1–11.

Solé-Leris, A. "The Theory of Love in the Two *Dianas*: A Contrast," *BHS*, XXXVI (1959), 65–79.

Soons, C. A. *Ficción y comedia en el siglo de oro* (Madrid, 1967).

——————— . "Poetic Elements in the plots of Tirso's novels," *BHS*, XXXII (1955), 194–203.

——————— . "Two historical *comedias* and the question of 'manierismo,' " *RF*, LXXIII (1961), 339–46.

Spurgeon, C. F. E. "Leading Motives in the Imagery of Shakespeare's Tragedies," in *Shakespeare Criticism 1919–1935*, compiled by A. Ridler, (O.U.P., 1965).

Stafford, L. L. "Historia crítica y dramática de *La prudencia en la mujer*," in *Estudios hispánicos. Homenaje a Archer M. Huntington* (Wellesley, Mass., 1952), pp. 575–84.

Sutherland, J. *English Satire* (Cambridge, 1962. 1st printed, 1958).

Sypher, W. *Four Stages of Renaissance Style. Transformations in Art and Literature. 1400–1700* (Anchor Books, New York, 1955).

Tamayo, J. A. "Madrid en el teatro de Tirso de Molina," *RBAM*, XIX (1950), 291–363.

——————— . "Los manuscritos de *Las Quinas de Portugal*," *Revista de Bibliografía Nacional*, III (1942), 36–63.

Templin, E. H. "Another Instance of Tirso's Self-Plagiarism," *HR*, V (1937), 176–80.

——————— . "The *burla* in the Plays of Tirso de Molina," *HR*, VIII (1940), 185–201.

——————— . "The *encomienda* in *El condenado por desconfiado* and other Spanish works," *HBalt*, XV (1940), 465–82.

——————— . *The Exculpation of "yerros por amores" in the Spanish "comedia"* (Univ. of California Press, 1933).

——————— . "Night Scenes in Tirso de Molina," *RR*, XLI (1950), 261–73.

Tetel, M. *Étude sur le comique de Rabelais* (Florence, 1964).

Thompson, A. R. *The Dry Mock. A Study of Irony in Drama* (Univ. of California Press, 1948).

Trueblood, A. S. "The Baroque: Premises and Problems. A Review Article," *HR*, XXXV (1967), 355–63.

Tymms, R. *Doubles in Literary Psychology* (Cambridge, 1949).

Urtiaga, A. *El indiano en la dramática de Tirso de Molina* (Madrid, 1965).

Valbuena Prat, A. *Historia de la literatura española*, II (4th ed., Barcelona, 1953; 5th ed., 1957).

——————. *Historia del teatro español* (Barcelona, 1956).

——————. *Literatura dramática española* (Barcelona, 1930).

——————. "Sobre la creación de caracteres y la temática de Tirso de Molina," *Segis*, I (1965), 11–22.

——————. *La vida española en la edad de oro* (Barcelona, 1943).

Varey, J. E. "La campagne dans le théâtre espagnol au XVIIe siècle," in *Dramaturgie et Société* (Paris, 1968), pp. 47–76.

Viqueira Barreiros, J. M. *Coimbra en las letras española* (Coimbra, 1964).

——————. "La lusofilia de 'Tirso de Molina,' " *Biblos*, XXXVI (1960 [1965]), 265–489.

Vossler, K. *Algunos caracteres de la cultura española* (4th ed., Madrid, 1962).

——————. *Escritores y poetas de España* (Buenos Aires, 1947).

——————. *Introducción a la literatura española del siglo de oro* (Madrid, 1934).

——————. *Lecciones sobre Tirso de Molina* (Madrid, 1965).

——————. *Lope de Vega y su tiempo* (Madrid, 1933).

Wade, G. E. "Adición a *Three Centuries of Tirso de Molina* de A. H. Bushee," *NRFH*, V (1951), 414–7.

——————. "The Authorship and the date of composition of *El burlador de Sevilla*," *HispI*, no. 32 (1968), 1–22.

——————. "*El burlador de Sevilla*: The Tenorios and the Ulloas," *S*, XIX (1965), 249–58.

——————. "The Character of Don Juan of *El burlador de Sevilla*," in *Hispanic Studies in Honor of Nicholson B. Adams* (Chapel Hill, 1966), pp. 167–78.

——————. "La dedicatoria de Matías de los Reyes a Tirso de Molina," *Est*, VIII (1952), 589–93.

——————. "El escenario histórico y la fecha de *Amar por razón de estado*," *Est*, V (1949), 657–70.

——————. "Further Notes on *El burlador de Sevilla*," *BC*, XVIII (1966), no. 2, 29–32.

——————. "The Interpretation of the *comedia*," *BC*, II (1959), no. 1, 1–6.

——————. "The Literary Sources of *El castigo del penséque* of Tirso de Molina," in *South Atlantic Studies for S. E. Leavitt*, (Washington, D.C., 1953), pp. 81–96.

——————. "Mythological and other Classical Allusions in the Theatres of

Tirso, Alarcón and Vélez," *BC*, X (1958), no. 2, 6–9.

_____ . "Notes on Tirso de Molina," *HR*, VII (1939), 69–72.

_____ . "Notes on Two of Tirso's Plays," *BC*, XII (1960), no. 2, 1–6.

_____ . "On Tirso's *Don Gil*," *MLN*, LXXIV (1958), 609–12.

_____ . "The Orthoepy of the Holographic *Comedias* of Tirso de Molina," *PMLA*, LV (1940), 993–1009.

_____ . "*Tan largo me lo fiáis* and *El burlador de Sevilla y el convidado de piedra*," *BC*, XIV (1962), no. 1, 1–16.

_____ . "Tirsiana," *RoN*, IX (1967), 95–101.

_____ . "Tirso de Molina," *HBalt*, XXXII (1949), 131–40.

_____ . "Tirso's *Cigarrales de Toledo*: some Clarifications and Identifications," *HR*, XXXIII (1965), 246–72.

_____ . "Tirso's Friends," *BC*, XIX (1967), no. 1, 1–6.

_____ . "Tirso's *Santa Juana. primera parte*," *MLN*, XLIX (1934), 13–8.

_____ . "Tirso's Self-Plagiarism in Plot," *HR*, IV (1936), 55–65.

_____ . "The Year of Tirso's Birth," *HispI*, no. 19 (1963), 1–9.

Wardropper, B. W. "*El burlador de Sevilla*: A Tragedy of Errors," *PQ*, XXXVI (1957), 61–71.

_____ . "Calderón's Comedy and His Serious Sense of Life," in *Hispanic Studies in Honor of Nicholson B. Adams* (Chapel Hill, 1966), pp. 179–93.

_____ . "Lope's *La dama boba* and Baroque Comedy," *BC*, XIII (1961), no. 2, 1–3.

Webber, E. J. "The Shipwreck of Don Manuel de Sousa in the Spanish Theater," *PMLA*, LXVI (1951), 1114–22.

Weber de Kurlat, F. *Lo cómico en el teatro de Fernán González de Eslava* (Buenos Aires, 1963).

Welsford, E. *The Fool. His Social and Literary History* (London, 1968. 1st published, 1935).

Whinnom, K. *Spanish Literary Historiography: Three Forms of Distortion* (Univ. of Exeter, 1967).

Wilson, E. M. "Calderón and the Stage-censor in the Seventeenth Century: a provisional study," *S*, XV (1961), 169–71.

_____ . "Seven *Aprobaciones* by Don Pedro Calderón de la Barca," in *Homenaje a Dámaso Alonso*, III (Madrid, 1963), 605–18.

Wilson, E. M. and Sage, J. *Poesías líricas en las obras dramáticas de Calderón. Citas y glosas.* (London, 1964).

Wilson, M. "The Last Play of Tirso de Molina," *MLR*, XLVII (1952), 516–28.

_____ . "*La próspera fortuna de Don Alvaro de Luna*: An Outstanding Work by Mira de Amescua," *BHS*, XXXIII (1956), 25–36.

_____ . "Some Aspects of Tirso de Molina's *Cigarrales de Toledo* and *Deleytar aprovechando*," *HR*, XXII (1954), 19–31.

_____ . "Tirso and *Pundonor*: A Note on *El celoso prudente*," *BHS*, XXXVIII (1961), 120–5.

Wilson, W. E. "Did Tirso Hate the Girones?," *MLQ*, V (1944), 27–32.

——————. "A Note on *La moza del cántaro*," *HR*, X (1942), 71–2.

——————. "Tirso's *Privar contra su gusto*. A Defense of the Duke of Osuna," *MLQ*, IV (1943), 161–6.

Woodward, L. J. "*El casamiento engañoso y El coloquio de los perros*," *BHS*, XXXVI (1959), 80–7.

Worcester, D. *The Art of Satire* (Cambridge, Mass., 1940).

Zamora Lucas, F. "Evocación de Tirso en sus conventos de Soria y Almazán," *Est*, V (1949), 123–55.

Zamora Vicente, A. "Acercamiento a Tirso de Molina," in *Presencia de los clásicos* (Buenos Aires, 1951), pp. 33–74.

——————. "Portugal en el teatro de Tirso de Molina," in *De Garcilaso a Valle-Inclán* (Buenos Aires, 1950), pp. 87–148.

Zamora Vicente, A. and M. J. Canellada de Zamora. "Una nota sobre *El amor médico*, de Tirso," *Fi*, II (1950), 77–80.

EDITIONS CONSULTED

Anonymous. *La estrella de Sevilla*, eds. Reed, Dixon and Hill (Boston, 1939).

——————. *The Star of Seville*, transl. by H. Thomas (Oxford, 1950).

Arias Pérez, Lic. Pedro. *Primavera y flor de los mejores romances que han salido ahora nuevamente en esta corte, recogidos por el . . . Dirigido al maestro Tirso de Molina* (Madrid, 1623), ed. J. F. Montesinos (Oxford, 1954).

Calderón de la Barca, P. *Obras completas*, I, ed. A. Valbuena Briones (Madrid, 1959).

——————. *Obras completas*, II, ed. A. Valbuena Briones (Madrid, 1956).

Ledesma, A. de. *Juegos de Noches Buenas a lo divino* (Barcelona, 1605. Reprinted in B.A.E., XXXV, Madrid, 1885).

Quevedo, F. de. *El buscón*, ed. A. Castro (Madrid, 1965).

——————. *Obras completas. Verso*, ed. L. Astrana Marín (3rd ed., Madrid, 1952).

Tirso de Molina. *Comedias escogidas del maestro Tirso de Molina* (Madrid, Ortega y Cía., 1826–34), 4 vols.

——————. *Teatro escogido de Fray Gabriel Téllez*, ed. J. E. Hartzenbusch, (Madrid, 1839–42), 12 vols.

——————. *Comedias escogidas de Fray Gabriel Téllez*, ed. J. E. Hartzenbusch, (Madrid, 1848), B.A.E., V.

——————. *Comedias de Tirso de Molina*, ed. E. Cotarelo y Mori (Madrid, 1906–7), 2 vols. N.B.A.E., IV, IX.

——————. *Tirso de Molina. Obras dramáticas completas*, ed. B. de los Ríos (Madrid, 1946–58), 3 vols. (Vol. I, 1946; vol. II, 1952, 2nd ed., 1962; vol. III, 1958).

_____ . *Tirso de Molina. Comedias I*, ed. A. Castro (Clásicos Castellanos, 7th ed., Madrid, 1963).

_____ . *Tirso de Molina. Comedias II*, eds. A. Zamora Vicente and M. J. Canellada de Zamora (Clásicos Castellanos, Madrid, 1956, 1st ed., 1947).

_____ . *Antona García*, ed. M. Wilson (Manchester Univ. Press, 1957).

_____ . *El burlador de Sevilla*, ed. P. Guenon (Paris, 1962).

_____ . *El burlador de Sevilla*, eds. J. E. Varey and N. D. Shergold (Cambridge, 1954).

_____ . *Don Gil de las calzas verdes*, ed. B. F. Bourland (New York, 1901).

_____ . *Don Gil de las calzas verdes*, ed. I. Manuel Gil (Madrid, 1964).

_____ . *Marta la piadosa*, ed. E. Juliá Martínez (4th ed., Zaragoza, 1958).

_____ . *El melancólico*, ed. B. Varela Jácome (Madrid, 1967).

_____ . *Por el sótano y el torno*, ed. A. Zamora Vicente (Buenos Aires, 1949).

_____ . *La prudencia en la mujer*, eds. A. H. Bushee and L. L. Stafford (Mexico, 1948).

_____ . *La prudencia en la mujer*, ed. C. Samonà (Milan, 1967).

_____ . *La venganza de Tamar*, ed. A. K. G. Paterson (Cambridge Univ. Press, 1969).

_____ . *La villana de Vallecas*, ed. S. W. Brown (Boston, 1948).

_____ . *La villana de Vallecas*, eds. J. Lemartinel and G. Zonana (Paris, 1964).

Vega, Lope de. *El castigo sin venganza*, ed. C. A. Jones (Oxford, 1966).

_____ . *Obras escogidas. Teatro. I*, ed. F. C. Sainz de Robles (5th ed., Madrid, 1966).